CRUCIBLE OF
THE CIVIL
WAR

CRUCIBLE OF
THE CIVIL
WAR

Virginia

from Secession

to Commemoration

Edited by Edward L. Ayers, Gary W. Gallagher,
and Andrew J. Torget

University of Virginia Press • *Charlottesville and London*

University of Virginia Press
© 2006 by the Rector and Visitors of the University of Virginia
All rights reserved
Printed in the United States of America on acid-free paper

First published 2006
First paperback edition published 2009
ISBN 978-0-8139-2794-7 (paper)

1 3 5 7 9 8 6 4 2

The Library of Congress has cataloged the hardcover edition as follows:
LIBRARY OF CONGRESS CATALOGING-IN-PUBLICATION DATA

Crucible of the Civil War : Virginia from secession to commemoration / edited by
Edward L. Ayers, Gary W. Gallagher, and Andrew J. Torget.
 p. cm.
 Includes bibliographical references and index.
 ISBN-13: 978-0-8139-2552-3 (cloth : alk. paper)
 1. Virginia—History—Civil War, 1861–1865. 2. Virginia—History—Civil War, 1861–
1865—Social aspects. 3. Secession—Virginia. 4. Group identity—Virginia—History—
19th century. 5. Confederate States of America—Historiography. 6. Slavery—Virginia—
History—19th century. 7. Virginia—Race relations—Political aspects—History—19th
century. 8. Reconstruction (U.S. history, 1865–1877)—Virginia. 9. Memory—Social
aspects—Virginia. 10. United States—History—Civil War, 1861–1865—Social aspects.
I. Ayers, Edward L., 1953– II. Gallagher, Gary W. III. Torget, Andrew J., 1978–
E581.C78 2006
975.5'03—dc22

2006002243

Contents

Preface

This volume originated in the graduate history program at the University of Virginia. While working on an essay about Virginia's decision to secede from the Union, I found myself struck by how little attention the state had received in the literature on the American Civil War. Despite an overwhelming number of books on the battles, leaders, and armies that figured prominently in military events across the state, few works have examined the diverse scenes of life that played out on Virginia's home front. Indeed, for the state that held more slaves and sacrificed more soldiers to the Confederate cause than any other, Virginia has been strangely neglected.

At the same time, I began reading the work of current and former University of Virginia graduate students. Their research upended much of the conventional wisdom about the war, questioning assumptions historians often make about the Old Dominion, and convinced me that much of the story of Civil War Virginia had yet to be told. Turning away from the well-trod field of military events in the state, their work concentrated instead on the ways in which the war affected Virginia's economic, social, and political networks. Some of their essays challenged older interpretations by reexamining Virginia's secession, the development of Confederate nationalism, and how Virginians chose to remember the war after its close. Others addressed areas largely untouched by historians, such as the wartime intersection between race and religion, the development of Confederate social networks, and the war's effects on slavery in the state. All the essays pointed to the profound uncertainty that confronted men and women, black and white, throughout the era.

Their collected work revealed a Virginia that I had rarely seen in the literature on the war, a place where confusion and ambiguity reigned. From the secession crisis through Reconstruction, Virginians confronted difficult choices, widespread hardships, and often discord among themselves. Indeed, the secession crisis forced Virginians to make some of the most agonizing decisions of their lives, producing heated debates within the state. Once the fighting began, Virginians who went into the armies struggled to sort out what it meant to be a soldier and citizen of the Union or the new Confederacy. Those left behind dealt with the privations common to war, questioned how Virginia's cherished social and economic institutions would survive, and wondered whether their loved ones in the armies would ever return.

While embracing the confusion and turmoil of the era, the essays also pointed to common threads that ran throughout wartime Virginia. Slavery, for example, remained the central touchstone of the conflict in the Old Dominion. Driving everything from secession to the ways in which people later chose to remember the war, the institution continued to exert a powerful influence on the state throughout the conflict. In a similar way, the essays also revealed the remarkable commitment that white Virginians of all backgrounds demonstrated for their new Confederate nation. Though they often lamented the hardships of war, citizens across the state remained ardently committed to their country and cause, even in the years after 1865. In all of these things, it seemed to me, the essays offered new ways to approach and understand life in wartime Virginia.

Edward Ayers and Gary Gallagher quickly saw the potential of such a collection and agreed to help turn it into a book. Richard Holway, our editor at the University of Virginia Press, gave us his steadfast support from the beginning and helped marshal the manuscript to completion. Two anonymous readers reviewed the manuscript for the Press and offered insightful and supportive advice on strengthening the essays, for which we are grateful.

We believe the essays in this volume offer new windows into Civil War Virginia. Each piece considers a different aspect of wartime Virginia, breaking new ground by telling stories about the complicated choices that confronted those who lived through the conflict. Yet when placed beside one another, the collected essays also tell a larger story about the rhythms of life in Virginia from the time of secession through the decades after the war's end. What emerges is a portrait of the Old Dominion that dwells on the complex experience of life in the Confederacy's most important state during one of the most turbulent periods in American history.

—*Andrew J. Torget*

CRUCIBLE OF
THE CIVIL
WAR

Introduction

Gary W. Gallagher

Virginia offers a feast of subjects for anyone interested in exploring the Confederate experience or the Civil War more broadly defined. The state endured a bitter internal debate about secession in 1861 that eventually led to the loss of its mountainous western counties, which joined the United States as West Virginia in 1863. Yet even as their western brethren departed, most citizens in Confederate Virginia overcame prewar divisions to achieve a striking sense of national purpose. Armies campaigning within the state's borders fought a number of the most famous battles in American history, slaughtering each other in profusion and creating enormous disruption among the civilian population. To a degree unparalleled elsewhere during the conflict, Virginians in the most heavily contested areas of the state struggled to cope with a battlefront and a home front that literally blended together. Virginia's decision to join the Confederacy undoubtedly lengthened the conflict, opening the way for dramatic social and economic changes among its white and black residents that would have been unthinkable to most observers in 1861. From the opening engagement at First Bull Run on July 21, 1861, until the surrender of the Confederacy's principal field army at Appomattox on April 9, 1865, foreign observers, members of the rival national governments, and citizens in the eastern regions of both the United States and the Confederacy (where most of the populations lived) most often looked to Virginia to gauge the progress of the war. The state was thus central to expectations and fluctuations of morale on both sides—a phenomenon evident from the outset of the war.

Abraham Lincoln gave particular attention to Virginia in his message of July 4, 1861, to a Congress called into special session to deal with the breakup of the Union. Detailing his response to the process by which eleven states had formed a new slaveholding republic, the president singled Virginia out among the four Upper South states that had withdrawn from the Union following his call for volunteers in the wake of Fort Sumter. Pro-Union sentiment had been repressed in Tennessee, North Carolina, Arkansas, and Virginia, observed Lincoln, but "[t]he course taken in Virginia was the most remarkable—perhaps the most important." Virginia's leaders had ordered the seizure of U.S. military property at Harpers Ferry and Norfolk and "received—perhaps invited—into their state, large bodies of troops, with their warlike appointments, from the so-called seceded States." Most ominously, Virginia had allowed "the insurrectionary government" of the Confederacy to be transferred from Montgomery, Alabama, to Richmond. "The people of Virginia have thus allowed this giant insurrection to make its nest within her borders," remarked Lincoln with evident anger, "and this [U.S.] government has no choice left but to deal with it, *where* it finds it."[1]

Well might Lincoln direct hard words toward Virginia, for he knew that its actions dramatically altered the landscape of the looming conflict. Repressing a rebellion of seven Deep South states had posed enough of a challenge to the U.S. government and its loyal citizenry, but Virginia's secession undoubtedly enhanced Confederate chances for success. Less than three weeks after Lincoln's message went to Congress, the battle of First Bull Run, a smashing Confederate victory fought thirty miles from Washington near Manassas Junction, featured Virginia generals and soldiers and ended any thoughts of a quick end to the national crisis.

The fledgling Southern government similarly understood the Old Dominion's importance. On April 22, five days after Virginia's convention voted to leave the United States, Vice President Alexander H. Stephens had visited Richmond to make a case for the Confederacy. As part of the wooing, he held out the promise of making Richmond the new national capital: "The enemy is now on your border—almost at your door—he must be met. This can best be done by having your military operations under the common head at Montgomery—or it may be at Richmond. . . . [I]t is quite within the range of probability that, if such an alliance is made, the

seat of our government will, within a few weeks, be moved to this place. . . .
[S]hould Virginia become, as it probably will, the theatre of the war, the
whole may be transfered here. . . . We want the voice of Virginia in our
Confederate Councils."[2]

Stephens and other members of the Confederate government wanted
more than Virginia's voice—they wanted Virginia's impressive human, industrial, and agricultural resources.[3] A short catalog will underscore just
how much Virginia had to offer. In 1860, it boasted a white population
of approximately 1.1 million, the largest among the seceded states, and
during the war drew from its two hundred thousand military-age white
males to supply more soldiers than any other Confederate state. Its nearly
five hundred thousand slaves, again the largest number in any Confederate state, would figure prominently in the South's wartime economy. Virginia possessed one-fifth of both the Confederacy's railroad mileage and
its assessed value of farmland and buildings. Richmond stood as the new
nation's preeminent manufacturing center, with more than a dozen iron
foundries, several rolling mills, fifty iron and metal works, and huge flour
mills. The Tredegar Iron Works, easily the most important manufacturing
establishment in the Confederacy, would produce an enormous amount
of ordnance and other war-related matériel during four years of fighting.
Southwestern Virginia contained vital sources of salt, lead, and coal (some
of these lay in what would become West Virginia), and the Shenandoah
Valley and Piedmont region ranked among the most important granaries
in the South, growing wheat, corn, fruits, and other crops in abundance.
In sum, Virginia possessed vital logistical riches for a nation soon to be
waging a massive war.

Beyond men to don gray uniforms, factories to put muskets and ammu-
nition into their hands, and farms to produce food to fill their stomachs,
Virginia gave the Confederacy an invaluable tie to the generation that had
founded the American republic. Politicians on both sides of the Potomac
River cast themselves as inheritors and protectors of the revolutionary
tradition. How better for Confederates to bolster such credentials than
to claim the birthplace of George Washington—indisputably the central
figure of the Revolutionary period—and Virginia's three other presidents,
who had guided the American republic for thirty-two of its first forty
years? Whether in Patrick Henry's ringing words of defiance against en-
croaching British power or in George Washington's steadfast leadership
and immense symbolic stature, Confederates could find comforting reas-
surance that they had taken the high road in their own attempt at nation-
building. Virginia's importance in this regard scarcely can be overesti-

mated, as evidenced, most obviously, by the Confederacy's placing George Washington on its Great Seal.[4]

Virginia also supplied the man who would function as the Confederate equivalent of General Washington. During the course of the war, Robert E. Lee, the son of Revolutionary War military hero Henry "Light-Horse Harry" Lee, eclipsed Jefferson Davis and all other politicians and generals as the Confederacy's most admired figure. Many Confederates explicitly compared Lee to Washington. The general consciously patterned himself after Washington, and his wife, Mary Anna Custis Lee, was the great-granddaughter of Martha Washington. Writing in late 1862, for example, a Georgia woman expressed thanks "that in this great struggle the head of our army is a noble son of Virginia, and worthy of the intimate relation in which he stands connected with our immortal Washington." Similarly, Peter W. Alexander, an influential Confederate war correspondent, wrote of Lee: "Like Washington, he is a wise man, and a good man, and possesses in an eminent degree those qualities which are indispensable in the great leader and champion upon whom the country rests its hope." Alexander added that the Confederacy "should feel grateful that Heaven has raised up one in our midst so worthy of our confidence and so capable to lead"—the "grand-son of Washington, so to speak . . . the wise and modest chief who commands the Army of Northern Virginia." Lee and the Army of Northern Virginia, like Washington and the Continental army, became their country's most important national institution, a rallying point that inspired white Southerners to hope for independence.[5]

Virginia also accounted for a disproportionately high number of officers among the Confederacy's high and midlevel command. Of 425 Confederate generals, 91 were born in Virginia; Tennessee, with 50, and Georgia and South Carolina, with 48 each, ranked second, third, and fourth. Among Virginia's most important generals were Thomas J. "Stonewall" Jackson, second only to Lee as a Confederate military icon, the flamboyant cavalryman James E. B. "Jeb" Stuart, and infantry corps commanders Jubal A. Early, Richard S. Ewell, and A. P. Hill. The Virginia Military Institute sent more than eighteen hundred men into the Southern army, almost all of whom served under Lee. The presence of so many officers with a military background helped make the Army of Northern Virginia a formidable opponent for U.S. forces in the Eastern theater. No other Confederate state contributed a comparable body of soldiers with formal training.[6]

The Virginia countryside across which Lee and his army maneuvered and fought commanded attention beyond that of any other military arena.[7] Several factors conspired to create this phenomenon. Virginia's location on the national frontier opposite Washington, D.C., lent special significance to battles fought on its territory. The presence of the two largest and most famous armies of the war—the Army of Northern Virginia and the Army of the Potomac—further boosted Virginia's visibility, as did the frightful scale of human carnage. Of the roughly 1.1 million casualties suffered by the two sides, more than 350,000 fell in Virginia (the addition of Lee's battles in Maryland and Pennsylvania swells the number to nearly 450,000). Tennessee and Georgia, which witnessed just more than 100,000 and just fewer than 90,000 battle casualties, respectively, finished a distant second and third in this grim reckoning. The four major battles fought within fifteen miles of Fredericksburg exacted a more grisly butcher's bill than all the battles combined in any other state, highlighting Virginia's status as the bloody cockpit of the war.

Have historians fully exploited Confederate Virginia as a remarkably rich topic for description and analysis? The answer is yes and no. The military side of Virginia's war has been exhaustively examined. Beginning with publications by former Confederates and Federals, extending through influential work by Douglas Southall Freeman and Bruce Catton between the 1930s and the 1960s, and continuing down to the present in an array of popular and scholarly books and articles, Virginia's military campaigns and the men who orchestrated and fought them have received ample and sometimes mind-numbingly detailed attention. Scarcely any battle or skirmish of any importance lacks a monograph (many of the big battles have inspired multiple treatments), and biographers have explored the lives of even many second- and third-echelon commanders. Some of the best recent work, such as George C. Rable's massive study of the battle of Fredericksburg, has undertaken the necessary work of examining battles within a context that includes both military consequences and impact on the home fronts. Whatever a reader's appetite regarding military events in Virginia, the literature almost certainly has something to offer.[8]

The same cannot be said for other dimensions of Virginia's wartime experience. In an essay on scholarship relating to Virginia and the Confederacy published fifteen years ago, I noted "the availability of both excellent potential topics and ample sources with which to study them" but lamented the fact that Virginia was poorly represented in books devoted to the home front.[9] There has been some gratifying progress since I made those observations. William A. Link's work on late-antebellum Virginia politics, William Blair's on questions of popular will in the midst of severe hardship, Peter S. Carmichael's on generational attitudes toward secession and war, Ervin L. Jordan Jr.'s on African Americans, Anne Sarah Rubin's on Confederate national sentiment, and community and regional studies by Edward L. Ayers, Daniel W. Crofts, Carol Kettenburg Dubbs, Ernest B. Furgurson, Kenneth W. Noe, Daniel E. Sutherland, Steven Elliott Tripp, and Brian Steel Wills have contributed significantly to our knowledge about wartime Virginia. Yet much remains to be examined. For example, we need to know more about such subjects as the dynamics of Virginia's slaveholding society, the refugee experience, the role of religion, tensions between national and local sentiment and between different geographical sections of the state, and the ways in which postwar Virginians understood and explained secession and their Confederate experience. For all the wartime topics, connections between the military and nonmilitary spheres must be brought into sharpest relief.[10]

The contributors to this book add important brush strokes to a portrait in progress of Virginia during the era of the Civil War. Even veteran readers will find valuable material in the essays, which collectively muster new evidence, present fresh interpretations, and remind us of how much remains to be written about the Confederacy's most important state.

Notes

1. Abraham Lincoln, *The Collected Works of Abraham Lincoln*, ed. Roy P. Basler, 9 vols. (New Brunswick, N.J.: Rutgers University Press, 1953), 4:426–27.

2. Alexander H. Stephens quoted in Emory M. Thomas, *The Confederate State of Richmond: A Biography of the Capital* (Austin: University of Texas Press, 1971), 13.

3. For convenient summaries of data concerning Virginia's population, wealth, manufacturing potential, and agricultural production, see J. G. Randall and David Donald, *The Civil War and Reconstruction*, revised 2nd ed. (Lexington, Mass.: D. C. Heath, 1969), tables on pp. 5, 8; Richard N. Current et al., eds., *Encyclopedia of the Confederacy*, 4 vols. (New York: Simon and Schuster, 1993), 4:1663–64 (essay titled "Virginia" by James I. Robertson Jr.); U.S. Bureau of the Census, *Historical Statistics of the United States, Colonial Times to 1970*, 2 vols. (Washington, D.C.: Government Printing Office, 1975), 1:462; Thomas, *Confederate State of Richmond*, 21–24; Ella Lonn, *Salt as a Factor in the Confederacy* ([Tuscaloosa]: University of Alabama Press, 1965), 19–34.

4. The figure on the Great Seal copied the equestrian statue of Washington by sculptor Thomas Crawford, which was unveiled on the Capitol grounds in Richmond in 1858.

5. Mary Jones to Col. Charles C. Jones Jr., December 19, 1862, in Robert Manson Myers, ed., *The Children of Pride: A True Story of Georgia and the Civil War* (New Haven, Conn.: Yale University Press, 1972), 1001; Atlanta *Southern Confederacy*, December 5, 1862.

6. For states of birth for all Civil War generals, see James Spencer, comp., *Civil War Generals: Categorical Listings and a Biographical Directory* (Westport, Conn.: Greenwood, 1986). For the importance of the V.M.I. graduates, see Richard M. McMurry, *Two Great Rebel Armies: An Essay in Confederate Military History* (Chapel Hill: University of North Carolina Press, 1989), 98–105.

7. As with almost every dimension of the Civil War, historians have argued about which military theater was most important. Scholars such as Thomas L. Connelly, Richard M. McMurry, Herman Hattaway, and Archer Jones have insisted that Lost Cause writers, who placed Lee at the center of their interpretation of the war, attributed too much influence to events in Virginia. These arguments overlook compelling wartime testimony that leaves little doubt that most people at the time, North and South and in London and Paris, considered Virginia the theater of decisive action. Appomattox represented the unequivocal end of the conflict to almost all contemporary observers because, despite the presence of scores of thousands of Confederate soldiers under arms elsewhere, it marked the end of the war in Virginia and of Lee's ability to inspire hope among white Southerners.

8. See George C. Rable, *Fredericksburg! Fredericksburg!* (Chapel Hill: University of North Carolina Press, 2002). Shortly after Rable's book appeared, Francis Augustin O'Reilly published a detailed, well-researched tactical study of the battle titled *The Fredericksburg Campaign: Winter War on the Rappahannock* (Baton Rouge: Louisiana State University Press, 2003). Totaling more than thirteen hundred pages between them, these two books supply enough information about the one-day battle and its impact to satisfy even the most inquisitive readers, while at the same time underscoring the degree to which Virginia's military experience has inspired a large literature. For a sense of how prominently campaigns and commanders in Virginia have figured in writings about the war, see David J. Eicher, *The Civil War in Books: An Analytical Bibliography* (Urbana: University of Illinois Pres, 1997).

9. Gary W. Gallagher, "Home Front and Battlefield: Some Recent Literature Relating to Virginia and the Confederacy," *Virginia Magazine of History and Biography* 98 (April 1990): 135–36.

10. See William A. Link, *Roots of Secession: Slavery and Politics in Antebellum Virginia* (Chapel Hill: University of North Carolina Press, 2003); William Blair, *Virginia's Private War: Feeding Body and Soul in the Confederacy, 1861–1865* (New York: Oxford University Press, 1998); Peter S. Carmichael, *The Last Generation: Young Virginians in Peace, War, and Reunion* (Chapel Hill: University of North Carolina Press, 2005); Ervin L. Jordan Jr., *Black Confederates and Afro-Yankees*

in Civil War Virginia (Charlottesville: University Press of Virginia, 1995); Anne Sarah Rubin, *A Shattered Nation: The Rise and Fall of the Confederacy, 1861–1868* (Chapel Hill: University of North Carolina Press, 2005); Edward L. Ayers, *In the Presence of Mine Enemies: War in the Heart of America, 1859–1863* (New York: W. W. Norton, 2003); Daniel W. Crofts, *Old Southampton: Politics and Society in a Virginia County, 1834–1869* (Charlottesville: University Press of Virginia, 1992); Carol Kettenburg Dubbs, *Defend This Old Town: Williamsburg during the Civil War* (Baton Rouge: Louisiana State University Press, 2002); Ernest B. Furgurson, *Ashes of Glory: Richmond at War* (New York: Alfred A. Knopf, 1996); Kenneth W. Noe, *Southwest Virginia's Railroad: Modernization and the Sectional Crisis* (Urbana: University of Illinois Press, 1994); Daniel E. Sutherland, *Seasons of War: The Ordeal of a Confederate Community, 1861–1865* (New York: Free Press, 1995); Steven Elliott Tripp, *Yankee Town, Southern City: Race and Class Relations in Civil War Lynchburg* (New York: New York University Press, 1997); and Brian Steel Wills, *The War Hits Home: The Civil War in Southeastern Virginia* (Charlottesville: University Press of Virginia, 2001).

Unions of Slavery

Slavery, Politics, and Secession in the Valley of Virginia

Andrew J. Torget

Abraham Lincoln took great care in crafting his message to the special session of Congress on July 4, 1861. More than simply recounting the momentous events that had occurred since his inauguration, Lincoln wanted to explain why the nation's legislature had "convened on an extraordinary occasion." Lincoln blamed the secession crisis on a minority of Southerners who had overtaken their respective state governments, reiterating his position that the Union was older than the states and indissoluble. Rebels unsatisfied with a fair election, he insisted, had created the crisis and purposefully forced the Federal government into a war. "The assault upon, and reduction of, Fort Sumter, was, in no sense," Lincoln argued, "a matter of self defence on the part of the assailants." A minority of Southerners bent on secession, he believed, had forced the clash at Fort Sumter and pushed Southern Unionists into rebellion. Yet as he laid out the first draft of the war's history, Lincoln did not dwell on the events in South Carolina. "The course taken in Virginia was the most remarkable," he asserted, "perhaps the most important."[1]

Few historians have quarreled with Lincoln's assertion of Virginia's central importance in the secession crisis. As the largest slaveowning state in the American South, as well as its most populous and industrial, Virginia was pivotal to the allegiance of Upper South states during the crisis. Without Virginia in the Union, with her strategic resources and symbolic value, Unionists in Tennessee and North Carolina had little hope of keeping their states allied to the North. The border region would determine how secession redefined the country, and Virginia was the keystone of border state allegiance. Lincoln, and historians since, understood that the Old Dominion's decision on the question of secession would fundamentally shape the course of the coming civil war.

Historians of Virginia's secession, however, seem to have agreed on little else. Virginia, with the rest of the Border South, did not follow the lead of South Carolina and the Lower South states in leaving the Union immediately upon Lincoln's election in November 1860, resisting secession until April 1861. The Old Dominion's delay in joining the Confederacy has prompted some to assert that slavery was less important to Virginians by 1860 than it had been in years past. Arguing that "how deeply slavery had penetrated a given region" was the best indicator of how that region would react during the secession crisis, these historians claim that Virginia proved reluctant to secede because of the decreasing percentage of slaves in the state.[2] Virginia resisted secession, they contend, because Virginians were less committed to defending slavery than Lower South states. While these historians are correct to concentrate on the crucial role slavery played in the crisis, it nevertheless seems unlikely that residents of the state with the largest number of slaves and slaveholders in 1860 believed they had little stake in the future of the institution.

Other historians have sought to explain Virginia's resistance to secession in terms of the political system. Unlike states in the Lower South, they contend, the robust operation of party politics in the Upper South left Virginians with faith that the checks and balances of the American political system would protect them from the dangers of a Republican presidency, until the clash at Fort Sumter convinced them otherwise. While the political system had collapsed in the Lower South by the time of Lincoln's election, they assert, it was the continued strength of two-party politics, the very resilience of old party distinctions in the Upper South, that explained Virginia's delay in secession.[3] These historians are right to focus their attention on the role that politics played in Virginia's decisions on secession. They underestimate, however, the role that slavery played in the crisis, as well as the power of the institution to shape and reshape local politics.

At the heart of these disputes among historians are disagreements over the respective roles that slavery and politics played in the secession of Virginia. Newspapers, as the political centers of nineteenth-century communities, offer the best places to examine slavery's role in shaping the political debates of Virginians during the secession crisis. As the recognized voices of local political parties and interests, newspapers document most clearly the changing political tones and concerns that swirled within Virginia's counties during the secession crisis. The shifts in county political sentiments that they illuminate, moreover, are borne out by the returns from the November 1860 election, the February 1861 election for delegates to the Virginia state convention, and the enthusiasm for secession expressed by early April 1861. Within the pages of their local newspapers, Virginians struggled with one another over the place of slavery in the commonwealth and the wisdom of remaining in the Union with Abraham Lincoln.

Newspaper accounts and editorials emanating from the Valley of Virginia during the secession crisis paint a different portrait of secession-era Virginia than most historians have suggested. Commonly known as the Shenandoah Valley, the region sat in the heart of the Old Dominion, cradled on either side by the Blue Ridge and Allegheny mountains. The Valley was a twenty-mile-wide swath of rich farmlands and mineral resources, making its lands some of the most prosperous and profitable in the nation. The Valley itself stretched as far north as Vermont, but its heart in Virginia lay in the center of the state, in the three contiguous counties of Rockingham, Augusta, and Rockbridge.[4] "In this glorious 'Old Augusta,' in noble Rockbridge, and in Union-loving Rockingham," crowed one Valley newspaper, people were united by similar economies, a rich history, and the promise of a profitable future.[5]

The Valley found itself at the center of the secession crisis. Lincoln's election had divided Virginians into three groups: unconditional Unionists, who believed in preserving the Federal Union above all else; ardent secessionists, who saw Lincoln's election as a harbinger of the end of Virginia slavery; and conditional Unionists, who remained wary of Lincoln's Republicans while also fearful of what secession could bring. Comprising the majority of Virginia's voters, conditional Unionists held the balance of power during the crisis. Without them neither the Unionists nor the secessionists could succeed. Although present in all areas of Virginia, conditional Unionists found particular strength in the Shenandoah Valley, and in their hands rested Virginia's pivotal decision.

The secession crisis struck Rockingham, Augusta, and Rockbridge counties hard. The crisis atmosphere quickly collapsed the older, long-standing divisions that had marked antebellum politics in the counties, as local Whigs and Democrats abandoned traditional two-party politics and temporarily shifted to a new kind of politics—one centered on protecting their common interest in Virginia slavery from outside threats.

Rather than battling one another, local politicians and newspapers in the counties began to show remarkable uniformity in their politics and interests during the secession crisis. By the time of the February 1861 election of delegates to the Virginia secession convention, Rockingham, Augusta, and Rockbridge had entirely abandoned their old political ways, uniting around a new politics grounded in the defense of Virginia slavery.

Before the crisis began, however, the three counties had been anything but united in political matters. Rockingham, the northernmost of the three, had been a citadel for the Democratic Party in nearly every election since Andrew Jackson gained the White House in 1828. Agriculture dominated the county's economy, and its farmers embraced the Democratic ticket. Harrisonburg, the county's only sizable town, proved a party stronghold and helped make Rockingham one of the most staunchly Democratic counties in the entire state. Democrat James Buchanan had swept the county in the 1856 presidential election with an overwhelming 84 percent of the vote. In Virginia's 1859 gubernatorial election, Democrat John Letcher took a similarly lopsided 77 percent of the county's votes, with his American Party opponent barely registering among voters.[6] The Democratic Party dominated Rockingham's politics.

Although it shared Rockingham's southern border, Augusta County did not share in its political thinking. Augusta had a more urban population, centered around the growing and bustling county seat of Staunton, with smaller towns and villages scattered throughout the countryside. While Buchanan had easily taken almost every vote in Democratic Rockingham, he had been soundly defeated in Augusta. Augusta had always been a strong Whig county, and the American Party candidate Millard Fillmore easily won the county's 1856 presidential contest over Buchanan with 56 percent of the vote. After the national dissolution of their party, ex-Whigs continued to oppose Democrats in Augusta County elections and, unlike in Rockingham, Democrat John Letcher lost the county in his 1859 bid for the Virginia governorship. A full 60 percent of Augusta voters supported the Opposition candidate over Letcher and, though the national Whig Party itself had faltered, the anti-Democratic voting patterns of Augusta remained steady.

Rockbridge, to the immediate south of Augusta, was a political amalgam of the other two counties. Lexington was its only real town, but villages dotted the county's landscape. Rockbridge often vacillated between Democratic and Whig candidates, usually leaning toward the Whig Party. The county endorsed Buchanan in the 1856 election by a margin of only 88 votes out of more than 2,000 cast. In the 1859 contest for governor, the county gave the American Party candidate a razor-thin 22-vote victory over Democrat John Letcher out of 2,438 votes recorded. Letcher was a resident of Rockbridge, but even that proved insufficient to marshal any sort of clear majority out of Rockbridge's mixed voting patterns. While Rockingham remained a Democratic stronghold, and Augusta staunchly Whig, Rockbridge straddled the middle ground between the two as a moderately Whig county.

True to old patterns, the 1860 presidential election began with partisan bickering and fighting within all three counties. Rockingham once again put its full faith in the Democratic Party. The county's two newspapers, each published out of Harrisonburg, endorsed Stephen A. Douglas as their choice for president. Augusta found itself split in its loyalties. No clear "Opposition" candidate had emerged for the 1860 contest and the county's newspapers divided their loyalties between the Democrat Douglas and the Constitutional Union candidate John Bell. Bell was as close to an anti-Democratic candidate as Augusta could find, and most in the county stood behind his candidacy. Rockbridge experienced a split similar to Augusta's: one of the county's newspapers endorsed Douglas, while the other touted Bell as the county's best choice for president. In alliance with their past Whiggish tendencies, Rockbridge voters tended to favor Bell over Douglas.

As summer faded into fall, however, the political prospects for both Stephen Douglas and John Bell appeared bleak. Abraham Lincoln's campaign, running against the hopelessly fractured Democratic Party, seemed poised to capture most of the North and thereby the presidency. Hamstrung by the Southern Democrat John Breckinridge's efforts in the South, Douglas remained unable to attract the national support necessary to defeat Lincoln. Bell's campaign had proven itself unable to establish any meaningful following beyond the border states and seemed to be siphoning votes away from the Democratic candidates rather than Lincoln. The fractured opposition appeared likely to guarantee Lincoln's election.

By October 1860, most county newspapers in the Valley conceded that Lincoln's election appeared almost certain. "The elections which have recently taken place in the Northern States, have resulted disastrously to the Democratic party, and indicate the election of a Black Republican President on the 6th of November," reported a paper from Rockingham. Some in the Valley prayed that either Bell or Douglas could still muster a miracle defeat of Lincoln, or that somehow the political splintering of the country would force the election into the Southern-controlled U.S. House of Representatives. County newspapers promoted their candidates right up to Election Day. But hope dimmed as November neared, and every Valley editor acknowledged the "almost certainty of defeat."[7]

With Lincoln's victory seemingly unavoidable, Valley editors began writing editorials for purposes other than electing Stephen Douglas or John Bell president. Redirecting their efforts at producing majorities in their counties for Unionism over sectionalism, the local newspapers began to focus their political energies on preventing the secession of Virginia. The editors continued to champion either Stephen Douglas or John Bell, but rarely denigrated the other candidate. Rather, Rockingham, Augusta, and Rockbridge newspapers hurled their political barbs almost exclusively against John Breckinridge, whose supporters advocated the secession of slave states should Lincoln win the presidency. If they were going to lose the presidency to Lincoln, the local newspapers hoped Election Day would produce enough Union votes in Virginia to preempt secession in the state and send a warning to the Lower South about Virginia's Unionist intents.

The Southern sectional appeal of Breckinridge, the newspapers argued, was even more sinister than the Republicans' attempt to win without the South. There was nothing overtly unconstitutional about Lincoln's probable election, yet the Breckinridge campaign proposed to sunder the Union nevertheless. "To break up the Government under these circumstances, simply because Lincoln should be elected, would be adding madness to treason.—The danger is in the Cotton States, and not in the North," argued Augusta's *Spectator*. Secession hardly seemed like a safeguard to people living along the border with the North, and Valley residents feared what a war would produce. The prospect of a Republican president was ominous, but no more so than the realization that the "aim of the leaders of the Breckinridge movement in the South is Revolution . . . and involving the country in bloody war."[8]

One newspaper spelled out people's fears with unusual clarity. "Be not deceived by this insane cry" from the Breckinridge campaign, Rockingham's *Valley Democrat* urged. "Slavery institutions are in no peril. Congress cannot *force* or *reject* slavery against the will of the people."[9] Indeed, people in Rockingham County knew they could hardly afford threats to Virginia slavery. At the time of the election, slaves made up 10 percent of the county's population.[10] Slavery was integral to Rockingham's agricultural economy, and farmers in the county had invested nearly $3 million in the slaves who made their farms and fields so profitable.[11] Augusta and Rockbridge held similar stakes in the institution. With twice the slave population of Rockingham, Augusta's farmers had almost $7 million invested in their enslaved laborers. Rockbridge was the smallest of the three counties, but boasted the highest percentage of slaves per capita of all three. Slaves made up 23 percent of the county's population and represented an investment of nearly $5 million.

Between them, Rockingham, Augusta, and Rockbridge counties had more than $14 million invested in their collective slave workforce, and profitably managed more than $26 million worth of developed farmlands. Rockingham was more rural, Augusta more urban, and Rockbridge more industrial, but the three counties shared the same economic foundation. Agriculture based in slavery was the mainstay of each, and a civil war could destroy it all.

Valley editors exhorted people to vote against Breckinridge sectionalism. "A heavy majority cast for Bell and Douglas over Breckinridge," argued one Valley newspaper, would demonstrate that the state could not easily be dislodged from the American Union. Local politicians scrambled to ward off Virginia's secession before it could begin, and Rockingham's *Valley Democrat* declared the election "a contest between . . . Union and Disunion." Nothing would so surely destroy Virginia slavery, they believed, as jettisoning the Constitutional protections of the institution and enveloping the country in a bloody civil war. In the last days before the election, the Rockbridge *Valley Star* urged its readers, "Never, never let it be said that the Bolters had ever a resting place among us. We want a majority that will silence forever the cry of Disunion."[12]

Far more than a majority of voters turned out on Election Day. Despite Lincoln's almost certain victory, Democratic Rockingham saw nearly two-thirds of its voters record their voices in the contest. True to the predictions of the two county newspapers, Stephen Douglas won handily. The final count gave Douglas 1,354 votes, followed by a strong showing for Bell with 883 votes, and 676 for Breckinridge.[13] As expected, Rockingham produced a solid Democratic victory for Douglas. Yet the strength of the non-Democratic candidate John Bell over Breckinridge signaled an important shift in the county's politics. Despite Rockingham's historical antipathy to any non-Democrat, the Unionist appeal of Bell now held more weight for county voters than Breckinridge's party affiliation as a Democrat. The combined votes for Douglas and Bell demonstrated that almost 78 percent of the county voted against sectional candidates. Rockingham still endorsed a Democratic candidate, but voters' interest in preserving the Union allowed John Bell to best the other Democrat on the ballot.

Voting against sectionalism required no change in Augusta's voting patterns. About three-quarters of the eligible white men of Augusta made their way to the polls on Election Day and registered their interests overwhelmingly with Bell. Bell garnered 2,553 votes to the 1,094 cast for Douglas, and a mere 218 recorded for Breckinridge. The two newspapers of the county had split their support between Bell and Douglas, but Bell's powerful victory demonstrated that voters in Augusta remained true to their past Whig voting patterns. Moreover, those in the county who voted Democratic overwhelmingly chose Douglas over Breckinridge, and the Bell and Douglas campaigns accounted for fully 95 percent of Augusta votes.

The results in Rockbridge mirrored those in Augusta. There was no razor-thin victory in the historically undecided county; three-fourths of Rockbridge's eligible voters gave Bell a dominating margin of victory similar to Augusta's. Overall, Bell had taken 1,231 votes in the county, with Douglas drawing 641 and Breckinridge attracting only a paltry 361. Though the two Rockbridge papers had split their support between Bell and Douglas, the county's tradition of moderate-Whig voting gave Bell the victory. Rockbridge's *Lexington Gazette* reveled in the news, printing the Bell and Douglas returns for the county under the banner: "Union majority."[14]

When "the smoke and *dust* sufficiently cleared away," the Valley learned that Abraham Lincoln had been elected president.[15] John Bell had won Virginia and only two other states, Tennessee and Kentucky, both of which were facing the same difficult situation as the Old Dominion. Despite his relative strength in the Valley, Stephen Douglas had made a poor showing both in Virginia and across the nation. Rockingham was one of only four counties in Virginia that Douglas won, and nationally he had only taken Missouri outright, splitting New Jersey with Lincoln. Worse, John Breckinridge had swept the Lower South and demonstrated considerable strength even in Virginia.[16] With a Republican about to become the nation's president and Breckinridge's supporters threatening immediate secession, Valley residents braced for the coming storm. "We are upon the heels of a crisis," cried Rockbridge's *Valley Star*, as many in the Valley felt trapped between unstable extremism to both their north and south.[17]

In the immediate aftermath of Lincoln's election, political leaders in the Valley preached calm. "Let the true and patriotic people of Virginia . . . patiently and dignifiedly await the development of events," counseled Augusta's *Vindicator*. As unsettling as Lincoln's election was, editors urged the counties' citizens to retain composure in the wake of his election. "The election of Abraham Lincoln is a calamity," acknowledged a Rockingham paper, but "it is the duty of all good citizens to submit to an election fairly conducted under the forms of the Constitution." No laws had been broken; and while repugnant, Lincoln's election was still constitutional. Until the Republicans committed an overt breach of the law, most in the counties agreed, "We can well afford to wait."[18]

People in the Valley took consolation in the fact that the national elections had not brought total victory to the Republicans. Democrats sympathetic to the South still held the sway of power in Congress and would be able to prevent the new Republican president from meddling with slavery. "They have the Executive, but no other branch of the Government, and will, consequently, be impotent for mischief . . . however much disposed they may be to do so," an Augusta newspaper reassured its readers. "We have the Senate, the House of Representatives and the Supreme Court in our favor, either one of which would of itself be a sufficient protection of our rights."[19] It would be impossible for the Republicans to attack Southern institutions with two-thirds of the Federal government under Southern control.

"The danger is in secession," warned the *Spectator*. Only if the Lower South forced a political fight with the Republicans, agreed the Valley newspapers, would Virginia stand in jeopardy. "If several of the Southern States secede, they will leave us in a minority in Congress, where we now have a safe majority," warned the Augusta newspaper. The possible secession of South Carolina, and any number of other Lower South states who chose to follow her out of the Union, would immediately dissolve the political safeguards that currently protected Virginia from overbearing Republican legislation. Many in the Valley feared that South Carolina and her cohorts intended to use that leverage to force Virginia to join the Lower South in secession. "They think that if they secede and leave us at the mercy of a Black Republican majority in Congress, that we will secede likewise," grumbled the *Spectator*. "This is the way in which they expect to drag us into a like destiny with them."[20]

Despite their shared stake in slavery, the people of the Valley saw fundamental differences between their own economic interests and those of the Lower South. "Cotton is not king in the border States" explained Rockingham's *Valley Democrat*. "Wheat, corn, tobacco, hemp, cattle &c., are the monarchs here, and demand to be consulted before they are precipitated into revolution." Even their interests in slavery differed markedly. Geographically isolated from the North, the Lower South states had little reason to fear that secession would imperil their investment in slavery. If Virginia seceded, however, there would be no way for the state to recover slaves who slipped into the North; the proximity of freedom would spark a mass exodus among the enslaved. "The negro property of the border

States will be worthless" if Virginia were to secede, warned one Valley paper; "every facility will be afforded the negro to escape."[21]

While politics remained at the center of Valley life in the first months after Lincoln's election, parties and elections carried a different tenor than in years past. For the first time in decades, the newspapers of Rockingham, Augusta, and Rockbridge spoke with a single voice. Democrats and ex-Whigs in the counties found themselves preoccupied with Virginia's particular geo-political interests in the crisis, temporarily ignoring what had previously divided them. Partisan squabbling hardly seemed important to Virginians facing the possible dissolution of their nation. "From the beginning of this movement," remarked the *Lexington Gazette,* "there has been a very general disposition to ignore party differences and to act as one people."[22] Local politics were no longer about particular parties for voters in the Valley, but about their common cause in defending Virginia slavery.

The pace of the new Valley politics did not slow in the aftermath of the 1860 election. Citizens in each of the counties held Union meetings throughout November and December to decide how best to defuse the threat of secession to Virginia. "The Court House was literally packed" one early December day in Rockbridge as "some gentlemen of Lexington" assembled "to discuss the affairs of the nation." As at most Union meetings throughout the Valley, men stood to make speeches and argued over tactics, but nearly all agreed that their energies were "for saving the Union."[23] Passing resolutions in support of the Union, Valley residents hoped to save Virginia from secession.

Most of the Union meetings determined that the practical solution to the current crisis would be "a Convention of all the States." Sectionalism, arising from both the North and South, had caused the crisis. A sectional convention, such as the Southern convention proposed by the Lower South, would do nothing to alleviate the problem. "The more rational and statesmanlike policy of a *National* Convention," Augusta's *Vindicator* argued, was the best means for defusing the explosive situation.[24] The Rockbridge *Valley Star* threw its support behind the call of Virginia governor John Letcher for a national convention. Rockingham and Augusta newspapers quickly voiced their agreement. If all the states could compromise together, perhaps disunion and civil war could be averted.

In the meantime, South Carolina edged closer toward secession. Since the election, residents of the Valley had followed with rapt attention as the Palmetto State put the machinery of secession into motion. Daily telegrams were reprinted as they arrived in the Valley newspapers, detailing South Carolina's convening of a state convention. While South Carolina held its own convention, several Lower South states proposed holding a convention of all slaveholding states, hoping to present a unified front to the incoming Republican administration. Citizens in the Valley, however, soundly rejected such proposals as a thinly veiled effort to force Virginia and the border states into "the glittering delusion of a Southern Confederacy."[25] For the Valley, joining a Southern Confederacy would be the first step toward their own ruin.

South Carolina's secession, however, changed the political calculus of the Valley. "ONE STAR LESS!" ran the headline in one Valley newspaper when word reached Virginia in late December that the long-anticipated event had finally arrived.[26] South Carolina's exit from the Union surprised no one, but it forced the Valley to face a gritty new reality. With one state already gone, and the rest of the cotton South preparing to follow, the Valley counties realized that Virginia could no longer count on Southern strength in Congress to check the anti-Southern whims of a Republican president. Every seceding state that followed South Carolina's lead left Virginia more at the mercy of the incoming Republican administration. Democrats in the Valley, moreover, now had to abandon any hope that a reunited national party base could remove the Republicans from power in 1864. The political safeguards that made a Republican presidency bearable were being dismantled one Southern state at a time.

As the crisis dragged into 1861, reports poured in over the telegraph wires of states that had either left the Union or were preparing to do so. No national conference of states appeared to be materializing, and the stream of seceding states made such a conference increasingly unlikely. Union meetings cropped up throughout each county as Valley residents began looking for other solutions. Some discussed the possibility of holding a border state conference. Others put their hopes into compromise legislation. The conciliatory efforts of Kentucky's Senator John Crittenden drew each county's particular attention. His proposal offered the South a guarantee that slavery could expand west, while also prohibiting it from entering the northern part of that new region, giving ground to both Southern desires and Republican ideology. Newspapers from all three counties embraced the proposition, and in early January a Rockingham paper reported with optimism that soon "Senator Crittenden will propose his resolutions in the Senate."[27]

In the meantime, Virginia's state legislature finally met for the first time since Lincoln's election in November. As widely expected, one of their first acts was to call for a state convention to determine Virginia's course of action in the national crisis. Legislators announced that a special election would be held in early February in which the counties would select representatives for a state convention. The election would also determine whether the decisions of the state convention would be referred back to the voters for final approval, or if the convention would have a free hand to decide the actions of Virginia in the crisis.

The legislature's call for a state convention divided opinion in the counties. "What can a Convention do at present more than the Legislature can do, except it be to declare us out of the Union?" asked a man in Rockingham. Many in the Valley shared this voter's fear that the convention was simply a ploy by Breckinridge supporters to sweep the commonwealth out of the United States under the guise of popular sentiment. Others in the counties believed that a state convention should meet "at the earliest possible period," arguing that the state needed to act in a unified and swift manner rather than allow outside events to determine its destiny.[28] Augusta's *Vindicator* and Rockingham's *Register* applauded the calling of a state convention and wanted action taken by Virginia before Lincoln's inauguration on March 4, 1861. The Rockbridge papers and Augusta's *Spectator,* while equally frustrated, argued against holding a state convention, but agreed that if one were called its decisions must be subject to the voters' final approval.

The debates within the counties over the merits of a Virginia state convention revealed the extent of political change in the Valley since the previous November. Partisan identification had in large measure ceased to influence political issues in Rockingham, Augusta, and Rockbridge. While almost all previous elections had elicited arguments over the true platforms of particular parties, people now debated politics almost exclusively in terms of Virginia's interests and geographic position as a border state in the crisis. The Valley counties found "common interests and a common necessity" among themselves far more politically compelling during the secession winter than shared party allegiance with white men in Maine or Mississippi.[29] Politics still mattered, perhaps more so now than ever before, but the Valley's focus had shifted profoundly since November 1860. Past partisan identification, while never fully discarded, had to be subordinated.

The Valley newspapers, long recognized as the engines of party loyalty in the counties, abandoned partisan rhetoric. By January, the newspapers evaluated political options solely in regard to "the perpetuation of the Union." The Rockbridge *Valley Star* urged its readers in early January to focus on "the rights and interests of Virginia before all other considerations."[30] By the time of the legislature's call for a special election, newspaper editorials in Rockingham, Augusta, and Rockbridge had ceased to argue the party ideals that had consumed them for decades, concerning themselves now entirely with Virginia's place in the Union.

Men throughout each county stepped forward during January to announce their candidacy for delegate to the upcoming state convention. Potential representatives dashed back and forth within each county during the month-long campaign, debating one another in taverns and courthouses. Some argued that, without the Lower South, Virginia could no longer depend upon the safeguards of the Union against Republican intrusions and stated bluntly that the commonwealth should "stand alongside of our sister States of the South." Other candidates counseled that Virginians "can obtain redress for our present grievances, and security against further aggressions without resorting to secession." These candidates accused their secessionist opponents of "resorting to revolution."[31] The contest quickly divided between those who would take Virginia out of the Union and those who still saw hope within it.

White men in Rockingham, Augusta, and Rockbridge swarmed the polls on February 4, 1861, and an overwhelming majority gave their votes to Unionist candidates. The margins of victory were staggering. Unionist candidates defeated secessionists with more than 74 percent of the vote in Rockingham, 87 percent in Augusta, and 91 percent in Rockbridge.[32] "The delegates elect are all conservative *Union* men," the *Rockingham Register* announced triumphantly, and the Valley rejoiced that voters had soundly rejected candidates urging secession.[33] Equally heartening, the counties learned that voters had produced even more lopsided margins in favor of referring the decisions of the state convention back to the voters.[34] Any effort to withdraw Virginia from the Union would now have to gain final approval from the state's voters. Augusta's *Spectator* reveled in the news, exclaiming, "Nearly the whole people are with us, working to 'harm' the schemes of the disunionists!"[35]

In Rockingham, historically one of the most staunchly Democratic counties in Virginia, voters had even elected ex-Whig John Lewis over secessionist Democrats as one of the county's three convention delegates. The *Rockingham Register* attributed the anomaly to the fact that past "politics were ignored in the canvass." Similarly, Whig-dominated Augusta elected the Democrat George Baylor to represent them. Baylor himself recognized that his election was the product of changed Valley politics. "It has been my fortune . . . to belong to a party in politics that was always in a minority in the county of Augusta," he told the convention in Richmond. "But for the fact that my people rose above party in electing delegates here, your humble speaker never would have been honored with a seat in this body."[36]

While all of the elected delegates from the Valley, and indeed most across the state, favored preserving the old Federal Union, sentiment was changing in the three counties. The Valley continued to support Unionism out of fear that secession would imperil Virginia's interests, the heart of which was the continued security of slavery. "As [Virginia] wishes to preserve slavery, she wants to preserve the Union," observed the *Lexington Gazette*, although many Virginians had begun to question the wisdom of entrusting the institution's future to Abraham Lincoln. During the campaign for the state convention, Unionist candidates had voiced their virulent opposition to any Federal attempt "to coerce a State by force of arms" to rejoin the Union, demonstrating their growing fears of Lincoln's intentions.[37] Almost every elected delegate had predicated his Unionism on a peaceful solution to the crisis, which would be based on a conciliatory Republican Party. Yet the Republicans had made no apparent effort to ward off the continued flight of Lower South states, and the incoming administration seemed to be taking no steps to ensure peace.

Wariness settled over the Valley, despite the recent election results. "I think the times have changed since the Presidential contest," wrote one man to Augusta's *Vindicator*. "If they have not, I for one have."[38] Many in the three counties shared his growing concern for the Valley's future. The *Vindicator* itself had developed a more pessimistic tone concerning efforts to preserve the American Union and by February was near advocating Virginia's secession. Frustrated by the failure of conference initiatives and the lack of Republican efforts to calm Southern fears, the newspaper and its editor had become convinced that the incoming Republican administration would likely pose greater threats to Virginia's interests than secession would.

The failure of compromise legislation had given them little reason to believe otherwise. The entire Border South had embraced John Crittenden's proposal, yet "hardly any Republican of stature would accept the Crittenden Compromise." Lincoln himself continued to have little to say publicly on any issue, and the Republicans who were talking had little good to say about most of the compromise legislation. "The fate of the Crittenden Resolutions in the Senate ought to satisfy any reasonable man of the slightness of a hope of a satisfactory settlement of affairs before the inauguration of the new President," wrote the *Vindicator*.[39] Several other compromise measures appeared destined for similar fates, and, though the counties followed all compromise proposals with hope, the Republicans seemed determined not to compromise anything at all. While they had rejected immediate secession in the February election, Rockingham, Augusta, and Rockbridge were no longer certain their safety lay within the Federal Union.

The Virginia state convention began in mid-February in Richmond, but the Valley found itself far more concerned with the impending presidential inauguration. Abraham Lincoln would take office in fewer than two weeks, and his inaugural speech would be the new president's first public address since the crisis began. People across Rockingham, Augusta, and Rockbridge counties braced to see whether Lincoln would take a conciliatory stance in his speech that would calm the nation, or betray his intent to forcibly reclaim the seceded Lower South and thereby inaugurate a sectional war. "The gist and marrow of the question that now threatens to plunge our country into civil war, will be settled in a very short time," predicted Augusta's *Vindicator.* "It is whether the doctrine of *coercion* or *secession* is to be recognized by Lincoln's administration."[40]

Inaugurated with Federal sharpshooters scanning from surrounding rooftops for possible assassins, Abraham Lincoln took the oath of office and finally broke his silence on the issues that had enveloped the nation's attention for the last four months. Lincoln acknowledged Southern fears "that by the accession of a Republican Administration their property and their peace and personal security are to be endangered," but he tried to assure them that he had no intention of interfering with slavery in any of the states where it already existed. Lincoln maintained, however, that no state had the right to secede from the Federal Union, and he denied that the United States had been broken. He promised "to hold, occupy, and possess the property and places belonging to the government, and to collect the duties and imports" of the Federal government in the seceded states. Lincoln's message promised peace, but couched the promise in terms that sounded threatening to Southern ears. "In your hands, my dissatisfied fellow-countrymen, and not in mine, is the momentous issue of civil war," he warned. "The Government will not assail you. You can have no conflict without being yourselves the aggressors."[41]

Lincoln's speech cast a long shadow over the Valley. For many, his vow "to hold, occupy, and possess the property and places belonging to the Government" foretold a military approach to secession that shot fear into their hearts. Few in Rockingham, Augusta, or Rockbridge could find assurances of peace in a message promising that Republicans would directly challenge the sovereignty of the seceded states. The Lower South's new government had already espoused its willingness to defend Confederate independence, and many residents of the three counties believed that the Republicans were now purposefully moving the country toward civil war. The prospect of Republicans using the crisis as a pretext for marching Federal troops against the slaveholding South shook even the staunchest Valley Unionist.

For many, the fundamental threat to Virginia slavery had shifted north with Lincoln's speech. *"War has been declared against us of the South by Abraham Lincoln,"* screamed the *Rockingham Register.* The newspaper bristled at Lincoln's language, believing that a military clash between the Federal government and the seceded states would be soon in coming. The address had "realized the worst apprehensions of those who dreaded the inauguration of a Black Republican President," and the newspaper bemoaned that it had "hope no longer for a favorable result." Augusta's *Vindicator* took a similar line, predicting that "Lincoln will proceed, without delay, to adopt hostile measures against the South." For the *Vindicator,* the only question that remained was whether this would "grow out of an attempt to collect revenue at the South, to reinforce Forts Sumter and Pickens, or retake other places."[42] Neither paper made any attempt to distinguish Virginia from the seceded states, believing that all slave states were now in danger.

Augusta's other newspaper, the *Spectator,* tried to spin the peaceful message underlying Lincoln's address. "We cannot believe that any President would willingly involve the country in civil war," the paper reasoned. But even the *Spectator* was unsure that peace would be anywhere in Virginia's future, stating that no one could conclusively know the intentions of Lincoln until "the policy of the administration shall be more clearly indicated by its acts." In Rockbridge, the *Valley Star* tried to tread neutral ground, only offering the bland comment that "we fear there are squatty times ahead." But the newspaper's editor omitted Lincoln's pointed statement that there could be "no conflict" without Southerners being "the aggressors" when the paper reprinted his speech, belying the newspaper's outwardly calm response.[43]

Over the next few weeks, compromise measures continued to be discussed and discarded, with little hope remaining that they would resolve anything. The Rockbridge *Valley Star* reported the death of the Peace Conference compromise with a hint of the inevitable: "So ends that effort to adjust our difficulties." Virginia's state convention had yet to act in any concerted manner and most people had no expectation that that would change. In the weeks following Lincoln's address, the convention seemed bogged down in endless speechmaking rather than taking active steps to influence Virginia's course in the crisis. "The Convention has as yet come to no conclusion," reported a frustrated *Rockingham Register,* "and will probably come to none for a considerable time."[44]

The frustration in the counties toward the convention was not due to a lack of effort by their delegates. Since the convention began, representatives from the Valley had made numerous speeches in hopes of preventing Virginia's secession. Underlying every Valley delegate's argument was a preoccupation with the preservation of slavery in Virginia. Augusta's George Baylor asserted that Virginia's interest in its slaves and economy should be considered apart from those of the cotton South. "We have at least half a dozen Kings here," Baylor announced. "We have got King Wheat, King Corn, King Potatoes, King Tobacco, King Flax and King Hemp" and "when you put all these Kings together, they far over-ride King Cotton, with all the powers that he may possess." Samuel Moore of Rockbridge did not bother to bring economics into his defense of Virginia slavery. "I have been satisfied upon reflection that a greater blessing was never conferred, by kind Providence, upon any portion of the African slaves," he proclaimed, "than in establishing the institution of slavery as it exists in Virginia."[45]

When Augusta's John Baldwin took the floor of the convention three weeks after Lincoln's inaugural, he cut to the heart of the matter. "There is but one single subject of complaint which Virginia has to make against the government under which we live," he thundered, "a complaint made by the whole South, and that is on the subject of African slavery." For Baldwin, any threat to slavery—whether it came from Lincoln, secession, or another quarter—could not be tolerated. "As a Southern man, as a slaveholder in Virginia," Baldwin declared, "I never can consent that this great interest, this great institution of the South, shall be placed under the ban of government." While the Valley's delegates voiced their unbending support for slavery's future in Virginia, that did not translate into support for secession. Baldwin's fellow delegate from Augusta, Alexander H. H. Stuart, summed up the shared perspective of the Valley representatives. "In my opinion," he told the convention, "secession is not only war, but it is emancipation; it is bankruptcy; it is repudiation."[46]

The Virginia convention, however, failed to take any action. Indeed, by late March none of the options that had seemed so promising in November appeared to offer any more hope for the white residents of Rockingham, Augusta, and Rockbridge. Neither national nor border conferences had ever materialized. Political safeguards that would have checked threatening Republican ambition had dissolved with the secession of the Lower

South. The Valley's repeated calls for compromise measures had died at the hands of Republicans apparently too stubborn to yield anything for the good of the Union. Their final prayer had been for Lincoln to adopt a conciliatory and nonconfrontational approach in the crisis, thereby avoiding a military clash with the Lower South that would produce war. But Lincoln's speech made even that seem unlikely and added the specter of an invading Republican army. The Valley's particular geo-political interests in the crisis now appeared to be threatened by the very Union that once seemed their best protection. For the three counties, "everything has failed and the question now is shall we unite with the prosperous South— or shall we starve with the Northern Black Republicans?"[47]

In Rockbridge, the attitudes of the residents shifted away from Unionism faster than those of Lexington's *Valley Star,* which continued to argue against secession as April approached. On March 28, the owner of the newspaper—apparently under pressure from readers—ceased writing Unionist editorials and hired a new editor more in line with the shift in popular opinion that had occurred since Lincoln's speech. In his first editorial, William McCorkle announced the newspaper's changed perspective with a plain reference to slavery: "It is very plain to our mind that the interests of Virginia does not lay in the direction of the free States. The course of this paper in the future, therefore, will be in accordance with the interests of Va."[48] By late March, the newspaper had determined that Virginia's interest in slavery would best be protected outside of the Federal Union.

Rockingham and Augusta had experienced a similar change, and the county newspapers reflected the mood of the Valley. "There is but one way to prevent universal war and destruction too horrible to contemplate," argued Rockingham's *Register.* "And that one course is for Virginia and every border slave state, *at once* to unite with the States of the South." The paper reported the appearance in late March of a secession flag floating over the Exchange Hotel in Harrisonburg, "the work of a portion of *the gallant fair ladies of our town,* who are in favor of joining the Confederacy." In Augusta, the *Vindicator* had long ceased any arguments favoring the Federal Union and now urged its readers that "separation is our only safety." The benefits of Unionism had lost their luster for many in the three counties who believed that a powerful and aggressive Republican president meant that war was eminent, despite all their efforts to prevent it. "The golden hour, when all this train of horrors could have been avoided," concluded the *Vindicator,* "has been lost."[49]

A few still held out desperate hope that secession and war could be avoided. Rockbridge's *Lexington Gazette* reiterated its position that secession would mean the end of Virginia slavery. "Our opposition to Virginia's going into a Southern Confederacy, has been on account of the institution of slavery," the paper explained. "We are devoted to that institution." The newspaper still believed there was no surer way to destroy Virginia slavery than to abandon the protections of the Constitution and involve Virginia in a civil war. "We have believed from the first, that if the Southern States unite together in a Southern confederacy," the paper maintained, "slavery will be driven out of Virginia." But even the *Gazette* had become disillusioned with Lincoln and the Republicans, fearing that soon "we shall come to the conclusion that separation is inevitable."[50]

The other holdout, Augusta's *Spectator*, agreed. "Nothing that has occurred," the paper argued, "has served to change or even shake the conviction, that we have interests in the Union which are paramount—interests that the Cotton States have not." The *Spectator* still believed that secession was the surest road to slavery's extinction in the Valley, and the paper continued to hold out desperate hope for a peaceful end to the crisis. But that position no longer held for most in Rockingham, Rockbridge, or even Augusta. By early April, most in the Valley would have agreed with the *Vindicator*'s gloomy pronouncement: "We pray we may be mistaken, but we do not see a hope—a ray of light—a straw to grasp at."[51]

The Valley region still disapproved of the Lower South's sectional approach to the 1860 presidential election. It still believed the secession of South Carolina with six other Gulf-Coast states had been rash and imprudent. But by early April 1861, the Valley had also come to believe that their slave-based economy could not coexist with a Republican president willing to wage war on slaveholders. For Rockingham, Augusta, and Rockbridge it had become clear that Lincoln would force a war by provoking the Lower South, and Valley newspapers began to fill with calls for militias to be formed in defense of the state.

The clash that Valley residents had been bracing for came in the predawn of April 12, 1861. Confederate general P. G. T. Beauregard ordered his men to fire on Fort Sumter in response to Lincoln's attempt to resupply the fort's beleaguered Federal troops, inaugurating the American Civil War. In the immediate aftermath, Rockingham, Augusta, and Rockbridge embraced statewide calls for secession, and meetings sprang up in each county, where "an overwhelming majority declared enthusiastically in favor of immediate Secession." Any timidity about secession had long since passed, as people of the Valley showed their fervent support for the new Southern Confederacy. "Another large and imposing secession flag now floats from atop of the Exchange Hotel," the Rockingham newspaper proudly reported. Below them in Rockbridge, the stars and stripes had been removed from the Lexington courthouse and replaced with a secession flag, "amid the cheers of the assembled multitude."[52]

There had been nothing short of a revolution in the sentiment of Rockingham, Augusta, and Rockbridge since November 1860. Decades of partisan rancor had dissolved over a period of five and a half months as the counties united in defense of their particular geographic and economic interests in protecting Virginia slavery. In the wake of Lincoln's election, each county had fought zealously to prevent the secession of the Lower South from dislodging Virginia, believing their homes, property, and rights would be protected by a united nation but destroyed by a sectional war. Yet throughout the secession winter those safeguards had been lost and the Union had been sundered. Every state that seceded left Virginia increasingly at the mercy of the incoming Republican administration; every compromise measure that failed demonstrated to the Valley that Republicans could not be trusted. By late March, the Valley had come to believe that Unionism was now Virginia's greatest threat and secession their only recourse.

The political transformation within the three counties had been extraordinary. Nearly every past election had divided Rockingham, Augusta, and Rockbridge along deeply entrenched party lines. But the presidential contest of 1860 and the crisis that followed it had produced an entirely new political climate within the Valley. The Valley had not embraced Unionism at the start of the crisis out of an ingrained faith in the second party system or out of a loss of faith in slavery, as some historians have claimed, but out of self-interest and dedication to the endurance of Virginia slavery. As one Augusta newspaper observed, "everything like old party lines was obliterated" by the time of the February elections for state convention delegates.[53] For the people of Rockingham, Augusta, and Rockbridge, political options had come to be judged not on the basis of tired party rhetoric, but on the ability of those options to preserve the basic pillars of their lives.

Indeed, if anything characterized the Valley during the crisis it was the cautious nature with which the counties approached their political choices. No single event jarred the Valley into secession. They chose first to embrace the Union, and then later to reject it, only after careful calculation. Taken separately, the secession of the Lower South, the failure of any conference to materialize, the Republican rejection of compromise proposals, or Lincoln's inaugural promise to challenge the Lower South would not have dislodged the three counties from their commitment to the Union. But taken together, the Valley counties came to believe they could not ignore the growing dangers of a Republican presidency. The shelling of Fort Sumter and Lincoln's call for troops did not shock Valley residents; it merely validated what they had already come to believe. Though it eventually destroyed everything they had hoped to save, the Valley's zealous desire to protect their investment in slavery had produced its own logic. For Rockingham, Augusta, and Rockbridge, slavery was placed above both partisanship and the Union.

In the last weeks before the firing on Fort Sumter, only Augusta's *Spectator* and Rockbridge's *Gazette* had maintained any hope that a peaceful solution was still possible. The clash at Sumter, however, convinced even them that life with Republicans would be intolerable, allowing the newspapers to join the secession consensus that predominated the three counties. Within weeks, J. S. McNutt, editor of the *Lexington Gazette*, declared himself a candidate for the Confederate Virginia legislature.[54] The *Spectator* greeted secession with the enthusiasm of a new convert, prompting the paper to predict in late April: "This county, we have no doubt, will send more [Confederate] soldiers to the field than any county in the State, though Rockingham and Rockbridge will nobly do their duty. These three counties, we venture to predict, will furnish more soldiers than any other three adjoining counties in the State."[55]

For the Valley, there was no more need for talk of saving the Federal Union; they saw nothing left for Virginians in a pact that tied them to Republican whims. Secession was not what voters in the Valley wanted, but they believed they had been given no other choice. For Rockingham, Augusta, and Rockbridge, the time had come to unite with the Lower South and face the Republicans with a unified and common front. "Let all stand together," shouted the *Spectator*. "We are still for Union—a Union of brave and patriotic men for the defence of our State."[56]

Notes

I would like to thank Ed Ayers, Gary Gallagher, and Alexandra Torget for their careful and insightful readings of earlier drafts of this essay. Tom Torget, Vanessa May, Calvin Schermerhorn, and Erik Alexander also gave valuable advice on revising and sharpening the arguments.

1. Michael P. Johnson, ed., *Abraham Lincoln, Slavery, and the Civil War: Selected Writings and Speeches* (Boston: Bedford/St. Martin's, 2001), 126, 129.

2. William Freehling, *The South vs. The South: How Anti-Confederate Southerners Shaped the Course of the Civil War* (New York: Oxford University Press, 2001), 42. Freehling is the most vocal proponent of this perspective on Virginia's secession, stressing the role that the steady "draining" of slaves out of Virginia to fill the labor needs of plantations in the Lower South states played in Virginia's approach to the secession crisis. The steady decrease in the percentage of slaves relative to the white population, Freehling argues, made the long-term endurance of the institution less important to Virginians by 1860 than it was for Lower South states, producing a Virginia that was less willing to take extreme measures—such as secession—to protect the institution than places like South Carolina or Mississippi.

3. See Michael Holt, *The Political Crisis of the 1850s* (New York: W. W. Norton, 1978), and Daniel Crofts, *Reluctant Confederates: Upper South Unionists in the Secession Crisis* (Chapel Hill: University of North Carolina Press, 1989). Holt is the leading proponent of the political perspective on Virginia's secession, arguing that slavery was far from the primary catalyst in the secession crisis. Holt asserts that the breakdown of the second party system in American politics dissolved the Lower South's faith in the political system, prompting the region to secede upon Lincoln's election. In Virginia and other Upper South states, however, Holt argues, two-party politics remained in place as late as 1861—albeit in beleaguered form—and prevented the border states from seceding with the Lower South. Daniel Crofts takes a similar line. Concentrating on the plight of conditional Unionists during the secession crisis, Crofts attributes Virginia's resilience against secession to the continued presence of two-party politics within the border states. On the second party system in Virginia, see William Shade, *Democratizing the Old Dominion: Virginia and the Second Party System, 1824–1861* (Charlottesville: University Press of Virginia, 1996).

4. The Valley of Virginia consisted of many more counties, most of which lay to the north of Rockingham, Augusta, and Rockbridge. This essay, however, concentrates on Rockingham, Augusta, and Rockbridge as representatives of the diversity of the Valley. Each of the three counties differed in political affiliation, population densities, and the amount of manufacturing in their local economies. Thus while all references to the Valley in this essay refer specifically to Rockingham, Augusta, and Rockbridge, their experiences suggest processes that were likely also at work in the northern Valley counties.

5. *Staunton Spectator*, February 12, 1861, page 2, column 2. All quotations retain their original grammar and spelling, unless bracketed for clarity. All quotations from the *Staunton Spectator* and the *Staunton Vindicator* are taken from the online archive *The Valley of the Shadow: Two Communities in the American Civil War*, http://valley.vcdh.virginia.edu.

6. All county vote totals for 1856 in this and the following two paragraphs are from the *Richmond Enquirer,* November 18, 1856, page 2, column 2. All county vote totals for 1859 are from the *Richmond Enquirer,* June 14, 1859, page 2, column 2. For Rockingham, Augusta, and Rockbridge's historical voting patterns, see William Shade, *Democratizing the Old Dominion,* 138–42. Shade attributes the historical political differences between the counties to the different ethnic groups that originally settled each county: Rockingham was dominated by Germans; Augusta by the Scotch-Irish; and Rockbridge by a mix of Scotch-Irish, English, and Welsh.

7. *Valley Democrat,* October 19, 1860, page 2, column 1; *Rockingham Register and Advertiser,* October 12, 1860, page 2, column 1. During the nineteenth century, state and local elections were often held earlier in the year than the national elections and were carefully observed as indicators of how well the national candidates would fare in November.

8. *Staunton Spectator,* October 23, 1860, page 2, column 4; *Valley Democrat,* November 2, 1860, page 2, column 1.

9. *Valley Democrat,* November 2, 1860, page 2, column 1 (emphasis is the *Valley Democrat's*).

10. Inter-university Consortium for Political and Social Research, "Historical, Demographic, Economic, and Social Data: The United States, 1790–1970," http://fisher.lib.virginia.edu/census, accessed May 19, 2004. All census statistics for 1860 taken from the Inter-university Consortium for Political and Social Research study based on the U.S. decennial censuses.

11. The capital invested in slaves for each county was calculated by multiplying the aggregate number of slaves by the average slave price in 1860 of $1,200: Rockingham, $2,864,400; Augusta, $6,739,200; Rockbridge, $4,782,000.

12. *Lexington Gazette,* November 1, 1860, page 2, column 1; *Valley Democrat,* November 2, 1860, page 2, column 2; *Valley Star,* October 25, 1860, page 2, column 1.

13. The 1860 vote totals for Rockingham, Augusta, and Rockbridge in this and the following two paragraphs are from the *Rockingham Register and Advertiser,* November 16, 1860, page 2, column 2.

14. *Lexington Gazette,* November 8, 1860, page 2, column 2.

15. *Valley Star,* November 15, 1860, page 2, column 1 (emphasis is the *Valley Star's*).

16. Breckinridge garnered almost as many votes in Virginia as Bell, even winning some counties in the northern part of the Shenandoah Valley. Whereas the residents in Rockingham, Augusta, and Rockbridge hoped to send a message to the Lower South with a strong showing for Union candidates in the counties, it seems that Virginians who voted for Breckinridge were trying to send a similar message of warning to Abraham Lincoln rather than endorsing the possible secession of Virginia from the Union. Indeed, the widespread support for Unionist

candidates in the February 1861 election for delegates to the Virginia state convention suggests that the support Breckinridge enjoyed in November 1860 was not indicative of support for Virginia's secession upon Lincoln's election. In both cases, Virginians attempted to preempt threats to Virginia slavery by sending a political message to those whom they considered to be the greatest threat to slavery in the state, hoping to prevent a crisis that could force Virginia to leave the Union.

17. *Valley Star,* November 29, 1860, page 2, column 1.

18. *Staunton Vindicator,* November 16, 1860, page 2, column 3; *Rockingham Register and Advertiser,* November 9, 1860, page 2, column 2; *Valley Star,* November 29, 1860, page 2, column 1.

19. *Staunton Spectator,* November 13, 1860, page 2, column 1.

20. Ibid.

21. *Valley Democrat,* December 21, 1860, page 2, column 2.

22. *Lexington Gazette,* December 5, 1861, page 2, column 1.

23. *Valley Star,* December 6, 1860, page 2, columns 1, 2.

24. *Valley Democrat,* December 21, 1860, page 2, column 1; *Staunton Vindicator,* November 23, 1860, page 2, column 2 (emphasis is the *Vindicator's*).

25. *Valley Democrat,* December 21, 1860, page 2, column 1.

26. *Rockingham Register and Advertiser,* December 28, 1860, page 1, column 6.

27. *Rockingham Register and Advertiser,* January 4, 1861, page 2, column 2.

28. "C" to *Rockingham Register and Advertiser,* January 4, 1861, page 2, column 3; *Rockingham Register and Advertiser,* January 4, 1861, page 2, column 4.

29. "A" to *Staunton Spectator,* January 22, 1861, page 1, column 5.

30. *Rockingham Register and Advertiser,* January 4, 1861, page 2, column 1; *Valley Star,* January 3, 1861, page 2, column 1.

31. Robert Bowman to *Rockingham Register and Advertiser,* January 25, 1861, page 2, column 2; Samuel Coffman to *Rockingham Register and Advertiser,* January 25, 1861, page 2, column 5; John F. Lewis to *Rockingham Register and Advertiser,* January 25, 1861, page 2, column 5.

32. Interestingly, the percentage of slaves in each county corresponded to the percentage of votes in favor of Unionist candidates, with the higher percentage of slaves in the county corresponding to higher votes in favor of Unionists.

33. *Rockingham Register and Advertiser,* February 8, 1861, page 2, column 1 (emphasis is the *Register's*).

34. The county returns in favor of reference were 80 percent in Rockingham, 93 percent in Augusta, and 90 percent in Rockbridge.

35. *Staunton Spectator,* February 12, 1861, page 2, column 2.

36. *Rockingham Register and Advertiser,* February 8, 1861, page 2, column 1; George Baylor, February 28, 1861, quoted in George Reese, ed., *Proceedings of the Virginia State Convention of 1861, February 13–May 1,* 4 vols. (Richmond: Virginia State Library, 1965), 1:272.

37. *Lexington Gazette,* February 7, 1861, page 2, column 2; John F. Lewis to *Rockingham Register and Advertiser,* January 25, 1861, page 2, column 5.

38. "Augusta" to *Staunton Vindicator,* February 8, 1861, page 2, column 7.

39. Crofts, *Reluctant Confederates,* 199; *Staunton Vindicator,* February 8, 1861, page 2, column 2.

40. *Staunton Vindicator,* March 1, 1861, page 2, column 4 (emphasis is the *Vindicator's*).

41. *Lexington Gazette,* March 7, 1861, page 2, column 2; *Valley Star,* March 14, 1861, page 1, column 1; *Valley Star,* March 14, 1861, page 1, column 2; *Staunton Vindicator,* March 8, 1861, page 3, column 1.

42. *Rockingham Register and Advertiser,* March 8, 1861, page 2, column 1 (emphasis is the *Register's*); *Staunton Vindicator,* March 15, 1861, page 1, column 3. Rockingham's other newspaper, the *Valley Democrat,* had been absorbed by the *Register* during February and its editor now worked for the *Register* as a correspondent at the Virginia state convention.

43. *Staunton Spectator,* March 12, 1861, page 2, column 3; *Valley Star,* March 7, 1861, page 2, column 6; *Valley Star,* March 14, 1861, page 1, column 4.

44. *Valley Star,* March 7, 1861, page 2, column 1; *Rockingham Register and Advertiser,* March 29, 1861, page 2, column 2.

45. George Baylor, March 1, 1861, quoted in Reese, ed., *Proceedings of the Virginia State Convention of 1861,* 1:289; Samuel Moore, March 1, 1861, quoted in Reese, ed., *Proceedings of the Virginia State Convention of 1861,* 1:278.

46. John Baldwin, March 21, 1861, quoted in Reese, ed., *Proceedings of the Virginia State Convention of 1861,* 2:139; John Baldwin, March 23, 1861, quoted in Reese, ed., *Proceedings of the Virginia State Convention of 1861,* 2:216; Alexander H. H. Stuart, April 16, 1861, quoted in Reese, ed., *Proceedings of the Virginia State Convention of 1861,* 4:16.

47. *Valley Star,* March 28, 1861, page 2, column 1.

48. Ibid., page 2, column 2. The owner of the *Valley Star,* Samuel Gillock, had acted as the newspaper's editor during the entire crisis until late March. No reason for hiring a new editor was given in the newspaper, but the abrupt shift in editorial style and the fact that Gillock remained the proprietor of the paper strongly suggests that the new editor, William McCorkle, was hired to appease readers who no longer agreed with Gillock's Unionism. Most likely, Gillock made the change in order to appease the base of subscribers and advertisers who allowed the newspaper to remain profitable

49. *Rockingham Register and Advertiser,* March 8, 1861, page 2, column 1 (emphasis is the *Register's*); *Rockingham Register and Advertiser,* quoted in John Wayland, *A History of Rockingham County, Virginia* (Dayton, Va.: Ruebush-Elkins Company, 1912), 132–33 (emphasis in the original); *Staunton Vindicator,* April 5, 1861, page 2, column 5; *Staunton Vindicator,* April 12, 1861, page 2, column 2.

50. *Lexington Gazette,* March 7, 1861, page 2, column 1; *Lexington Gazette,* March 14, 1861, page 2, column 2.

51. *Staunton Spectator,* April 2, 1861, page 1, column 6; *Staunton Vindicator,* April 12, 1861, page 2, column 2.

52. *Rockingham Register and Advertiser,* April 19, 1861, page 2, column 2, and page 2, column 1; *Valley Star,* April 18, 1861, page 2, column 2.

53. *Staunton Vindicator,* February 22, 1861, page 2, column 1.

54. *Lexington Gazette,* May 9, 1861, page 2, column 1.

55. *Staunton Spectator,* April 23, 1861, page 2, column 1.

56. Ibid.

"I Owe Virginia Little, My Country Much"

Robert E. Lee, the United States Regular Army,
and Unconditional Unionism

Wayne Wei-siang Hsieh

Douglas Southall Freeman, perhaps Robert E. Lee's greatest biographer, has called Lee's decision to wage war against the Federal flag he had so faithfully served before the Civil War the "Answer He Was Born to Make." Freeman's biography remains a monumental work of scholarship, and popular perceptions of Lee's secession rarely deviate from Freeman's unquestioning acceptance of Lee's decision. For example, on January 19, 1907, Charles Francis Adams, son of the wartime American minister to England and himself a former officer in the Army of the Potomac, delivered to Washington and Lee University an address marking the centennial of Lee's birth that absolved Lee of the charge of treason, for "I do not see how I, placed as he was placed, could have done otherwise."[1] Lee's presumably guiltless course also excuses by extension all of the serving and retired U.S. Army officers who drew their swords for the Confederate banner. Nevertheless, from the perspective of the U.S. government, Lee's resignation from its service and immediate commission in the army of a hostile government can only be described as treasonous. Although Freeman and Adams cited Lee's Virginia loyalties as reason enough for his conduct, many other Virginians with regular army backgrounds stayed loyal to the government that they had all at one point or another sworn to serve. These Unionist officers raise important questions about whether or not we can cite regional origin to explain and, at times, to justify an individual's conduct during the secession crisis. After all, many of these men experienced the same personal and regional pressures to secede that Lee experienced, but they chose familial estrangement and regional ostracism for the sake of the uniform that Robert E. Lee repudiated.[2]

Lee, after all, had held a colonel's commission in the U.S. Army at the time of Virginia's secession and had received an excellent education at West Point at government expense. Indeed, Lee owed much of his well-deserved prominence to a military career supported by the U.S. government. Perhaps constitutional ideas about state's rights or loyalties due to the Old Dominion justify Lee's course in the final analysis, but surely the question requires more serious consideration than it has received.

Forty-four out of 126, or a little over a third, of living regular army "Virginians"—defined as West Point graduates who were born in Virginia or who claimed the state as either their place of appointment or residence on admission to the academy—chose to actively affirm their loyalty to Union over state in the midst of the Civil War. To use another measure of Unionist sentiment, twelve of eighteen (67 percent) Union generals born in the Old Dominion (including what later became West Virginia) were former regular army men, and out of those twelve, ten had graduated from the U.S. Military Academy at West Point. A far higher percentage of Union generals from Virginia had regular army backgrounds than did Union generals as a whole (44 percent of all Union generals had held commissions as regular army officers). Four of the remaining six Union generals from Virginia without regular army experience had served as volunteers during the Mexican War, in which regulars had served as the core cadres of the American armies. These figures impress all the more in light of the widespread willingness of other former officials of the Federal government to support secession.[3] The antebellum regular army exerted a powerful nationalizing influence on its members that was duplicated in no civilian institution.[4]

The U.S. Military Academy can serve as a rough proxy for the regular army's officer corps due to both its institutional prominence in the U.S. Army and the substantial biographical data available on West Pointers. West Point had established a strong institutional dominance within the regular army's officer corps beginning in the 1820s, and academy graduates held about 75 percent of regular army commissions in 1860. Furthermore, Academy-trained officers also tended to be more strongly Unionist: of Southern-born West Pointers in the service at the time of secession, 162 stayed with the Union and 168 joined the Confederacy, while of serving

West Pointers' behavior in the secession winter

	Union	Confederate	Resigned	Stayed out	Total
Virginia	44 (35%)	70 (56%)	3 (2%)	10 (8%)	126
All slave-state residents	173 (36%)	251 (52%)	10 (2%)	57 (12%)	487
Upper South residents	159 (43%)	162 (44%)	9 (2%)	40 (11%)	366
Lower South residents	14 (12%)	89 (74%)	1 (1%)	17 (14%)	121
Unionist state residents	113 (60%)	51 (27%)	5 (3%)	21 (11%)	187
Confederate state residents	60 (20%)	200 (67%)	5 (2%)	36 (12%)	300

This table indicates how West Pointers of different regional backgrounds behaved during the secession winter—whether or not they continued their allegiance to the Federal Union, joined the Confederacy, resigned to avoid the conflict, or continued their inactive military status (for those graduates who had left the army before the secession winter).

Upper South is defined as: Arkansas, Delaware, Kentucky, Maryland, Missouri, North Carolina, Tennessee, Virginia, and Washington, D.C.

Lower South is defined as: Alabama, Florida, Georgia, Louisiana, Mississippi, South Carolina, and Texas.

Union is defined as those slave states (including the District of Columbia) that stayed in the Union: Delaware, Kentucky, Maryland, Missouri, and Washington, D.C.

Confederate is defined as those slave states that joined the Confederacy: Alabama, Arkansas, Florida, Georgia, Louisiana, Mississippi, North Carolina, South Carolina, Tennessee, Texas, and Virginia.

Please see note 4 for a fuller account of how the figures in this table were derived.

Southern officers appointed directly from civil life, only one stayed loyal to the Union and 129 joined the Confederacy.[5]

The regular army Virginians who chose Union over state were not anonymous never-do-wells, free from the distinguished Old Dominion heritage of Marse Robert that has made his decision so obvious and pre-determined to many historians. It was, after all, Winfield Scott—a fellow Virginian and the finest American field commander until the Civil War—who had hoped during the secession crisis that Lee would take a high position in the Union army.[6] And it was George Henry Thomas of Southampton, generally ranked by historians as the fourth-most prominent Union general, who played a key role in preventing the Union defeat at Chickamauga in September 1863 from becoming an outright rout and who presided over the destruction of the Confederate Army of Tennessee in the winter of 1864.[7] Most importantly for our purposes, both Thomas and Scott, in addition to Philip St. George Cooke, another prominent Virginian who stayed with the Union, have left historians enough evidence of their Unionism to show that Robert E. Lee's decision to secede was not carved in stone upon his birth.[8]

Thomas, like Lee, showed some hesitation during the secession winter, but he chose the Federal Union over the Old Dominion. Like Lee, Thomas had a distinguished career in the Mexican War, earning two brevet promotions to captain and major for gallantry at Monterey and Buena Vista. In the fall of 1860, he served in Texas with Lee, where Thomas, himself a slave-holder, probably expressed pro-Southern sentiments in the wake of John Brown's failed raid and the upcoming presidential election. He left Texas on a leave of absence that began on November 12, and while on his way east, he severely injured his back in a train accident.[9]

While convalescing from his back injury, and with Virginia's fate regarding the Union seeming doubtful, Thomas contemplated resigning from the army and applied for an instructor's position at the Virginia Military Institute. In March, with his back improving, Governor John Letcher of Virginia offered Thomas the position of Chief of Ordnance for Virginia. The commonwealth had not yet seceded, and Thomas refused the appointment, writing "that it is not my wish to leave the service of the United States as long as it is honorable for me to remain in it, and, therefore, as long as my native state remains in the union, it is my purpose to remain in the army, unless required to perform duties alike repulsive to honor and humanity." Thomas's statement was hardly an affirmation of unconditional Unionism, and at that point he seems to have left his options open.[10]

Nevertheless, when Thomas found himself faced with the painful prospect of irrevocable decision, he chose the old Union over the new Confederacy. On April 4, Virginia still affirmed its opposition to secession, and on April 6, Thomas willingly returned to active service long before his leave's original date of expiration and despite continued problems with his back. On the way to Carlisle Barracks in Pennsylvania to meet his regiment, Thomas received word of the firing on Sumter. In Carlisle, he voluntarily reaffirmed his oath of allegiance to the United States before a magistrate. After the Virginia convention passed an ordinance of secession, Thomas also sent word to his wife and sisters of his decision to stay with the Union.[11] He cast his die and never seems to have regretted it in either word or deed.

Indeed, after the war, Thomas B. Van Horne recorded a conversation in which Thomas "said there was no excuse whatever in a United States officer claiming the right of secession, and the only excuse for their deserting the government was what none of them admitted, having engaged in—a revolution against a tyranny, because the tyranny did not exist, and they well knew it.'"[12] Van Horne also plausibly claims that Thomas "believed that there was a moral and legal obligation which forbade resignation, with a view to take up arms against the Government," and even "condemned the National authorities for accepting the resignation of officers, when aware that it was their intention to join the rebellion as soon as they were in this way freed from the obligation of their oath of allegiance." For whatever reason, Thomas never uttered these words in public, and his only public reference to his decision to stay loyal referred to the gratitude he felt to the Federal government for a free West Point education. Nevertheless, toward the end of the war, in March 1865, he was willing to write these harsh words on the Confederacy as a whole: "Their cause was cursed in the beginning but their infatuation has led them on in their suicidal course until they now see nothing before them but disgrace & infamy. God grant that our land may be [illegible word] freed from the likes of them."[13]

Thomas was no Republican, however. After the war, George L. Hartsuff, a West Pointer from New York and future Union major general who conversed with Thomas in late 1860, claimed that "General Thomas was strong and bitter in his denunciations against all parties North and South that seemed to him responsible for the condition of affairs. . . . But while he reprobated very strongly, certain men and parties North, in that respect going as far as any of those who afterward joined the rebels, he never in my hearing, agreed with them respecting the necessity of going with their States; but he denounced the idea, and denied the necessity of dividing the country, or destroying the Government." Such sentiments square well with the characteristically conservative Unionism of most regular army officers.[14]

Furthermore, Thomas did not totally renounce his Southern identity during the war. Even toward the end of the conflict, he still spoke fondly of his service in the Lower South. In a letter to a fellow Unionist, he wrote: "I often think of the pleasant time we had at New Orleans Bks where I was always so cordially welcomed at your house, also of Fort Moultrie where the who[le] garrison lived on as cordial and friendly terms as the members of a family, and where we also had so many sincere friends as I thought among the inhabitants of Charleston and [the] neighboring country. I often wonder what has become of them." Thomas even waxed nostalgic with that other notorious Southern sympathizer, William Tecumseh Sherman, and reported that he and Sherman "have frequently talked over our pleasant and happy tour of service on Sullivan's Island & I find he looks back to those happy days with as much pleasure as I do." Both Sherman and Thomas, Ohioan and Virginian, were political conservatives; both had Southern sympathies; and both had acquired an absolutely inflexible Unionism in the antebellum regular army.[15]

Thomas's decision to stay with the Union did not have exclusive origins in ideological considerations. Thomas was, after all, married to a Northern woman he had met while serving as an instructor at West Point in the early 1850s. Although Frances Kellogg Thomas claimed after the war that her husband had independently chosen Union over state, her Northern background probably had some effect. Due to his regular army obligations, moreover, Thomas had also spent fewer than eighteen months at home in the quarter century before the Civil War, which probably affected whatever affective bonds he once held for his native state and county.[16]

Thomas still had much family in Virginia, however, and the residents of Southampton County still saw Thomas as one of their own when they presented him a ceremonial sword in 1848 for his service in the Mexican War. The harsh reaction of Thomas's sisters in Southampton to their brother's Unionism in 1861 certainly implies an expectation among his kinfolk that he would follow the Old Dominion. Southampton legend contains many stories of familial wrath: the demand that Thomas change his name; the symbolic rebuke of turning the errant brother's portrait to the wall in the ancestral home; the refusal of his sisters to even acknowledge Thomas's existence when Union officers brought aid out of courtesy to their comrade-in-arms; and a few other colorful if sad anecdotes.[17] Thomas's brother, Benjamin, reconciled, but he was the exception, and there is no record of any member of Thomas's blood relations being present at his military funeral in 1870.[18] Many former Confederate officers also seemed to reveal an earlier expectation that Thomas would secede when they claimed after the war that he had openly declared his intention to join the Confederate cause before he reversed himself.[19]

Other anecdotal evidence supports the assertion that regular army Virginians who stayed with the Union incurred real personal costs. William Rufus Terrill, West Point Class of 1853 and a brigade commander killed at the battle of Perryville in Kentucky, saw his brother James Barbour join the Confederate service. Family tradition has it that William discussed the issue with his father and resolved to stay with the Union as long as he did not have to serve in Virginia, and Terrill did spend most of his career in the Western theater.[20] His father declared, however, "Do so, and your name shall be stricken from the family record, and only remembered in connection with your treachery to the country that gave you birth."[21]

Philip St. George Cooke, the antebellum regular army's leading authority on cavalry, may have carried a burden of familial estrangement even more severe than Thomas's and Terrill's. James Ewell Brown Stuart, husband of the elder Cooke's daughter, Flora, took such offense at his father-in-law's Unionism that he changed the name of his son, Philip St. George Cooke Stuart, to James Ewell Brown Stuart Jr. Stuart wrote his wife, "Be consoled . . . by the reflection that your husband & brothers will atone for the father's conduct." Stuart referred to the fact that John Rogers Cooke, Philip St. George Cooke's son and a regular army officer (although not a West Pointer), had joined the Confederate cause along with both of Cooke's sons-in-law (Stuart himself and Charles Brewer, a former regular army surgeon). Only one of the Cooke children, Julia Turner Cooke, did not become estranged; she married Jacob Sharpe, an officer in a New York volunteer regiment during the war. The war's conclusion did not end the estrangement; only Cooke's nephew, John Esten Cooke, a novelist and writer of some note, proved willing to reconcile himself to the old soldier.[22]

Cooke, unlike Thomas and Lee, never wavered during the sectional crisis. He had been stationed in Utah during the secession winter, and he changed the name of his post from Camp Floyd (named after the ardently pro-Southern secretary of war John B. Floyd) to Fort Crittenden, in honor of the old Kentucky senator who was trying to iron out a sectional compromise. When he heard of the resignations of his son and two sons-in-law in Missouri, Cooke is reported to have exclaimed, "Those mad boys! If I only had been here!" When he found his own loyalty questioned, Cooke mournfully wrote Washington on June 17, 1861: "Instead of sympathizing with the unhappiness of my family disunion, they taunt and impute it as a crime! The Department, I doubt not, knew of the acts of my far distant, long absent, unhappy sons . . . But I dismiss the subject—with loathing."[23] Eleven days earlier, Cooke had also written a public letter to the *National Intelligencer* in Washington declaring his true loyalties.

Indeed, Cooke even disclaimed any strong bonds to Virginia in that letter: "At fourteen years of age I was severed from Virginia; the National Government adopted me as its pupil and future defender; it gave me education and a profession, and I then made a solemn oath to bear true allegiance to the United States of America, and to 'serve them honestly and faithfully against all their enemies or opposers whatsoever.' This oath and honor alike forbid me to abandon their standard at the first hour of danger." Cooke claimed he was now a man of the West, unsurprising in light of his decades of service on the frontier. Taking a conservative Unionist position, Cooke wrathfully denounced the conduct of Southern extremists, with special invective against South Carolina. He also chided Northern actions, though with much less heat, and did not totally disavow his bonds with Virginia. Cooke admitted that "if I had been on the ground I might have felt tempted to shoulder a musket in defence of the mother of *dead* statesmen, 'right or wrong,'" but he finally declared, "I owe Virginia little, my country much."[24]

Lee's image as the quintessential gentleman bound by honor and duty carries in it more than a kernel of truth, but General Lee held no monopoly on virtue in the Old Dominion. Philip St. George Cooke had graduated from West Point in 1827 and had as fine a reputation as any other officer in the regular army. In a volume of memoirs published in 1857, Cooke gave an almost mystical description of his calling to the colors as a young officer: while standing on a flatboat, "The scabbard of my sword (fastened to the belt by a ring) unaccountably became detached, and fell into the river and disappeared, leaving the blade still more strangely suspended: it was an omen. Thenceforth I was devoted to the service of the Republic." Other Regulars would not have shared Cooke's romantic sensibility, but most would have shared Cooke's self-image as a disinterested and responsible guardian of legitimate national authority. Indeed, during the Kansas crisis before the Civil War, Cooke had served as a fairly impartial Regular who attempted to suppress sectional violence. Ten years after Appomattox, Cooke looked back on a potentially violent sectional confrontation in Kansas and reminisced: "It was part of the education of both parties that they still respected national authority. There was one flag yet! At Lecompton I rode alone—leaving my forces far behind—in front of an army of thousands, which, with cannon-matches lighted, were about to attack the territorial capitol, and ordered them to retire, and the nation's representative was obeyed!"[25]

Winfield Scott, another old soldier from Virginia, also believed that the Union colors deserved compulsory obedience. Like Cooke, he mixed unconditional Unionism with a conservative political attitude that emphasized the orderly and nonviolent resolution of sectional conflicts. In the fall of 1860 Scott called for a policy of measured restraint. He wrote Secretary of War Floyd a letter in October in which he affirmed the right of a state to secede *and* the right of the Federal government to force it back into the Union. Scott also seemed to assume the loyalty of the Federal army, believing that that loyalty combined with a firm but moderate administration policy would head off secession.[26] Scott was clearly trying to steer a middle course, but as events would show, his loyalties to the Union remained preeminent.

Scott was not so conciliatory when he heard rumors that Southerners would try to disrupt the Electoral College balloting on February 13, 1861, declaring that anyone interfering "should be lashed to the muzzle of a twelve-pounder gun and fired out of a window of the capitol. . . . It is my duty to suppress insurrection—*my duty!*" Scott throughout the secession winter strengthened some Federal posts in the South, took various other precautions, and in March carefully guarded Lincoln's inauguration. He cited Jackson's reinforcement of the Charleston garrison during the Nullification Crisis in 1833 to try to persuade President James Buchanan to reinforce Charleston's Fort Moultrie in December 1860. Scott also heartily approved of Major Robert Anderson's bold withdrawal of his Charleston garrison to the more secure Fort Sumter in late December 1860.[27]

Scott was still no abolitionist, however. His conservative attitudes toward secession could be summed up by what he claimed in his memoirs (written during the Civil War) to have told his soldiers during the Nullification Crisis: "These nullifiers . . . have, no doubt, become exceedingly wrong-headed, and are in the road to treason; but still they are our countrymen, and may be saved from that great crime by respect and kindness on our part. We must keep our bosoms open to receive them back as brothers in the Union." He advised Lincoln in late March 1861 to abandon both Fort Sumter in Charleston and Fort Pickens in Florida as a sign of conciliation toward the South.

Lincoln resolved instead to reinforce Sumter in April after word reached Washington that Fort Pickens's reinforcement had miscarried due to a garbled order, leaving Sumter as the only remaining Federal post that could be reinforced.[28] Scott acquiesced to his commander-in-chief's policy and participated in early Union war planning. When Lee refused the Federal field command, Scott told him, "you have made the greatest mistake of your life; but I feared it would be so." The loyal Virginian held his position as General-in-Chief until a brief power struggle with George B. McClellan forced him to resign on October 31 at the age of seventy-five, ending a military career that had begun before the War of 1812.[29]

Cooke, Thomas, and Scott stood in stark contrast to, and even waged war against, Robert E. Lee. Like those Virginians who stayed with the Federal service, Lee strongly opposed secession. On January 23, 1861, he wrote, "The framers of our Constitution never exhausted so much labor, wisdom and forbearance in its formation, and surrounded it with so many guards and securities, if it was intended to be broken by every member of the Confederacy at will. . . . It is idle to talk of secession. Anarchy would have been established, and not a government, by Washington, Hamilton, Jefferson, Madison, and the other patriots of the Revolution." Unlike his former comrades-in-arms, however, there were limits to Lee's Unionism; the previous day, he wrote to Martha Custis Williams, "there is no sacrifice I am not ready to make for the preservation of the Union save that of honour."[30] For Lee, of course, honor demanded that he stay with the Old Dominion above all else.

But what of Philip St. George Cooke's honor? Cooke had cited both his oath to the United States to "serve them honestly and faithfully against all their enemies or opposers whatsoever" and his honor as the touchstone of his decision to stay with the Union. Historian Alan Nolan has pointed out that Lee had taken the same oath, which makes no provision for state's rights or loyalties to the Old Dominion, no matter how strongly felt.[31] George Thomas, like Lee, had also qualified his loyalties with a reference to honor, but he clearly decided that suppression of the rebellion did not fall under his own escape clause. The aged Scott had declared it his "duty" to put down the rebellion, which Lee himself believed to have no legal justification. Did honor and duty truly stand with Robert E. Lee during the secession winter? Scott, by Lee's own account, was an intimate friend of Lee; surely he would not have consented to offering Lee field command of the Federal army if he did not think it plausible, even expected, that Lee would stay with the Union.

Furthermore, Lee's resignation from the U.S. Army leaves open many questions. Southern-born officers believed that the resignation of their commissions released them from their oaths to the Federal government, and even during the Civil War, American officers in both sections could resign their commissions. All officers agreed, however, that resignation was only honorable under certain conditions. For example, no self-respecting Regular would have looked well on a colleague who resigned his commission right after being ordered to lead an assault. In a less extreme example, even Douglas Southall Freeman admits that Lee could not have resigned his commission "under orders" without bringing disgrace to himself.[32] The crucial judgment posterity must give is whether or not Thomas's contention was correct—that resigning with the intent to take up arms against the United States could not possibly be seen as honorable.

Defenders of Lee cannot claim that he resigned his commission with no idea that he would join Virginia's armed forces. Lee submitted his resignation on April 20, 1861; on the same evening, a Saturday, before his resignation had become public knowledge, he received a request to meet with a representative of Virginia's state government. The meeting occurred on April 22, when Lee accepted a commission as a major general of Virginia. Even if Nolan's circumstantial case of preresignation contacts between Lee and Virginia state authorities do not reflect reality, the swiftness of Lee's actions after his resignation surely shows that the thought of taking up arms against Washington had more than crossed his mind.[33] Lee resigned from the Federal service precisely because he knew war was imminent; he then almost immediately joined a military force that had already opened hostilities with the Federal government.

Moreover, when Lee accepted his state commission, he was still bound by his oath to the Federal army, since the army's general regulations stipulated that a resignation did not take effect until it was "duly accepted by the proper authority." That did not occur until April 25. Furthermore, the regulations also stipulated that "in time of war, or with an army in the field, resignations shall take effect within thirty days from the date of the order of acceptance." Surely Lee knew after Sumter that the U.S. government was at war, whether he thought that war just or unjust. The regulations were obviously designed to prevent resignations from harming the service during times of crisis, which is exactly what Lee's resignation did.[34]

Even Freeman admits that Lee may have stood with the Union if he had not been replaced by David Twiggs as department commander of Texas, since he would have been honor-bound to defend his post when secessionist Texans demanded its surrender before Virginia seceded. Regular army officers, Unionist and secessionist, agreed that Twiggs's surrender of his department was an unconscionable breach of faith, and most Confederate West Pointers made sure to resign their commissions before they joined the Confederate army.[35]

Nevertheless, one can wonder if there really was much of a difference between Twiggs's surrendering his post outright and Lee writing a letter of resignation before taking up arms against the Federal government. Lee did not even bother to follow army regulations to the letter with regard to resignations, never mind Thomas's more serious charge that any reasonable construction of the regular army oath could not sanction such conduct. Finally, if coercing his home state back into the Union was unbearable—perhaps Cooke and Thomas were simply made of sterner stuff—Lee could have simply resigned and joined neither the Union nor the Confederate war efforts. As distinguished a regular army officer as Alfred Mordecai of North Carolina, perhaps the leading ordnance specialist of the antebellum period, chose that path, and considering Lee's advanced age and political opinions, that option may have been the most compatible with both his familial ties and his obligations toward the U.S. government.[36]

Even Virginia's secession does not totally immunize Lee. Some Deep South officers remained loyal to the Federal service.[37] For example, Kentucky-born William P. Sanders, a West Pointer of the Class of 1856 who had moved to Mississippi at the age of seven, possessed strong Southern credentials but remained with the Union. Jefferson Davis himself had interceded for him while a cadet at West Point and prevented his dismissal for academic failings. Edward Porter Alexander, a Confederate West Pointer from Georgia, served with Sanders on the West Coast and described him as "intensely Southern in all his views of it [secession], more so I think than any other Southern officer in the army with whom I met during the whole period of the initiation of hostilities. His family were from Kentucky & Mississippi, & he frequently claimed connection or relationship with Jefferson Davis." When Alexander left to join Confederate forces, he fully expected Sanders would be a future comrade; Sanders instead rose to the rank of brigadier general in the Federal army and would be killed in action while fighting troops under Alexander's own command at Knoxville in November 1863. Sanders must have strained relations with his family over his Unionism, since three of his brothers served in Mississippi cavalry regiments. Sanders, with his Mississippi connections, was in some ways even more "born" for the Confederate cause than Robert Edward Lee; indeed, he came within an ace of making the same decision, but in the end, he did not.[38]

Looking at all Southern officers affiliated with states that seceded, 60 out of 300 stayed with the Union, 200 rallied around the Confederate colors, 5 serving officers resigned, and 36 stayed out of the conflict.[39] Of the 487 graduates of West Point with some kind of affiliation with any slave state, 173 stayed loyal to the Federal colors, while 251 supported the new Confederacy. Ten officers still in the service resigned their commissions during the secession winter and seem to have played no active role in the war, while 57 (mostly older) officers who had resigned before the war stayed out of the fratricidal conflict. Clearly, most Southerners chose the new Confederate nation over the old Union, but a sizable minority were willing to go as far as drawing their swords against their native states.[40]

Indeed, in some ways, Lee's age, length of service, and Upper South background actually make a decision to stay in the Union more expected than secession. Twenty-seven of 90 slave-state West Point graduates (30 percent) of the Classes of 1830 and before joined the Confederacy (Lee was in the Class of 1829), while 224 of 397 graduates (56 percent) of the classes of 1831 to 1860 did the same. Even when we only look at Virginians, the statistics continue to point to Lee staying with the Union. While 9 of 27 (33 percent) Virginian graduates of the West Point classes up to and including the class of 1830 went Confederate, a higher percentage of older graduates stayed with the Union: 13 of 27 (48 percent). Lee's behavior better fit the profile of a younger West Pointer from Virginia. Sixty-one of 99 (62 percent) Virginian graduates of the Classes of 1831 to 1860 went Confederate, while 31 of 99 (31 percent) stayed with the Union.[41]

More important than simple age, however, was length of time and achievement in the service, i.e., rank. Although all three slave-state West Pointers with general's stars joined the Confederacy, 10 of 13 full colonels stayed loyal to the Union, while only 3, including Lee, joined the Confederacy. Forty-three of 85 (51 percent) field-grade officers (colonels, lieutenant-colonels, and majors) stayed loyal, while 34 (40 percent) joined the Confederacy. In contrast, of the slave-state West Pointers who only held the lowest commissioned rank of second lieutenant in the antebellum regular army, 100 of 167 (60 percent) rebelled, while 34 (20 percent) served under the Federal colors.[42]

Looking only at Virginians, the one West Pointer who had a general's star in 1861—Joseph E. Johnston, a brigadier general in the Quartermaster's Bureau—went on to a prominent Confederate career, but of the six colonels, five stayed with the Union, while *only* Lee joined the Confederacy. Eighteen of 31 (58 percent) field-grade officers stayed loyal to the Old Union while 10 of 31 (32 percent) joined the Confederacy, which almost perfectly reverses the proportions of Unionist and Confederate among West Point graduates from Virginia as a whole. Of the West Point graduates who only held a second lieutenant's commission in the antebellum U.S. Army, 21 of 27 (78 percent) served in the Confederate army, while 2 of 27 (7 percent) served under the Union colors.[43]

The lower the rank an officer had acquired in the antebellum regular army, the weaker his ties to the U.S. Army uniform. Lee acquired high rank and prominence in the regular army, and his fellow Virginian and mentor, Winfield Scott, the greatest living American soldier at the time, remained loyal to the Federal government. From this perspective, Lee should have followed his aged chief. At the very least, by no stretch of the imagination was Robert E. Lee foreordained at birth to be a Confederate.

Beyond punctilious—if deadly serious—questions of honor, Lee's actions also contravened the long-standing American tradition of civil supremacy in military affairs. Ever since George Washington quashed the Newburgh Conspiracy in 1783, an attempt by disgruntled Continental army officers to cow the Continental Congress into funding officers' pensions, perhaps the most sacred principle in the American military tradition has been complete obedience to the civil authorities.[44] Like most principles, civil supremacy has not always been given the full measure of its due by American officers, but even by Lee's time American military professionals had a long record of carrying out orders they considered unpalatable, whether it was invading Mexico or dispossessing native peoples in causes some officers saw as unjust.[45] Antebellum regular army officers' commitment to civil supremacy also represented a pragmatic reaction to the long-standing American suspicion of standing armies, but self-interest need not be incompatible with strongly held principles.

Indeed, Lee's own excellent relationship with his civilian commander-in-chief during the Civil War, Jefferson Davis, redounded to both their benefit precisely because he recognized the political reality of civilian supremacy in American military practice. In contrast, Confederate general Joseph Johnston mismanaged his own relationship with his civilian chief and Union general George B. McClellan refused to fully concede the political reality of civil supremacy. Lee did provide counsel on a wide range of issues during the Civil War, ranging from conscription to the arming of slaves as troops, but he never attempted to dictate to civil authorities the proper solutions to vexatious questions of national policy.[46]

But Lee did precisely that during the secession winter. In order to protect the republic from the man on horseback, American political culture had always jealously safeguarded the exclusive authority of constitutionally mandated political leaders to decide major political questions, whether it be war, peace, states' rights, or some other major point of controversy. By this principle, American soldiers were only the loyal agents of the sitting Federal government, agents who would carry out their duties regardless of their own political beliefs.[47] American republicanism feared that without special checks, professional soldiers with special access to powerful instruments of coercion would play a disproportionate, even despotic, role in national councils.

In April 1861, Robert E. Lee threw off those checks and decided to use military skills developed at government expense to influence a political controversy that by a strict construction of civilian control should have been left to the politicians. Lee's acceptance of a commission in the Virginia state forces was an inherently political act in de facto defiance of his constitutional superiors. As a citizen, Lee had every right to believe coercion illegal; as a soldier, it is less clear if Lee had the right to attempt to coerce his own erstwhile political leaders, the Lincoln administration, into agreement with his views by offering his sword to another group of politicians. Southern secessionists conceded the Lincoln's administration's legitimacy as the duly elected president of the United States when they formed their own government. In their defense, of course, they believed that American constitutional doctrine had always allowed for secession; unfortunately, Lee's oath of loyalty to the Federal government included no such escape clause.

Long-standing American distrust of standing armies has led to countless problems in American military policy and some justifiable bitterness among American military professionals, but it has provided a powerful bulwark against military dictatorship capturing the republic. At the core of this principle is the belief that civilian political leaders are the final arbiters of political questions: not soldiers, priests, nobles, or some other such group not strictly regulated in the Constitution. Robert E. Lee was not only a citizen when Virginia seceded and the constitutional question came to a head; he was also a commissioned officer in the U.S. Army bound by custom, tradition, and law to the service of his commander-in-chief, Abraham Lincoln. American traditions of civilian control did not ask soldiers to forfeit entirely their individual moral consciences, but Lee himself had admitted that he thought secession illegal and unwarranted. If that was true, was Federal coercion so obviously immoral and heinous that it could justify the breaking of his oath?

In Lee's defense, the scope and severity of the Civil War washed away so much of the antebellum status quo that the breaking of the old regular army's fellowship of service may seem understandable, perhaps even inevitable. Lee also certainly did not choose to cast his lot with the Confederacy out of avarice; the Lincoln administration after all had offered him the chance to be the Union's leading general and a hero to all the North. Nevertheless, is honor still honor and are oaths still oaths if they can be so easily explained away by "context"?

Finally, one need not use anachronistic early twenty-first-century criteria to find Robert E. Lee wanting in April of 1861. There is no need to cite his slaveholding or his indifference toward racial and gender equality or some other form of morality yet to be articulated; the sad example of the Dragoon of Lynchburg, Philip St. George Cooke, stands as a powerful witness against Robert E. Lee. The case may not be decisive, but the regular army Virginians who remained true to the strictest construction of their solemn oaths of service deserve more than the obscurity heretofore granted to them by posterity.

Whatever duty and honor really meant to regular army officers during the secession winter, the creation of a viable Confederate government made the question abstract and academic. Lee and his fellow Confederates had all chosen their loyalties, right or wrong, and now only battle could decide the physical fact of states' rights and secession. In the end, historians and posterity would for the most part exonerate them of the charge of treason and mutiny, whether justly or unjustly, but even Douglas Southall Freeman could not erase the verdict of Union arms—that the Lost Cause would indeed be lost.

Notes

1. Charles Francis Adams, "Lee's Centennial," in *Studies Military and Diplomatic, 1775–1865* (New York: Macmillan, 1911), 295.

For one example of popular representation, the recent movie *Gods and Generals* portrays Lee's decision to secede as essentially uncontested. The movie opens with Lee's well-known interview with Francis Blair where he was offered the primary Federal field command, but it omits Lee's even more well-known interview with Winfield Scott, Lee's longtime mentor and a fellow Virginian, who put the Union ahead of the Old Dominion.

2. Douglas Southall Freeman, *R. E. Lee: A Biography,* 4 vols. (New York: Charles Scribner's Sons, 1934–1935), 1:431–47. For a contrary opinion, see Alan T. Nolan, *Lee Considered: General Robert E. Lee and Civil War History* (Chapel Hill: University of North Carolina Press, 1991), 30–58. For the most part, I find Nolan's treatment far more persuasive, although on factual matters Freeman's treatment still holds up very well; I only differ with Freeman on the crucial question of whether or not Lee had a choice during the secession crisis. My primary goal is to supplement Nolan's account with a treatment of those regular army Virginians who chose a course different from Lee's.

3. James Spencer, *Civil War Generals: Categorical Listings and a Biographical Directory* (New York: Greenwood Press, 1986), 68–70, 114–20; William B. Skelton, *An American Profession of Arms: The Army Officer Corps, 1784–1861* (Lawrence: University Press of Kansas, 1992), 361.

One of the non–West Pointer Regulars, Lawrence Pike Graham, had three brothers who all graduated from West Point, and one was a brother-in-law of George Gordon Meade, the future Union commander at Gettysburg. All four Graham brothers stayed with the Union. See Ezra J. Warner, *Generals in Blue: Lives of the Union Commanders* (Baton Rouge: Louisiana State University Press, 1964), 180.

It should also be acknowledged that two of the Virginia-born generals, Jesse Lee Reno and Jacob Ammen, moved to free states while they were children. Reno's family moved to Pennsylvania when he was about nine (Warner, *Generals in Blue*, 394), while Warner gives nothing more specific with regard to Ammen beyond the statement that he "grew up in Ohio" (6). Of course, a simple move would not necessarily have obliterated all Southern sympathies and manners.

If West Virginia counties are excluded, eleven of fourteen Union generals from Virginia have regular army backgrounds. Of those eleven, nine are West Point graduates. All three non–regular army generals were volunteers in the Mexican War.

On the easy transfer of much of the Federal government's bureaucratic apparatus to the Confederacy, see Richard Franklin Bensel, *Yankee Leviathan: The Origins of Central State Authority in America, 1859–1877* (Cambridge: Cambridge University Press, 1990), 99–103.

For one point of comparison using William B. Skelton's figures for Upper South officers (defined for him as Virginia, Tennessee, and Arkansas) in the army at secession, the figures are 58.9 percent joining the Confederacy, 36.1 percent staying in the Federal service, and 5.1 percent withdrawing from the conflict altogether (Skelton, *American Profession of Arms*, 356).

4. The primary source for my database of slave-state West Pointers is George W. Cullum, *Biographical Register of the Officers and Graduates of the U.S. Military Academy at West Point, N.Y., from its Establishment in 1802, to 1890, with the Early History of the United States Military Academy*, 3rd ed., 3 vols. (Boston: Houghton, Mifflin, & Company, 1891). I went through every West Point Class from 1802 to 1860 to find every graduate still living in 1861 who was born, appointed from, or possessing a place of residence at time of admission in a slave state (including Washington, D.C.). For the sake of the database, all such cadets were considered "Southerners." I also reviewed cadets with Northern birth states and at-large appointments to see if their place of residence at admission was a Southern state, with the caveat that I excluded those cadets who seemed obviously "Northern"—i.e., they received Northern volunteer commissions (Civil War volunteer commissions below the rank of general were handled by the states) and retired north of the Mason-Dixon line. States of residence for at-large appointed cadets can be found in "Cadet Cards Arranged by State," Archives and Special Collections, U.S. Military Academy Library, West Point, N.Y.

Also note that not all the numbers sum up correctly since several graduates served with the Union army for a time and then later resigned to join the Confederacy. Also note that when graduates had dual affiliations within the South, I gave priority to either the state of appointment or place of residence at time of appointment: for example, if a graduate was born in Kentucky but was appointed from Louisiana, I have taken the state of appointment, Louisiana, as the more correct marker of regional identification. This is a hardly perfect measure, but since appointments to the academy were made by members of Congress, the recipients of such appointments generally had at least some influence with whatever regional partisan networks supported their application. For at-large appointments, I have applied the same principle to the state of residence at the time of appointment. It must be pointed out that these are not exact figures, but my assumption has been that graduates whose "true" regional affiliations do not match their place of residence or birth will more or less cancel each other out.

5. James L. Morrison Jr., *"The Best School in the World": West Point, the Pre–Civil War Years, 1833–1866* (Kent, Ohio: Kent State University Press, 1986), 15; Bensel, *Yankee Leviathan*, 119.

6. Freeman, *Lee*, 1:432, 437. Another great scion of a distinguished Old Dominion family, James Monroe (USMA 1815), a nephew of President Monroe, served as Scott's aide-de-camp during a fairly distinguished military career. He resigned from the service in 1832 and participated for a time in politics in New York, which became his adopted state. During the secession crisis, he returned to his native Virginia to argue against secession, but failed. He returned to New York City, where he became a leading figure in the Union Club, and died at Orange Mountain, N.J., on September 7, 1870, aged seventy-one. See Cullum, *Biographical Register*, 1:133–37.

7. A concise summary of Thomas's military career can be found in Cullum, *Biographical Register*, 2:33–35.

8. Though the decision-making processes of most regular army Virginians during the secession winter has left little or no historical evidence, biographical data available through sources such as George W. Cullum's *Biographical Dictionary of West Pointers* and the academy's own cadet records provide revealing clues.

9. Francis F. McKinney, *Education in Violence: The Life of George H. Thomas and the History of the Army of the Cumberland* (Detroit: Wayne State University Press, 1961), 82, 85–93.

Simon Cameron, Lincoln's first secretary of war, had doubts about Thomas's loyalty early in the war. See John A. Garraty and Mark C. Carnes, eds., *American National Biography*, 24 vols. (New York: Oxford University Press, 1999), 21:507.

Thomas later reported that he had warned Winfield Scott of General David Twiggs's plans to surrender the Department of Texas. Thomas B. Van Horne, *The Life of Major-General George H. Thomas* (New York: C. Scribner's Sons, 1882), 20, is the only source I have found for Thomas's warning to Scott of Twiggs's treachery, and Van Horne presumably received his information from Thomas himself. Considering the tensions between Twiggs and Thomas in Texas, and the treasonous nature (in Thomas's view) of Twiggs's conduct there, it is not unreasonable to think that Thomas's memory may have added this embellishment after the fact. For Thomas's difficulties with Twiggs, see McKinney, *Education in Violence*, 75–77.

10. McKinney, *Education in Violence*, 86, 88 (quote). On the issue of Thomas's wavering, also see Don Piatt, *General George H. Thomas: A Critical Biography, with concluding chapters by Henry V. Boynton* (Cincinnati: Robert Clarke & Co., 1893), 82–83.

11. McKinney, *Education in Violence*, 88–89; Wilbur Thomas, *General George H. Thomas: The Indomitable Warrior* (New York: Exposition Press, 1964), 133; Van Horne, *Life of Major-General George H. Thomas*, 28.

After the war, Mrs. Thomas recalled that her husband had written her that "turn it every way he would, the one thing was uppermost, his duty to the government of the United States," quoted in McKinney, *Education in Violence*, 89.

Thomas's decision must have come after Virginia's secession on April 17 in response to Lincoln's call for volunteers, although Van Horne is not explicit in giving the timing as such.

12. Van Horne, *Life of Major-General George H. Thomas*, 26. Van Horne's punctuation is somewhat confusing, since there is no single opening quotation mark, but the single closing quotation mark seems to indicate that he meant this statement to be a direct quote. Furthermore, although Thomas may not have been as blunt in April 1861 as he was after the war, his wartime conduct speaks well enough to his consistency.

13. Ibid., 27; Freeman Cleaves, *Rock of Chickamauga: The Life of General George H. Thomas* (Norman: University of Oklahoma Press, 1948), 67; George H. Thomas to A. A. Draper, March 22, 1865, A. A. Draper Letters, Special Collections, U.S. Military Academy Library, West Point, N.Y. (cited hereafter as A. A. Draper Letters).

14. Hartsuff quoted in Thomas, *Indomitable Warrior*, 134. On the conservatism of the antebellum regular army officer corps as a whole, see Skelton, *American Profession of Arms*, 350.

15. George H. Thomas to A. A. Draper, March 4, 1865, A. A. Draper Letters. On Sherman's Southern sympathies, see Charles Royster, *The Destructive War: William Tecumseh Sherman, Stonewall Jackson, and the Americans* (New York: Alfred A. Knopf, 1991), 126–27.

16. Henry Coppée, *General Thomas* (New York: D. Appleton & Company, 1893), 23, 27–28; McKinney, *Education in Violence*, 91. On the importance of family considerations, see Skelton, *American Profession of Arms*, 357.

17. James Maget to Elizabeth Thomas, Southampton County, February 7, 1848, Mss2/M2723/a/1, Virginia Historical Society, Richmond, Virginia; McKinney, *Education in Violence*, 90–91; Richard O'Connor, *Thomas: Rock of Chickamauga* (New York: Prentice-Hall, 1948), 111.

18. McKinney, *Education in Violence*, 90–93, 473. McKinney indicates that there is a record of twenty-five members of Mrs. Thomas's family being present, so presumably none of General Thomas's own family were present, because none were listed. Mrs. Thomas also chose to bury Thomas in her own hometown of

Troy, New York, while then General-in-Chief William T. Sherman had unsuc-cessfully asked that Thomas be interred at West Point. There was no proposal to return his body to his home state. Also see Cleaves, *Rock of Chickamauga,* 306–7.

19. O'Connor, *Thomas,* 115–16; Thomas, *Indomitable Warrior,* 133; Piatt, *General George H. Thomas,* 84–85. Among Thomas's biographers, only Cleaves and McKinney have recognized the slight hesitation Thomas felt in deciding for or against the old Federal Union (see Cleaves, *Rock of Chickamauga,* 67; McKinney, *Education in Violence,* 89).

20. Warner, *Generals in Blue,* 496–97. Whatever the merits of the family tradi-tion, there is some evidence that Terrill was given duty in the West out of defer-ence to his Virginian family (A. D. Bache to G. W. Cullum, May 20, 1861, Special Collections, U.S. Military Academy Library, West Point, N.Y.).

21. Father to William Rufus Terrill, May 13, 1861 [copy], Alexander Dallas Bache Papers, Special Collections, U.S. Military Academy Library, West Point, N.Y.

22. Emory Thomas, *Bold Dragoon: The Life of J. E. B. Stuart* (New York: Vin-tage Books, Random House, 1988), 95 (includes quote of Stuart); Otis E. Young, *The West of Philip St. George Cooke* (Glendale, Calif.: Arthur H. Clarke Company, 1955), 322, 328, 346.

23. Young, *West of Philip St. George Cooke,* 322–24 (quotes on 323, 324).

24. P. St. George Cooke to Washington National Intelligencer, June 6, 1861, re-printed in *The Rebellion Record: A Diary of American Events, with Documents, Narratives, Illustrative Incidents, Poetry Etc.,* vol. 2, ed. Frank Moore (New York: D. Van Nostrand, 1866), 171–72.

25. Philip St. George Cooke, *Scenes and Adventures in the Army, or, Romance of Military Life* (Philadelphia: Lindsay and Blakiston, 1859), 40; Theo. F. Roden-bough, ed., *From Everglade to Canon with the Second Dragoons, (Second United States Cavalry): An Authentic Account of Service in Florida, Mexico, Virginia, and the Indian Country, including the Personal Recollections of Prominent Officers, with an Appendix Containing Orders, Reports and Correspondence, Military Rec-ords, Etc., etc., etc.* (New York: D. Van Nostrand, 1875), 184.

The earlier episode is supposed to have occurred in 1829, two years after his graduation from the academy. The historian Durwood Ball has characterized the conduct of regular army commanders in Kansas as "even-handed" (Durwood Ball, *Army Regulars on the Western Frontier, 1848–1861* [Norman: University of Oklahoma Press, 2001], 187).

26. Timothy D. Johnson, *Winfield Scott: The Quest for Military Glory* (Law-rence: University Press of Kansas, 1998), 223; Winfield Scott, *Autobiography of Lieut.-Gen. Winfield Scott,* 2 vols. (New York: Sheldon & Company, 1864), 2:610–11. On the loyalty of the Federal army, see the latter citation.

27. Quoted in Johnson, *Winfield Scott,* 224–25 (quote on 224); Scott, *Autobi-ography,* 2:614–15; Benjamin Franklin Cooling, ed., *The New American State Papers: Military Affairs,* 19 vols. (Wilmington, Del.: Scholarly Resources, 1979), 19:37, 46–47.

28. Scott, *Autobiography*, 1:248; David Morris Potter, *Lincoln and His Party in the Secession Crisis* (New Haven: Yale University Press, 1942), 360–63. I am following Potter's argument that Lincoln had originally hoped to give up Fort Sumter but stay firm on Fort Pickens (358–59). On Scott's conservative and conciliatory Unionism, also see his letter of March 3 to Seward, reprinted in Scott, *Autobiography*, 2:625–28.

29. Freeman, *Lee*, 1:437; Johnson, *Winfield Scott*, 226, 233.

30. Lee quoted in Nolan, *Lee Considered*, 33–35.

31. Nolan prints the full text of the oath on ibid., 37.

32. Freeman, *Lee*, 1:438. After Twiggs took over command of the Department of Texas, Lee had no duty assigned to him.

33. Nolan, *Lee Considered*, 42–44.

34. U.S. War Department, *Regulations for the Army of the United States, 1857* (New York: Harper & Brothers, [1857]), 4. For Nolan's similar treatment of this issue, see Nolan, *Lee Considered*, 39.

35. Freeman, *Lee*, 429; Ball, *Army Regulars*, 192; Skelton, *American Profession of Arms*, 357.

36. On Mordecai, see Skelton, *American Profession of Arms*, 355.

37. My analysis of Cullum's *Biographical Dictionary of West Pointers* resulted in sixteen Lower South West Pointers who stayed with the Union. How many were "true" Southerners is open to question—seven had associations of some sort with non-Southern locales, either as their birthplaces or their residences at the time of appointment. We do not have enough biographical data to make firm conclusions with regard to the group as a whole. A Northern state of residence may not, after all, indicate any real shedding of a Southern identity. Since some Northern-born officers ended up in the Confederate service due to family ties and connections with the South, I have simply assumed that such cases more or less washed each other out.

38. Gary W. Gallagher, ed., *Fighting for the Confederacy: The Personal Recollections of General Edward Porter Alexander* (Chapel Hill: University of North Carolina Press, 1989), 27–28; Warner, *Generals in Blue*, 419–20, 657 n. 553; Cullum, *Biographical Dictionary*, 2:668. Alexander in his memoirs wrote that when he left California, Sanders had told him that he only felt honor-bound to return a clutch of deserters he had captured to his post, but that he would then resign his commission. Something obviously changed in Sanders's state of mind, but Alexander unfortunately did not know what exactly triggered that change.

39. See table 1 and its associated citations.

40. I also counted as loyal any individuals who made public professions of loyalty to the Union, even if they did not serve in a military capacity. Most of the individuals counted, however, did serve in uniform. Furthermore, I have denoted all slave-state residents as Southerners, even though every slave state did not secede. I have felt justified in doing this because one might expect a West Pointer from a border state that did not secede to be still reluctant to wage war on the Confederacy.

41. Adams makes much of historical background and context to explain away the Unionist loyalties of such officers as Thomas and Scott. He claims that Thomas's and Scott's examples could not apply to Lee (Adams mentions no other Virginians who stayed loyal), because Lee's connections with Virginia were so much stronger (Adams, "Lee's Centennial," 302–5). Although it is true that Lee had especially strong familial connections to Virginia, other aspects of Lee's background, such as his career track in the antebellum regular army, pointed toward continued Federal allegiance. Lee's complicated character does not simply reduce to his identity as a Virginian—he was also a soldier in the service of the United States of a specific background, station, and rank.

42. Rank and age were closely related, since seniority was the primary determinant for promotion in the antebellum regular army. However, brevet ranks were given out for meritorious conduct, and in my database I have made no distinction between regular and brevet ranks.

Jefferson Davis (USMA 1828), Albert Sidney Johnston (USMA 1826), and Joseph Eggleston Johnston (USMA 1829) were the generals. I have included Davis even though he declined his brigadier's commission, since I am using rank as a proxy for achievement in the regular army. The Unionist colonels were: John J. Abert, John J. Abercrombie, Lorenzo Thomas, Edmund B. Alexander, Dennis Hart Mahan, Dixon S. Miles, Washington Seawell, William H. C. Bartlett, Philip St. George Cooke, and Henry H. Lockwood. The Confederate colonels were Edward G. W. Butler, Robert E. Lee, and Jones M. Withers.

Note that I have considered professors at either West Point or the U.S. Naval Academy as being equivalent to colonels: D. H. Mahan and William H. C. Bartlett for the former, Henry H. Lockwood for the latter. I have felt justified in doing this because the academies played such an important role in their respective services, although the Naval Academy at this time had a weaker footing. Nevertheless, Lockwood was one of the Naval Academy's most prominent early instructors and would go on to become a brigade commander at Gettysburg (Charles Todorich, *The Spirited Years: A History of the Antebellum Naval Academy* [Annapolis, Md.: Naval Institute Press, 1984], 57–59, 77–78, 199).

Using data drawn from only officers still in the U.S. Army in 1860, Skelton finds rank to be a minor factor in the decision of serving officers to resign and join the Confederacy, except for field-grade and general officers (Skelton, *American Profession of Arms*, 355–56). My own data is different in that it includes all living West Point graduates, as opposed to just those still in the regular army in 1860.

43. The Unionist Virginian colonels were John J. Abert, Edmund B. Alexander, Dennis Hart Mahan (the most important West Point professor of his generation), Washington Seawell, and Philip St. George Cooke.

44. For an excellent discussion of Washington, Newburgh, and the American tradition of civilian control, see Don Higginbotham, *George Washington and the American Military Tradition* (Athens: University of Georgia Press, 1985), 96–105.

45. Some officers had moral qualms over both the regular army's campaigns of Indian pacification and the Mexican War, but almost all paid due deference to

civilian political leaders. See Ball, *Army Regulars*, 23; Skelton, *American Profession of Arms*, 332.

46. On Lee's good relations with civilian leaders, see Freeman, *Lee*, 4:179–81. For Lee's unwillingness to overstep his bounds with regard to the arming of slaves, see Robert F. Durden, *The Gray and the Black: The Confederate Debate on Emancipation* (Baton Rouge: Louisiana State University Press, 1972), 134. On McClellan's disastrous command relations with Lincoln, see, for example, Stephen W. Sears, *George B. McClellan: The Young Napoleon* (New York: Ticknor and Fields, 1988), 338–39. On Johnston's troubles with Davis, see James M. McPherson, *Battle Cry of Freedom: The Civil War Era* (New York: Oxford University Press, 1988), 365–66, 691, 753–54.

47. Skelton, *American Profession of Arms*, 304.

"It Is Old Virginia and We Must Have It"

Overcoming Regionalism in Civil War Virginia

Aaron Sheehan-Dean

The unity of the American South was a product of the Civil War, not a precedent for it. Before the war, every Southerner recognized differences between lowcountry and upcountry folk, between coastal regions and the Black Belt. Antebellum leaders could not even assume unity within individual states. Among the most problematic states was Virginia, which distinguished itself as a place where regional tensions, predicated on an east-west division dating to the earliest days of European settlement, presented serious obstacles to political and social unity. From the 1830s through the 1850s, state leaders struggled to resolve the contradictory trends in the state. The modest success they achieved drew on three elements: an increasingly democratic politics, growing prosperity, and the continuing profitability of slavery. With the exception of a handful of counties along the state's northwestern border, most white Virginians participated to some degree in all these trends. But the process of seceding, and the tepid response of northwestern counties in particular, rejuvenated regional antagonisms across the state. The experience of fighting and the continuing problems of defining the boundaries of Confederate Virginia further inflamed the problem. During the war, enlisted men, officers, and civilians all responded by seeking ways to ameliorate regional tensions. Drawing on a sense of shared sacrifice and common interest during the war, Virginians forged new connections between the state's

many communities. The emerging solidarity, though by no means universal, provided an important foundation for Virginians' confidence in and
devotion to their new Confederate nation.[1]

By the 1850s, Virginians understood their state as consisting of five regions—the Tidewater, the Piedmont, the Valley, the southwest, and the
northwest—separated by ecology, geology, and weather patterns, as well
as distinct and generally complementary economic systems and political orientations.[2] The Tidewater held many of the state's oldest and most
prestigious families, although land values had fallen by the second quarter
of the nineteenth century. Virginia's Piedmont rose to dominance during this period. Piedmont families capitalized on the fertile soil of their
region to produce a broad array of crops and products. Relying heavily
on slave labor, many Piedmont counties had populations evenly split between black and white residents. The families in this region controlled
more wealth than anyone else in Virginia. Although rates of slaveholding
were lower than in the Tidewater, Valley citizens pursued many of the
same strategies as their neighbors to the east and possessed impressive resources. Farmers in the southwest region of the state possessed few slaves
compared to their Piedmont and Tidewater colleagues, but during the late
antebellum era these men began to expand their use of slaves, especially
in the production of tobacco. They also reached out more aggressively to
deliver their products to markets, particularly into western North Carolina and Tennessee.[3] As a result of these decisions and trends, Virginians to the south and west of the Shenandoah Valley identified themselves
with the interests of the Lower South. The opposite was true for people
in the fast-growing northwest region of the state, who invested little in
the slave economies that dominated the rest of Virginia. Glass, coal, and
agricultural products produced in the region flowed along the Kanawha
River toward Pittsburgh and markets in southern Pennsylvania and Ohio.
People in this region identified more closely with Northern interests than
with Virginians in other parts of the state.

Despite the geographic and human diversity of the commonwealth,
until the 1850s, the Alleghany Mountains marked the single main division between eastern and western Virginia. Easterners and westerners
argued over the future of slavery and the proper allocation of political
power within the commonwealth. The majority of complaints came from
westerners angry over the unequal distribution of power within the state's
General Assembly, particularly the disproportionate share of political
power granted to eastern representatives.[4] In response to the demands
of westerners and white workingmen in the east, the General Assembly

of 1850 reluctantly called a constitutional convention.[5] This time, unlike during previous efforts, conservative lawmakers yielded to the demands of yeomen and removed all property restrictions on voting and transformed a wide array of state and local offices from appointed to elected positions.[6] Virginia's middle- and lower-middle-class white men thus began the 1850s with greater political rights than ever before. During the coming years they exercised those rights actively, participating in politics in increasing numbers.[7] As a result of their new responsibility and authority, yeomen in the state came to conceptualize themselves as independent men. Political empowerment drew these men into a shared defense of a slaveholding republic, a commitment that state leaders called upon when they worked to build support for the Confederacy during the Civil War. For the state, the result of this engagement produced a period of regional reconciliation and security.[8]

A strong economy also facilitated the lessening of regional tensions in the 1840s and 1850s. During these decades, agricultural reformers, urban boosters, and industrial developers all worked tirelessly to transform Virginia's economy.[9] By the 1850s, these agents of change, and the hundreds of thousands of Virginia families who adjusted their economic practices or changed occupations, had substantially diversified the state's economic base. Combined with a general upswing in prices for agricultural goods in the 1850s, Virginians enjoyed a new period of prosperity and success. Even those parts of the state that had been firmly committed to mono-crop production added new cereal grains or learned to complement farming with successful animal husbandry.[10] Entrepreneurs pursued the use of new technologies and heavy industry.[11] Aiding the agricultural and industrial development was a rapidly growing transportation network. Over the decade and a half following the Mexican-American War, Virginia laid more miles of railroad track than any state in the Union and could boast more total miles than any state except New York and Pennsylvania. Virginians of all classes and backgrounds made substantial investments in turnpikes, canals, and expanded ocean ports as well as the new technology of the railroad.[12] Along these new channels to national and global markets flowed agricultural goods from all around the state, iron from forges in the Shenandoah Valley and the enormous Tredegar Iron Works in Richmond, salt from the mines in the southwestern part of the state, and glass from factories in the northwest.

Virginia's economic growth in the antebellum decades was fueled by slave labor, deployed not just in agriculture but all across the economy. Even as slaveholders from eastern Virginia overworked their land and sold slaves south to the Lower South, Piedmont, Valley, and southwest residents increased their stake in the system by purchasing more slaves and investing them in a diverse array of enterprises.[13] Farmers used slaves in all types of agricultural production in the state, from the tobacco plantations of the central and southern Piedmont to the wheat and corn fields of the Valley.[14] Slaveowners also used their slaves in a growing number of industrial pursuits, from the Kanawha saltworks to the Shenandoah iron mines to the forges of Richmond.[15] The shared use of slave labor by city and country employers helped tie urban and rural places together around the institution of slavery. While the debates of the 1830s over the structure of Virginia's democracy and the policies of urban development had often pitted urban residents against rural ones, the cross-traffic in slave labor between these two "regions" in Virginia offered incentives for unity.

Although abolitionists and free labor advocates argued otherwise, the prominent role of slavery in the Virginia economy neither depressed the Southern economy nor ensured that nonslaveholders remained mired in poverty. To the contrary, many nonslaveholders benefited from living in a society enriched by slave labor.[16] In most rural communities, slaveowners loaned and rented out their slaves to poorer neighbors during harvest time or other periods of high labor demand. Further, the use of slave labor by slaveowners to produce valuable crops and goods stimulated the demand for internal improvements, such as turnpikes and railroads, that gave yeomen families greater access to the market. The continual demand for foodstuffs for slaves stimulated local and regional economies and gave nonslaveholding farmers places to sell their goods. Virginia's economic success in the 1840s and 1850s, and especially the fact that a broad middle class shared in that prosperity, ensured that most white residents remained committed to the state and the infrastructure, both human and mechanical, that they had worked so hard to develop. This was particularly true for the southwest, which invested heavily in slavery and a slave-based economy in the 1840s and 1850s. The northwest, by contrast, expanded with little reliance on slavery. Thus, residents of this section did not possess the same commitment to preserving the conditions responsible for Southern success in the decades before the war as the rest of the state.

The 1850s thus presented a contradictory picture to observers of Virginia. Powerful social and economic trends—the simultaneous growth of free and slave labor and patterns of in- and out-migration—seemed destined to pull Virginia apart. At the same time, the political responses to these challenges and the continuing profitability of slavery helped mitigate intra-state divisions. As the presidential election of 1860 and the secession debate of 1861 demonstrated, Virginians remained divided over certain issues. But those same events also revealed that most white Virginians recognized a fundamental unity of purpose among themselves. In their defense of a newly democratized political system and the prosperity of the 1850s, knowingly built on slave labor, most Virginians endorsed the new Confederate States of America.

In terms of national politics, Virginians' own ambivalence, the conservatism of many leading politicians, and the unifying pull of defending slavery helped unite the state around a policy of protecting Virginia slavery from the dangers of secession. These factors ensured that the state did not follow the Lower South out of the Union after Lincoln's election. Virginia's secession remained uncertain, even unlikely, well into 1861. As Deep South states exited the Union after Lincoln's election, Virginia Unionists slowed the process within their regions, and moderates dominated the convention that convened in early February 1861. The strongest pro-secession sentiment in the state was in the east, and these partisans blamed westerners for impeding secession. One ardent fire-eater complained to a friend that if Virginia failed to secede, "we remain in the Union to be abolitionised. Western Va. has us down."[17] His friend described the layout of the secession convention in a letter from mid-February, noting, "the numbers are 42 on our side 111 against." He, too, identified westerners as the ones responsible for slowing down the momentum toward secession, but held out hope for a change. "There is a rumour that Congress has passed a force bill," he noted, "which, it is to be hoped will bring these Western men to their senses."[18]

The distribution of Unionist and secessionist strength, however, was by no means so clear cut. On April 4, convention delegates voted against secession, and though secessionists drew considerable strength from eastern Piedmont and Tidewater counties, Unionists too could count friends in all regions of the state. Conservative businessmen who dominated places like Richmond, Norfolk, and Danville as well as a wide stretch of northern Virginia counties joined most westerners in opposing secession. These conditional Unionists feared the economic and social instability that might accompany secession, but they also feared the North's increasing economic strength and apparent hostility toward slavery.

Following the brief fight at Fort Sumter, South Carolina, on April 12 and, more importantly, Lincoln's April 15 decision to call up seventy-five thousand troops, the majority of Virginia's conditional Unionists felt they could no longer stay in the Union. The shift of support was sudden, widespread, and deeply felt. James Dorman Davidson, a prominent Lexington

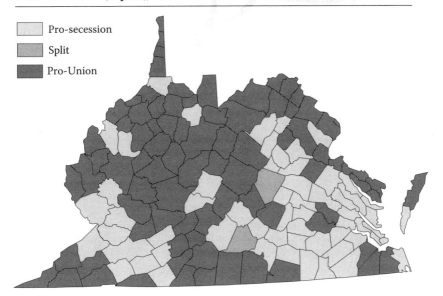

Votes on secession, April 4, 1861

- Pro-secession
- Split
- Pro-Union

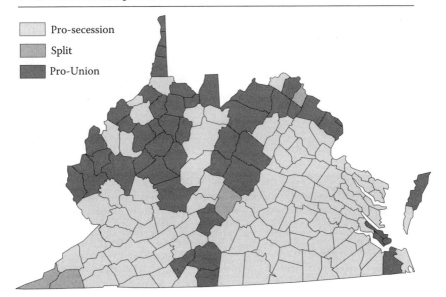

Votes on secession, April 17, 1861

- Pro-secession
- Split
- Pro-Union

lawyer, remained strongly pro-Union until the fifteenth. Having praised Lincoln's inaugural address as essentially "a message against Coercion," the militia call shocked Davidson.[19] His response, and that of his community, typified the transformation made in most parts of Virginia. "Rockbridge was revolutionized at once," he wrote, "and now our secession friends say, they are true conservatives now, and that we are the fire eaters."[20] On April 17, secession convention delegates voted eighty-eight to fifty-five to approve Virginia's secession. The pattern of support for secession, which included nearly all the Tidewater, Piedmont, southwest, and upper Valley counties revealed the beginning of a new coherence within the state, one predicated on loyalty to the Confederacy.[21] The places outside the triangle of Confederate country were largely those counties in the northwest that had not benefited from the economic growth of the 1850s. If they had prospered, that success was based on the use of free not slave labor. The secession debate thus unintentionally revitalized the main regional cleavage within the state at a point when internal tensions were at a relatively low ebb.

The legislation authorizing the secession convention required that Virginia voters confirm any decision of the convention to secede. The statewide ratification vote occurred on May 23, and although most Virginians knew the outcome in advance, many voters took the opportunity to express their dissatisfaction with the actions of the convention. Northwestern residents, in particular, opposed the secession ordinance and voted accordingly. But the very process of voting, which state leaders conceived as a way to ensure popular support for any decision made, generated new strains. Eastern soldiers sent west observed the heightened regional tensions immediately. Thomas Broun, a Piedmont volunteer, contemptuously described the situation in Putnam County, on Virginia's western border, a week before the vote. "A great excitement prevailed in camp Monday night," Broun reported, "disaffected people living here and near the Ohio (Virginians too) ordered us to leave, gave us 24 hours to depart, otherwise they would compel us, &c." Broun's reaction revealed the arrogance for which westerners had criticized their eastern brethren for generations: "these disaffected creatures are about like the Ragged mountain people (in Albemarle County)." Broun observed the political nature of the problem Confederates confronted, but offered no way to alleviate it. "Designing persons had made them believe that we were sent here to compel them to vote for secession &c.," he reported.[22]

Some local officials used Confederate soldiers to ensure peaceful conditions at the polls that day, and no doubt some eager volunteers offered guidance to prospective voters. For those Confederates stationed in western counties, the politics of secession reinvigorated the old regional stereotypes. James Edmondson, stationed in Berkeley County in the lower Shenandoah Valley, informed his wife that "the better class of people here are for secession, but the other class (who outnumber them) are the other way."[23] After the ratification vote, Edmondson blamed the anti-secession majority on German workers, whom he deemed "very excitable on the subject." Nevertheless, Edmondson felt sure that the soldiers' presence protected the honor of the virtuous minority who stayed true to Virginia. "It is supposed by some of the citizens," he wrote, "that but for the presence of our company the good loyal citizens would not have been permitted to vote."[24] Broun and Edmondson were not alone in falling back into the unthinking condescension that characterized east-west relations in the early decades of the nineteenth century. Another Confederate on patrol in the region in mid-1861 offered the following assessment of mountain residents: "the men . . . of this county are a set of cowardly poltroons—and spend their time principaly in circulating rumors and trying to awaken the women and children."[25]

Residents of the northwest responded in kind to eastern Confederates sent to ensure the region's loyalty to the new slaveholding republic. The active role played by Unionist civilians in the region contradicted most of what eastern Confederates expected about warfare. One soldier described an unsuccessful attack on a Union position in a letter home. Federal forces, he recounted, trapped a small group from their regiment sent on a scouting party and killed several soldiers. The Confederates nonetheless managed to take a few prisoners, and information extracted from the Union soldiers confirmed their suspicion of the locals. "Those prisoners that was brought informed us they were apprised of the attack as much as we ware," wrote one soldier. "So much for union men we cannot have a fare chance heare," he continued, "and western Virginia are to be more dreaded than any other portion of the state on account of the union men. They have already done us great injury." Soldiers encountered civilians in this region with extreme trepidation, never knowing who would betray them, especially in those counties that formed the boundary between Union and Confederate territory in western Virginia. From this contested area, one soldier related the following episode: "Two of our picket guards were shot last week by a Union man and a very little boy. They rushed upon them and they ran upstairs and the pickets followed after them. They shot and killed one, wounded the other. The little boy shot one of the pickets. The pickets took them on to Staunton and placed them in prison." Despite the violence of this exchange, conditions worsened considerably in 1862, when Union and Confederate civilians and soldiers commonly engaged in bushwhacking. In later cases, Unionists who surprised and shot Confederate pickets and were captured would be tried and executed as guerrillas.[26]

This was not the war that Virginia men had volunteered to fight. John Winfield, a junior officer with the Seventh Virginia Cavalry, wrote home to his wife from Winchester, at the lower end of the Shenandoah Valley. "You observe from the caption of this letter that I am again back in this miserable hole Winchester," wrote Winfield, "we were called here suddenly on yesterday from Sheppardstown—to prepare for another wild goose chase in the mountains of Hampshire—called away from the face of a foe—to seek one in the jungles and hills of a poverty stricken region." Winfield's anger, and his disregard for both the enemy and the citizens of the region he was supposed to be defending, typify the frustration among Confederates after several months of defeat in the mountainous and heavily Unionist northwest. Many easterners who came west identified western Virginians as the enemy responsible for Confederate failures in the region and targeted them for destruction. "I believe we are surrounded by Unionists in this section," noted one man. "Though they are afraid to express their real sentiments—We have made but four arrests as yet. they have not had a trial—I hope to have the pleasure of shooting a few of them yet. . . . They are acting as guides to McClellans armey—& are responsible for our defeat."[27]

Aided by the Unionist majority in northwestern Virginia, the Federals advanced south and east toward the Shenandoah Valley. By July 1861, Union troops pushed the Confederates off of Rich Mountain, capturing hundreds, including the commanding officer. Another Confederate commander, General Robert S. Garnett, was killed on July 13, and his forces retreated thirty-five miles south to Monterey. The combined effect of the loss at Rich Mountain and the barely successful retreat devastated the Confederates involved. Many soldiers reacted by dismissing the region and its inhabitants. In a fit of anger, one volunteer wrote home from Pocahontas County in late July: "This is the meanest place that ever had a name and I wouldnt live here for anything in reason, and if it wasnt that the Yankees might get to Richmond through this way they are welcome to the whole country about here, as far as I am concerned." Another eastern soldier in the west calmly advocated giving up the whole region. "Although Western Virginia abounds in that grandest natural scenery," he remarked,

"I am perfectly disgusted with the country and think we would be benefitted and not injured by a division of the state."[28]

This assessment proved prescient. The withdrawal of the northwestern counties from Virginia and their return to the Union removed the most coherent block of Unionists from the state and eased the way for the secessionist Virginia to come together. Even as Union and Confederate soldiers battled through the upper northwest in early 1861, political leaders in the region organized its exit from Confederate Virginia. Meeting in Wheeling in May 1861, Unionists convened a "loyal" government of Virginia and petitioned the United States for recognition. President Lincoln seized on these actions as the latent Southern Unionism upon which he had staked so much hope and eagerly assented to recognition. By 1863, the U.S. Congress had created the new state of West Virginia, composed of a northern layer of strong Unionist places and a southern layer of more pro-Confederate counties.[29] For Lincoln and the North, this represented a significant political victory, a display that the Confederacy could be peeled apart as white Southerners returned to their senses. Unfortunately for Lincoln, his victory may have done more to prolong the war than end it, for the removal of the upper northwest left a much more unified Virginia in its place.

The opposition of Unionist residents in the upper counties of the trans-Alleghany region compelled most soldiers, if not Virginia's politicians, to accept the division of the state.[30] John Hill recorded his memories of marching through Taylor County: "at that place we were saluted by no welcome smiles; no wavings of handkerchiefs, but sullen derisive countenances told us plainly that we were in the enemy's country."[31] Greenlee Davidson, marching through the region in late 1862, revealed that little had changed in the first year of war. "After leaving Middletown we passed through a most beautiful country," he noted. "The lands are in the highest state of cultivation and every farm has a barn almost as large as Noah's Ark. But strange to say, none of these magnificent barns, or roomy smokehouses contain either corn or meat." Davidson determined that the residents were hiding their goods; he approached homes hoping to buy food, but no one would sell to him. "It is perfectly evident," he concluded, "that the people of this section of the State are as hostile to us as if we were north of the Mason and Dixon line."[32] For the rest of the war, most Confederates treated the upper tier of northwestern counties as enemy territory. Ideology and the musket together marked the boundary between Confederate Virginia and the Union.

Even as the Federals secured their control of northern West Virginia during the war, Confederate Virginians worked to retain the southern counties of the soon-to-be Union state. The loyalty of this region to the South had been apparent to some Confederates early in the war. A young volunteer from the Piedmont stationed in the western part of the upper Valley conveyed to his parents the tenor of the area in a letter home in mid-summer 1861. Writing from Dickinson's Hotel in Alleghany County, Addison Roler reported that "the sentiment for secession & for sustaining our rights against N. aggression seems very unanimous & decided in this County—though, the people don't make so many outward demonstrations of it as at Charlottesville & the Univ."[33] Roler's assessment proved quite accurate. Over the course of the war, Alleghany County sent nearly every one of its eligible men to fight in the Confederate military.[34]

Enlistment rates indicate the level of support for the Confederacy in a given county. Within northwest Virginia as a whole, only 17 percent of eligible men fought in Confederate forces. For southwest Virginia and the Shenandoah Valley, the rates were 76 percent and 66 percent, respectively.[35] The experience of war encouraged many westerners to support the Confederacy, and, as a result, the triangle of Confederate country faintly visible at the moment of secession expanded and encompassed nearly all of the state by 1865.

Confederate enlistment, 1861–1865

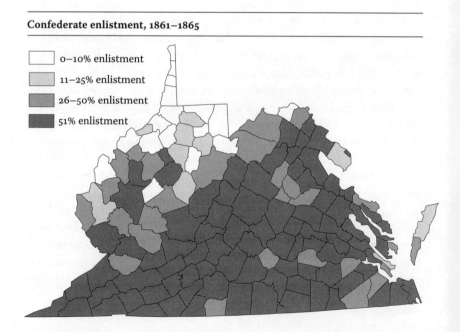

- 0–10% enlistment
- 11–25% enlistment
- 26–50% enlistment
- 51% enlistment

Commanders charged with defending the west sought to invigorate the latent Confederate majority they believed existed in the region. In an address "to the People of Western Virginia," General William Loring announced that "the Army of the Confederate States has come among you to expel the enemy, to rescue the people from the despotism of the counterfeit State Government imposed on you by Northern bayonets, and to restore the country once more to its natural allegiance to the State." Loring located his headquarters in Charleston, in the Kanawha Valley, a place under periodic Union occupation but with strong Confederate sympathies. Loring's rhetorical effort—asserting the "natural" allegiance of the area to the Old Dominion—reflected the political goals of generations of Virginia leaders who sought to unify the state along broad cultural lines while avoiding reference to the social and economic divisions that separated them. For those who neglected their natural obligations, Loring issued a stern warning. "Those who persist in adhering to the cause of the public enemy," he announced, "will be dealt with as their obstinate treachery deserves." Perhaps sensing that threats and appeals to blind obedience might not satisfy his need for men, Loring closed his proclamation with a reminder of the elements that bound all Virginians together in the struggle. He appealed to "all able-bodied men to join his army to defend the sanctities of religion and virtue, home, territory, honor and law."[36] Loring's conflation of ideological, emotional, and material interests reflected the ongoing efforts of Virginia leaders to build unity out of whatever materials proved suitable.

Some commanders made even more explicit linkages between the traditions of the west and the Confederacy. In an early 1862 address to his soldiers, General James Ewell Brown Stuart drew on the heritage of autonomous and free men in the west. "I appeal with confidence to men from my own section of the state," Stuart wrote, "Reared like you in plain view of the azure splendor of her blue mountains, we have a common veneration for yonder bulwark and temple of liberty."[37] Stuart's subtle evocation of the democratic traditions of the region resonated because of the changes in Virginia in the 1850s. The late antebellum political reforms were central to the mindset of Virginia's white men, and Confederate leaders wisely and effectively sought to convince these men that the liberties granted by Virginia could only be sustained by the Confederacy.

Just as generals like Stuart sought ways to alleviate regional tensions and generate enthusiasm for the Confederacy, so too did common soldiers. Early in the war, soldiers relied upon assumptions and stereotypes derived from antebellum political debates. Richard Waldrop, a Tidewater soldier, noted in mid-1861 that "some of the country companies called us parlour soldiers, kid glove & band box soldiers, etc." Like many soldiers, however, Waldrop observed that the sting of these accusations could be relieved by fulfilling their duties and earning the respect of others. "We have knocked the block out of them & left a good many of them on the side of the road every day, whether *we* were marching in front or rear of the column," he noted proudly, "& I don't think we will hear much more from them about that."[38] Waldrop's assumption may well have proved correct. Both Northern and Southern soldiers responded to evidence of physical courage and displays of martial acumen.[39] The process of fighting provided one way for Virginia soldiers to bridge gaps that had previously divided them.

Still, the experience of the war frequently required shifting troops out of their home regions. This often produced a sense of dislocation among the soldiers. In mid-1864, a newcomer to eastern Virginia recorded his impressions. "I am very much disappointed in E. Va.," wrote J. Kelly Bennette, "for I was always under the impression, from the way the Tuchahoes are in a habit of speaking to us backwoodsmen, that 'Old Fugginy' was the garden spot of all earth." Bennette's evaluation was substantially less charitable. "I find nothing but old worn out fields deeply washed in gullies & whose soil, if such a thing can be found, will not sprout black-eyed peas," he noted, "And then the water: it is miserable."[40] For some, the sense of geographic dislocation was enough to prompt thoughts of desertion. At the conclusion of a long letter of complaint about the impending draft, one soldier noted, "I hope if we are not drafted before we go out of service to see you about the first of may next. Or I shall make the attempt even at a risk. I will forget how the mountains look if I am forced to stay away two years more."[41] Others felt alienated by the urban places of the east. Edward Penick, a soldier from Pittsylvania County stationed in Richmond, described his amazement at the city and the capitol building, but found the prevalence of vice offensive. "Our boys are anxious to get from here on account of filth & not more so than myself," he wrote his wife. "I see degradation in almost every form you can think of."[42]

The antagonism that some soldiers felt toward their fellow Virginians, or at least toward places in their state, did not necessarily blind them to the necessity of protecting those people or those places. Over time, even those volunteers who showed signs of alienation or unhappiness with their posting began to rethink their outlooks. Despite his depressing stay in the state capitol, Penick continued to write home confident of imminent victory. J. Kelly Bennette accompanied Jubal Early's Army of the Valley on its raid into Maryland in late summer 1864. Though he disliked the burning of Chambersburg, Pennsylvania, Early's most infamous accomplishment, Bennette felt it justified by the Union misbehavior in the South. Crossing into Virginia in early August, he noted the destruction around Romney: "What a desolate looking, desolated place it is! A fine example of yankee rule! Who now looking at this will feel any compunction of conscience for the burning of Chambersburg?"[43] The atrocities to which Virginians had been subjected offered an important counterbalance to lingering notions of regional prejudice.[44]

Counteracting those men who found old suspicions confirmed, other Virginia soldiers had positive experiences as they traveled to new parts of the state. In letters home and in their diaries, soldiers from all regions recounted the novelty of being in parts of the state about which they had only read. Detailed sociologies of hardy westerners or wealthy Tidewater plantations filled the journals of soldiers as they struggled to splice together their actual experiences of Virginia with their prewar assumptions. James Henry Langhorne wrote home in a state of euphoria from Harpers Ferry. "This is one of the most picturesque places I ever saw," he wrote, "the Shanandone river comes pouring down the Valey of Va on the Southern side of the place, and just across it commanding every accessable point to the place are the Virginia heights. . . ." Like many soldiers, Langhorne delighted in the Shenandoah Valley. "I don't know that I ever enjoyed a travel more than I did the one down the Valey yesterday," he wrote, "the country is beautiful, undulating the land very rich, and everything looked flourishing & prosperous, I never had an idea of what a glorious state Va was until now."[45] On their travels, men thrilled at the sight of mountains or basked in the grandeur of the statues of Washington, Jefferson, and Madison around the capitol building in Richmond. These experiences provided a new sense of state solidarity and added strength to the belief that Virginia was a place worth preserving.

The fact that the Confederacy drew soldiers from all regions of the state stands as testimony that men understood the interconnectedness of their fortunes. The service of Valley soldiers in the swamps around Suffolk or of Petersburg men fighting their way across the Alleghany plateau demonstrated their commitment to a cause larger than themselves or their community interests. In mid-1864, Benjamin Lyons Farinholt commanded a small squad of men and a large contingent of local farmers in the successful defense of Staunton Bridge, in Halifax County. Following the repulse of Union troops, Farinholt appealed to citizens of the area for two hundred slaves to build defensive works. "This labor may be the means of saving your farms and homes from desolation and the foul presence of the enemy's vandals," he urged. Farinholt then drew on his own family's experience in a different part of the state to encourage these residents to preserve Virginia. "I who have seen my own section of the state laid waste and desolate by the enemy appeal to you," he wrote, "that your own homes may not meet a similar fate."[46]

The sympathy of shared sacrifice was most evident following the battle of Fredericksburg in late 1862. Although the Confederates bested the Union troops in battle, they remained confined south of the Rappahannock River through a harsh December. As bad as conditions were for the soldiers, many immediately organized relief efforts for Fredericksburg residents. In prewar Virginia, local elites had provided relief to worthy poor neighbors during severe times on an ad hoc basis.[47] Union artillery shells, however, had fallen on rich and poor residences alike in Fredericksburg and quickly destroyed the mechanisms and the means for providing aid to the less fortunate. The city and county governments were similarly incapacitated and unable to help. Soldiers formed their own charitable entities, submitting circulars among the camps to raise money for local residents. One colonel collected more than $2,000 in an hour, a testament, he felt, to the bravery and generosity of the soldiers who defended the families of Virginia on the battlefield and off. The contributions were also a testament, he believed, to the relatively strong position of Virginia Confederates and to soldiers' desire to sustain communities to which they were bound only by ties of state and national allegiance. The generosity of Southern soldiers for the victims of Fredericksburg revealed the remarkable success that Confederates had achieved in building a nation. Contributions came from communities all over the Confederacy. Those who contributed felt a common cause with the residents of this Virginia town, and their actions demonstrated the depth of Confederate nationalism at the conclusion of this awful year of war.[48]

Richard Waldrop embodied the transformation many Confederate Virginians experienced during the war. In the fall of 1864, he described to his wife the effectiveness of Sheridan's logistical raids in the Shenandoah Valley while unconsciously revealing that Sheridan failed in his larger goal of overawing pro-Confederate sentiment. He reported that "the Yankees have played sad havoc here: having burnt all the mills, barns, & workshops in their reach & night before last the country below here was illuminated by the burning houses. It is very trying to us to have to stand & look at their vandalism & not be able on account of our small numbers to punish them for their scoundrelism & relive our people from the galling trials to which they are subjected." Waldrop's concern revealed the successful consolidation of Confederate identity that had occurred during the war. In

1861, he had been posted to the northwest, where he complained bitterly about the land, the climate, and the people. Were it not that "the Yankees might get to Richmond through this way [the Valley]," he had pronounced in 1861, "they are welcome to the whole country."[49] Over the course of the war, and especially in the context of what seemed to him, and others, to be egregious violations of the code of civilized war, he could now speak unself-consciously about "our people" and mean western Virginians as well. This curious and entirely unintended side effect of Sheridan's oc-cupation mirrored the reactions Virginians expressed after the battle of Fredericksburg in 1862.[50] The dramatic suffering of one region helped mo-bilize support for the Confederacy as a whole.

Some soldiers offered explicit nationalist justifications for their con-tinued service despite lingering resentment over confinement in places unfamiliar to them. Alexander Pendleton, born and raised in the upper Shenandoah Valley, complained to his mother about the mountainous Appalachian region. "It is up one mountain and up another and so on for the whole road," he lamented. Pendleton resigned himself to defending a part of the state for which he did not care because he was acting on behalf of the state as whole, noting in the same letter, "this is the meanest coun-try I ever saw, but still it is old Virginia and we must have it."[51] Another Virginia soldier expressed a similar sentiment during his campaigning in the mountainous southwest. "Good gracious," this man wrote a friend, "did I ever expect to be in such a country candidly I would not live here for a million a year, however a sense of duty made me come & will make me stay."[52] That willingness to stay demonstrated a faith in the value of all parts of the Confederacy.

The new tendency among Virginians during the Civil War to focus on Confederate loyalty as the way to define regions, rather than the socio-economic and political distinctions used during the antebellum period, highlights the centrality of domestic concerns in considering the effect of the war on Virginia. The willingness of some Virginians to give up on what became West Virginia was shaped by prewar animosities between the northwest and other parts of the state. Conversely, the ability of most Virginians to overcome regional prejudices and fight for the protection of the state as a whole helped extend the conflict in time and space. Changes that had been occurring in the antebellum era—principally the consoli-dation of those places connected to slavery—accelerated during the war as a new Virginia defined its interests in harmony with those of the new Confederate slave republic.

Similarly, the hard work done by white Virginians to bring the state to-gether around a Confederate identity may have helped facilitate the build-

ing of a new racial coalition within the state later in the century. A favorite
tactic of Confederate veterans seeking either political office or support for
a policy was to recreate the sense of shared purpose that prevailed during the war. Without a doubt, these advocates invented and reimagined a
substantially more harmonious past than had actually existed. Nevertheless, most white Confederates had in fact abandoned antebellum regional
alignments in favor of ones based on a dedication to the Confederate
cause. In doing so, they both perpetuated war and created a new Virginia
for times of peace.

Notes

I would like to thank Andrew Torget, Ed Ayers, and Gary Gallagher for their helpful suggestions on this essay.

1. I am drawing here on the model of nationalism described by David Potter, in
which he argues that "national loyalty, far from being opposed to other loyalties,
is in fact strengthened by incorporating them." "It is self-evident," Potter wrote,
"that national loyalty flourishes not by challenging and overpowering all other
loyalties, but by subsuming them all in a mutually supportive relation to one another." See David Potter, "The Historian's Use of Nationalism and Vice Versa," in
The South and Sectional Conflict (Baton Rouge: Louisiana State University Press,
1968), 47–49.

2. The boundaries I have used to create the five regions described above come
from a report compiled by the state auditor, in response to a request from the
secession convention to enumerate the men available for military service. The
auditor issued a "report . . . exhibiting the White, Free and Slave Population, and
the value of real estate and personal property, arranged by districts," in November
1861. The report is document 37, table A, in *Journals of the Virginia State Convention of 1861*, vol. 3, *Documents*. (Richmond: Virginia State Library, 1966), 5–10. I
generated the economic and demographic conclusions reached in this paragraph
through analysis of the 1860 Census.

3. Kenneth Noe, *Southwest Virginia's Railroad: Modernization and the Sectional Crisis* (Urbana: University of Illinois Press, 1994).

4. See, for example, Alison Freehling, who, in her account of the debates over
slavery in the 1830s, posits a conflict between eastern and western Virginia so
powerful "as to preclude peaceful resolution." See Alison Goodyear Freehling,
Drift Toward Dissolution: The Virginia Slavery Debate of 1831–1832 (Baton Rouge:
Louisiana State University Press, 1982). Also, see George Ellis Moore, *A Banner in
the Hills: West Virginia's Statehood* (New York: Meredith, 1963).

5. For a brief overview of the general move toward more democratic state con-
stitutions in the South, see Fletcher M. Green, "Democracy in the Old South,"

Journal of Southern History, 12 (February 1946): 3–23. The most thorough coverage of Virginia's course to an unrestricted franchise and equal taxation can be found in Freehling, *Drift Toward Dissolution*, and William G. Shade, *Democratizing the Old Dominion: Virginia and the Second Party System* (Charlottesville: University Press of Virginia, 1996), 103. My summary of these events draws heavily on both of these accounts as well as Craig Simpson, *A Good Southerner: The Life of Henry A. Wise of Virginia* (Chapel Hill: University of North Carolina Press, 1985).

6. These continued to be apportioned on a "mixed" basis that considered both population and property-holding. See Daniel Crofts, *Reluctant Confederates: Upper South Unionists in the Secession Crisis* (Chapel Hill: University of North Carolina Press, 1989), 57, for a summary of the changes in the 1850–1851 convention.

7. William Shade chronicles the increase in political participation over the antebellum era, which he attributes mostly to the growth of parties as institutions. See especially chapter 7 of *Democratizing the Old Dominion*.

8. According to Daniel Crofts, the "political linkages between the disparate regions of Virginia tended to overcome the tenuousness of its material and cultural bonds" (Crofts, *Reluctant Confederates*, 57). For an analysis of western Virginia that reaches the same conclusion, see John Alexander Williams, "Class, Section, and Culture in Nineteenth-Century West Virginia Politics," in *Appalachia in the Making: The Mountain South in the Nineteenth Century*, ed. Mary Beth Pudup, Dwight B. Billings, and Altina L. Waller (Chapel Hill: University of North Carolina, 1995), 210–32.

9. David R. Goldfield, *Urban Growth in the Age of Sectionalism: Virginia, 1847–1861* (Baton Rouge: Louisiana State University Press, 1977), and William M. Mathew, *Edmund Ruffin and the Crisis of Slavery in the Old South: The Failure of Agricultural Reform* (Athens: University of Georgia Press, 1988).

10. Daniel Crofts shows this process in motion in his history of Southampton County, which was one of the few parts of the state with soil and climate suitable for growing cotton but which also produced the most highly prized pigs in Virginia, as well as a variety of grains and marketable vegetables. See Daniel Crofts, *Old Southampton: Politics and Society in a Virginia County, 1834–1869* (Charlottesville: University Press of Virginia, 1992), chapter 3.

11. No comprehensive history of Virginia's antebellum industrialization has been written, but numerous case studies provide valuable evidence on the wealth and diversity of approaches taken around the state before the Civil War. See John T. Stealey III, *The Antebellum Kanawha Salt Business and Western Markets* (Lexington: University Press of Kentucky, 1993), and Charles B. Dew, *Bond of Iron: Master and Slave at Buffalo Forge* (New York: W. W. Norton, 1994).

12. John Majewski, *A House Dividing: Economic Development in Pennsylvania and Virginia before the Civil War* (Cambridge: Cambridge University Press, 2000).

13. Claudia L. Bushman's study of an antebellum family in King and Queen County provides a good example of the multiple uses to which slaves were put

and of how some owners creatively integrated slavery and new technologies. See Claudia L. Bushman, *In Old Virginia: Slavery, Farming, and Society in the Journal of John Walker* (Baltimore: Johns Hopkins University Press, 2002). Other local studies emphasize this theme as well. See Lynda J. Morgan, *Emancipation in Virginia's Tobacco Belt, 1850–1870* (Athens: University of Georgia Press, 1992); Goldfield, *Urban Growth in the Age of Sectionalism;* Gregg D. Kimball, *American City, Southern Place: A Cultural History of Antebellum Richmond* (Athens: University of Georgia Press, 2000); and Frederick F. Siegel, *The Roots of Southern Distinctiveness: Tobacco and Society in Danville, Virginia, 1780–1865* (Chapel Hill: University of North Carolina Press, 1987).

14. For the view that slavery in Virginia was losing its appeal and its power, see the work of William W. Freehling. Freehling's interpretation is best expressed in an article on the Virginia secession convention: "The debates reveal all the anxiety of a declining society implicated in the ironies of its former greatness and convulsed by the internal contradictions which caused the Deep South to secede." See William W. Freehling, "The Editorial Revolution, Virginia, and the Coming of the Civil War," *Civil War History* 16 (March 1969): 64–72. See also William W. Freehling, *The Road to Disunion: Secessionists at Bay* (New York: Oxford University Press, 1990), 24; and William W. Freehling, *The South vs. The South: How Anti-Confederate Southerners Shaped the Course of the Civil War* (New York: Oxford University Press, 2001).

15. Dew, *Bond of Iron;* Charles B. Dew, *Ironmaker to the Confederacy: Joseph R. Anderson and the Tredegar Iron Works* (1966; reprint, Richmond: Library of Virginia, 1999); and Kimball, *American City, Southern Place,* chapter 5.

16. For instance, a study of Danville, Virginia, found a "sharply stratified society" but one that nonetheless offered a growing middle class a greater share of resources during the 1850s (see Siegel, *Roots of Southern Distinctiveness,* chapter 6). All of the elements elucidated in this paragraph can be seen in Augusta County, a county in the Shenandoah Valley with 25 percent slaveholding households. For a further elucidation of this argument, see Edward L. Ayers and William G. Thomas III, "The Differences Slavery Made: A Close Analysis of Two American Communities," http://www.vcdh.virginia.edu/AHR/ (December 2003), accessed January 2–10, 2004.

17. Charles L. C. Minor to John Hampden Chamberlayne, March 1861, in *Ham Chamberlayne—Virginian: Letters and Papers of an Artillery Officer in the War for Southern Independence, 1861–1865,* ed. C. G. Chamberlayne (Richmond: Dietz, 1932).

18. John Hampden Chamberlayne to Parke Chamberlayne, February 18, 1861, Bagby Family Papers, Virginia Historical Society, Richmond, Virginia (hereafter abbreviated as VHS).

19. James Dorman Davidson to James B. Dorman, March 6, 1861, in Bruce Greenwalt, ed., "Unionists in Rockbridge County: The Correspondence of James

Dorman Davidson Concerning the Virginia Secession Convention of 1861," *Virginia Magazine of History and Biography* 73 (January 1965): 78–102.

20. James Dorman Davidson to R. M. T. Hunter, May 2, 1861, in Bruce Greenwalt, ed., "Life Behind Confederate Lines: The Correspondence of James D. Davidson," *Civil War History* 16 (September 1970): 205–26.

21. Over the course of the war, Confederate civilians in the lower Shenandoah Valley strongly supported the Confederacy even as many in the region proudly remained loyal to the Union. Edward H. Phillips, *The Lower Shenandoah Valley in the Civil War: The Impact of War Upon the Civilian Population and Upon Civil Institutions* (Lynchburg, Va.: H. E. Howard, 1993).

22. Thomas L. Broun to Annie Broun, May 15, 1861, Catherine Barbara Broun Papers, Southern Historical Collection, University of North Carolina, Chapel Hill, North Carolina (hereafter abbreviated as SHC).

23. James K. Edmondson to Emma Edmondson, May 22, 1861, in *My Dear Emma: War Letters of Col. James K. Edmondson, 1861–1865*, ed. Charles W. Turner (Verona, Va.: McClure Press, 1978).

24. James K. Edmondson to Emma Edmondson, May 25, 1861, in Turner, *My Dear Emma*.

25. John Q. Winfield to Sallie Winfield, June 26, 1861, John Q. Winfield Papers, SHC.

26. John A. Garnett to William Gray, September 30, 1861, William Gray Papers, VHS; Tinsley Linsley Allen to Ellen Allen, November 13, 1861, in *The Allen Family of Amherst County, Virginia: Civil War Letters*, ed. Charles W. Turner (Berryville, Va.: Rockbridge Publishing Co., 1995), 4. For guerrilla warfare in western Virginia, see Kenneth W. Noe, "Exterminating Savages: The Union Army and Mountain Guerrillas in Southern West Virginia, 1861–1862," in *The Civil War in Appalachia: Collected Essays*, ed. Kenneth W. Noe and Shannon H. Wilson (Knoxville: University of Tennessee Press, 1997), 104–27.

27. John Q. Winfield to Sallie Winfield, September 16, 1861, John Q. Winfield Papers, SHC; William George Cabaniss to "Dear Pa," July 30, 1861, Moore Family Papers, VHS.

28. Richard Woolfolk Waldrop to Christopher Waldrop, July 27, 1861, Richard Woolfolk Waldrop Papers, SHC; Nimrod Brahaman Hamner to "Dear Ma," July 15, 1861, Hamner Family Papers, VHS.

29. The story of the breakaway counties in northwest Virginia and their rebirth as the state of West Virginia is told in Richard L. Curry, *A House Divided: A Study of Statehood Politics and the Copperhead Movement in West Virginia* (Pittsburgh: University of Pittsburgh Press, 1964), and George Ellis Moore, *Banner in the Hills: West Virginia's Statehood* (New York: Appleton, 1963).

30. For evidence of Governor John Letcher's reluctance to admit the separation of the state even in late 1862, see Roland Lee Sevy, "John Letcher and West Virginia," *West Virginia History* 27 (October 1965): 10–55.

31. John Lyon Hill, August 9, 1861, John Lyon Hill diary, VHS.

32. Charles W. Turner, ed., "Captain Greenlee Davidson: Letters of a Virginia Soldier," *Civil War History* 17 (September 1971): 197–221.

33. Addison Brown Roler diary, July 5, 1861, Addison Brown Roler Papers, VHS.

34. This figure comes from a database I created for my dissertation that includes enlistment information for all Virginia counties.

35. Aaron Sheehan-Dean, "The Family War: Motivation and Commitment in the American Civil War" (Ph.D. diss., University of Virginia, 2003), 282, table 1-1.

36. General William Loring, "To the People of Western Virginia," September 14, 1862, Broadside, Duke Special Collections, Duke University, Durham, North Carolina (hereafter abbreviated DSC).

37. James Ewell Brown Stuart, March 5, 1862, Box 262, James Ewell Brown Stuart Papers, Henry Huntington Library, Pasadena, California (hereafter abbreviated as HH).

38. Richard Woolfolk Waldrop to Christopher Waldrop, July 23, 1862, Richard Woolfolk Waldrop Papers, SHC.

39. Gerald F. Linderman, *Embattled Courage: The Experience of Combat in the American Civil War* (New York: Free Press, 1987).

40. J. Kelly Bennette diary, June 14, 1864, J. Kelly Bennette Papers, SHC.

41. Edward Camden to "Miss Porter," February 2, 1862, William H. Jones Papers, DSC.

42. Edwin Anderson Penick to "My Fond Wife," March 12, 1862, Edwin Anderson Penick Papers, VHS.

43. J. Kelly Bennette diary, August 4, 1864, J. Kelly Bennette Papers, SHC.

44. Several recent studies of Virginia stress the cohesive power of Confederate identity within the state. See Steven V. Ash, *When the Yankees Came: Conflict and Chaos in the Occupied South* (Chapel Hill: University of North Carolina Press, 1995); Steven Elliott Tripp, *Yankee Town, Southern City: Race and Class Relations in Civil War Lynchburg* (New York: New York University Press, 1997); William Blair, *Virginia's Private War: Feeding Body and Soul in the Confederacy, 1861–1865* (New York: Oxford University Press, 1998), 56, 141; Daniel E. Sutherland, *Seasons of War: The Ordeal of a Confederate Community, 1861–1865* (Baton Rouge: Louisiana State University Press, 1995), 355; Werner H. Steger, "'United to Support, But Not Combined to Injure': Free Workers and Immigrants in Richmond, Virginia, During the Era of Sectionalism, 1847–1865" (Ph.D. diss., The George Washington University, 1999); Michael Stuart Mangus, "'The Debatable Land': Loudoun and Fauquier Counties, Virginia, during the Civil War Era" (Ph.D. diss., Ohio State University, 1998).

45. James Henry Langhorne to "My own darling Mother," May 13, 1861, Langhorne Family Papers, VHS.

46. Benjamin Lyons Farinholt, "Appeal to the Citizens of Charlotte and Halifax," July 4, 1864, Benjamin Lyons Farinholt Papers, VHS.

47. Suzanne Lebsock, *The Free Women of Petersburg: Status and Culture in a Southern Town, 1784–1860* (New York: Oxford University Press, 1985).

48. Thomas T. Munford to "My Dear Nannie," December 22, 1862, Thomas T. Munford Papers, Lewis Leigh Collection, Military History Institute, Carlisle, Pennsylvania (hereafter abbreviated MHI). See also George S. Pickett diary, December 21, 1862, George S. Pickett Papers, Civil War Times Illustrated Collection, MHI, and George Rable, *Fredericksburg! Fredericksburg!* (Chapel Hill: University of North Carolina Press, 2002), 429. Montgomery Slaughter was the wartime mayor of Fredericksburg. The collection of his papers at the Henry E. Huntington Library contains numerous contributions from individuals and organizations all over the Confederacy.

49. Richard Woolfolk Waldrop to Ellen Douglas Waldrop, October 6, 1864; Richard Woolfolk Waldrop to Christopher Waldrop, July 27, 1861, both in Richard Woolfolk Waldrop Papers, SHC.

50. In her study of Loudoun County, Brenda Stevenson notes that civilian support for the Confederacy solidified after Sheridan's activities in the area. See Brenda Stevenson, *Life in Black and White: Family and Community in the Slave South* (New York: Oxford University Press, 1996), 36. This same response can be seen among the South Carolina civilians subjected to William T. Sherman's campaigns in late 1864-early 1865. See Jaqueline Campbell, *When Sherman Marched North from the Sea: Resistance on the Confederate Homefront* (Chapel Hill: University of North Carolina Press, 2003).

51. Alexander Pendleton to Anzolette Page Pendleton, May 10, 1862, in W. G. Bean, "The Valley Campaign of 1862 As Revealed in Letters of Sandie Pendleton," *Virginia Magazine of History and Biography* 78 (July 1970): 326–64.

52. Dick to Mr. Wren, January 22, 1861, Robert Alonzo Brock Collection, Box 283, HH.

Defining Confederate Respectability

Morality, Patriotism, and Confederate Identity in Richmond's Civil War Public Press

Amy R. Minton

On March 19, 1862, the *Daily Dispatch*, Richmond's most widely circulated newspaper, presented a question to its readers. It encouraged Richmonders to look around at their neighbors and "ask why it is that, with scarcely an exception, the best members of society are the most loyal in their devotion to the South; whilst those who are doubtful are, with scarcely an exception, men who are doubtful in the relations of social life, who are dissolute, or dishonest, or false in their private character, or, if not absolutely vicious, who are weak minded, eccentric, and unstable?" In posing this query, the *Dispatch* did two things. First, it equated social standing with "private character." Those "best members" of Confederate society were not necessarily the wealthiest or most politically prominent people, or those with highly placed family connections, but those whose characters were the most sound. Second, the *Dispatch* explicitly linked those sound character principles to Confederate patriotism. While people with disreputable characters and behaviors were most likely to be unpatriotic, those of good character, it claimed, stood unwaveringly by the South. By forging these connections between character and patriotism, the *Daily Dispatch* put before its readers a version of Confederate identity that linked moral, social, and political respectability.[1]

The *Dispatch* article was part of a larger effort by Richmond's Civil War newspapers to create and promote a sense of common Confederate identity and cause among their readers. The city's five major wartime newspapers—the *Daily Dispatch*, the *Richmond Whig*, the *Richmond Enquirer*, the *Richmond Daily Examiner*, and the *Richmond Sentinel*—differed greatly in their views on Confederate politics, economy, and military operations, but they all fervently supported the war. While innumerable examples from personal correspondence, diaries, petitions, and other sources indicate that Confederate identity was contested and often fractured along class, gender, or other lines, the newspapers relentlessly promoted a spirit of nationalism and commonality among the members of the fledgling Confederate nation. In 1862, in response to a debate concerning the military exemption status of printers, the *Daily Dispatch* highlighted the importance of the press to the war effort. It asked its readers, "who can estimate the value to the Southern cause of the daily appeals of a patriotic press?" Without the "incentives to patriotism and energy which the press daily pours forth," the public "would sink into apathy and inertion." Likewise, the *Richmond Sentinel* asserted that "whatever will promote the cause of public and private virtue, Christian morals, social happiness, popular elevation and intelligence, and a serene dignity of national character, shall at least find unvarying sympathy in the columns of the Sentinel. . . . We shall aim to inculcate correct tastes and sentiments, rather than to seek applause or profit by ministering to bad ones."[2]

In their attempts to foster patriotism, the papers tried to use language and ideas that would unify a diverse and rapidly changing city. At the time of secession, Richmond was both the largest city in Virginia and the state's social, cultural, political, and economic center. Railroad lines into the city had multiplied over the previous decade and a half, spurring an enormous growth of business, industry, and manufacturing that helped push Richmond's population to 37,910 people in 1860—23,635 white, 2,576 free blacks, and 11,699 slaves. Rapid expansion produced a voracious need for labor that enslaved African Americans alone could not fulfill, and the 1850s saw a growing population of white and immigrant laborers and artisans settle in the city. The numerous tobacco factories, manufacturing establishments, milling operations, railroads, and financial institutions all helped make Richmond the South's leading industrial and commercial center, and attracted not only laborers, but businessmen and merchants as well. As the capital of Virginia, Richmond also hosted a sizable number of government officials and clerks. Recognizing that their readership extended across the spectrum of society, the press tried to put forth an image of Confederate citizenship that could appeal to a large part of the many social classes of the Confederate capital.[3]

The Richmond wartime press worked tirelessly to promote the virtues of what might be termed a "patriotic" or "Confederate" respectability that simultaneously projected an image of Confederates as upstanding, moral people and sought to keep Confederate men and women from falling into the immorality and vices they felt would doom the Confederate cause. Common to all the papers, despite other differences, was the message that, in the Confederacy, patriotism and respectability were inseparable. By employing a rhetoric couched in the language of respectability, a concept familiar to all classes of Confederate society, the papers tried to unite everyone, regardless of their station in life, in a common cause. Winning the war, the papers recognized, would require the efforts of all citizens, rich and poor, men and women.

The press's use of respectability as the focal point of its discourse on Confederate identity would not have seemed strange or out of place to most of Richmond's citizens. In the decades prior to the Civil War, Richmonders of all classes increasingly viewed themselves and others around them in terms of respectability. A culture centered around the ideas of respectability began to emerge after the 1820s as Southerners sought to reconcile their society based on slavery with the larger American cultures influenced by evangelical Christianity and domesticity. Hierarchy, a critical element of the Southern slaveholding society, began to be portrayed in terms of a hierarchy of morals and character, rather than simply power. While the wealthiest men continued to hold most of the powerful positions in Southern society, wealth was viewed as an outward sign of respectability. Success, Southerners theorized, came from hard work and fair dealings, and those who had achieved success were deserving of its rewards. While an aristocratic culture of hierarchy and honor continued to exist in the South, many Southerners were also beginning to turn to a more democratic, individualistic culture that still managed to incorporate African American slavery.[4]

To antebellum Southerners, the behaviors that made someone respectable emanated from within. Often, the basis for what constituted respectable behavior was influenced by the morals and teachings of evangelical Christianity. Honesty, industriousness, sobriety, propriety, and decency all became hallmarks of what it meant to be a respectable person. While wealth and material prosperity were certainly seen as outward signs of respectability, one did not necessarily need to be wealthy to be respectable. Decent clothing, a neat and clean appearance, and a private residence were all markers of a respectable person, but it was not those material possessions alone which made someone respectable. Above all, respectability was based on character, morality, and conduct.[5]

For both white men and women, the contours of respectability often closely mirrored those of the culture of domesticity that gained strength in both the North and South during the antebellum era. Respectable men were to work hard at their chosen profession and earn sufficient wages to support their families. Failure to do so was often attributed by others to a lack of morals, character, and sense of duty that led the man into vice, sin, or simply sloth. For respectable women, the home was their focal point and special care. The natural piety and nurturing instincts that Southerners attributed to women made them the centers of private home life. An emphasis on the home did not mean that respectable women were never seen outside of it; on the contrary, women sought to better themselves by attending public lectures and exhibitions, and frequently donated their time and energy to charitable and religious causes, including their churches and teaching in Sunday schools. Paid work outside the home, however, was generally frowned upon, primarily because it left women with little time to perform the household responsibilities so necessary to the fulfillment of a respectable, moral home life for themselves and their families, but also because it potentially left women under the control of men outside those families.[6]

These ideas of respectability, while implemented by people according to their economic class and abilities, found resonance among many levels of Richmond's prewar society. Merchants, politicians, artisans, laborers, and professionals could all relate to an ethos that placed emphasis on the individual, and on the individual's ability to shape their place in society. It came naturally, then, for the Confederate press, in an effort to reach as many people as possible, to often use a language of respectability to convey their opinions about Confederate society. The press initially used a rhetoric of respectability to distinguish between true Confederates and other groups of people, whether they were Yankees, foreigners, or simply disreputable elements of Southern society. As the first excitement and passion of war gave way to the harsh realities of a long, punishing conflict, the press altered and redefined the elements of respectability to accommodate wartime conditions and circumstances, always correlating the new Confederate respectability with the patriotic behaviors and attitudes that they believed would help push the Confederate nation to victory. In the process of creating a positive portrayal of Confederates and Confederate behavior, the press often used the language of respectability to gloss over and hide the deep problems and class conflicts that confronted the Confederacy. Rather than opening up a real dialogue about those problems, the press avoided the underlying issues by simplistically portraying every patriotic act as stemming from a sound, respectable character, and every unpatriotic act as evidence of a disreputable character.

From the earliest days of the war, Confederates—and the Confederate press—tried to separate themselves culturally from Northerners. While Southerners had long drawn distinctions between themselves and Northerners on many levels, secession and the outbreak of the Civil War lent these efforts at self-definition and contrast a new urgency. In the fall of 1861, the *Richmond Enquirer* highlighted the importance of genteel conduct and behavior on the part of Confederates. The Confederate people, the *Enquirer* asserted, were establishing at this stage both their character and their reputation. "To a people," it proclaimed, "as well as to an individual, a good name is to be held as among the most valuable of possessions." To support their good name, Confederates characterized themselves as law-abiding, rational people who conducted their society with "perfect internal order . . . and harmonious co-operation" between its citizens. In the South, they claimed, "order, discipline, subordination, moderation, are everywhere and in everything apparent." The *Dispatch* also lauded the South as having "a state of society in which pauperism is unknown, criminals few, female virtue respected, and the physical and moral welfare of the people, as a whole, better than that of any equal number of people on any other part of the earth's surface." While these statements are obviously hyperbolic and too sweeping to be true, they highlight the importance the press placed on convincing all readers that the South—and by extension, the South's purpose in seeking independence—was inherently respectable and intelligent.[7]

Confederate soldiers early on appeared as paragons of virtue and respectability. The papers depicted Confederate volunteers as part of a "citizen soldiery" made up from only the "best sort" of men. The *Dispatch* observed that Richmond's Sturdivant's Battery was composed "entirely of young Virginians, of character and respectability," and that anyone wishing to join could be assured of spending time "with men of the right kind." In advertising the need for recruits for various companies, the *Dispatch* noted that a local unit, the Richmond Light Infantry Blues, only wanted "men of good character" to join. Significantly, the press's praise and admiration extended to companies from all levels of society: a battalion made up of workers from the Tredegar Iron Works that the *Whig* termed men "of the Right Stripe"; the Emmet Guard, a unit made up of laboring-class

Irish men; and the city guard, which the *Enquirer* observed contained many "respectable persons." The press maintained that true Confederate soldiers were upright, sober, churchgoing men.[8]

In contrast to the pictures of moral, decent, responsible Confederates that it painted, the Richmond press never lost an opportunity to characterize Northerners as devoid of social respectability and self-respect. Quite often, editorialists linked Northern society's demoralization with an unbridled pursuit of gain. As the *Daily Dispatch* argued, the North had decided to make money rather than character or moral worth "the standard of respectability." In doing so, Northerners had developed a "passion for show and fashion, which is a distinguishing characteristic of vulgarians and pretenders." In the North, "infidelity, fanaticism, wealth, and the greed of gain" had led to a "gradual corruption of manners." There, "individuals once respectable, by a long indulgence of evil passions, may become more like beasts than men"—a description they thought fit the Yankees perfectly. The *Richmond Whig* came to the same conclusions about Northern society. "In New York," it claimed, "the intense love of money getting" and "the rivalry and competition for ostentatious and luxurious distinctions" had "extinguished even the traces of that Spartan simplicity which made us and alone can keep us a free people. Luxury and the love of gain, which procures it, have corrupted their society to the core."[9]

Northern soldiers, the papers argued, could not compare to the Southern troops in terms of quality and character. The *Dispatch* asserted in exaggerated fashion that the Northern troops were "composed of the dregs of their cities, of all the reckless, brutal and licentious material that threatened the social structure at home." Several days later, the paper reiterated that "while the volunteer forces of the North contain a few regiments of men taken from the respectable classes in society, the great proportion of those who have enlisted are of the most lawless and abandoned character." Specifically, these recruits were "the refuse scum of its oderiferous, thieving, idle, abandoned, dissolute, God-forsaken, hell-deserving and gallows-tending subjects." While Northern society was degenerate as a whole, the papers claimed, the men making up the army displayed truly reprehensible characters.[10]

The press portrayed estimable Northerners as being either reluctant to make war on the South or completely opposed to any war at all. Respectable Northerners, just like respectable Southerners, saw the rightness in the Southern cause. Shortly after the war began, the *Daily Dispatch* observed of the North that "from the very nature of things, the better classes of that section will revolt from the invasion of a country, proposing no interference with them at home, claiming the simple boon of independence and separation from a Government to which they can no longer yield a loyal consent. The intelligent and better classes will feel . . . that this claim is too sacred" to be opposed. "Even during the present excitement and enthusiasm," the *Dispatch* continued, "we see indications in the more respectable of the Northern regiments . . . of an unwillingness to push their loyalty to the extent of invading the South. . . . It is only mercenaries and cut-throats that will enlist in the bloody programme of invasion." For the *Whig*, former Northern friends and supporters of the South lost their claims to respectability when they lacked the moral courage to maintain their conservative opposition to the war and oppose the popular "despotism" that ruled the North. What were once "decent, plausible, respectable, fair-weather friends," it asserted, had decided "to sacrifice . . . whatever respect may have heretofore been entertained for them in this quarter of the world" by capitulating to popular war fever and sentiment in the North.[11]

During the first months of the war, excitement and pageantry characterized the war effort as men flocked to volunteer for the army and women immediately set to work making uniforms and clothing for the soldiers. It was easy for the press at that time to sustain a rhetoric that emphasized both the respectability of Confederate citizens and the Confederate cause and nation in general. As early as the summer of 1861, but more intensively in the following years of the war, however, it became harder for the press to maintain the illusion of an upright, decent, sober, honest Confederate citizenry. The Confederate capital itself became so beset with crime, drunkenness, and rowdiness that President Jefferson Davis had to declare martial law in the city by March 1862, less than a year after the war began. Inflation, food shortages, and public protest added further to the city's problems. As the press struggled to reconcile the deplorable state of affairs in the city with the idea of a virtuous and moral Confederacy, it again relied on the language of respectability to help distinguish friend from foe, this time within the capital city. Characterizing all disruptive elements in the city as disreputable people, the press excluded these people, on the basis of their immorality and lack of patriotism, from the ranks of true Confederates.

Although the press acknowledged that some of the disreputable elements were of Virginian, and even Richmond, nativity, the papers frequently characterized the debased and criminal portion of the population as coming from without, rather than arising from within. In particular, the press often claimed that these elements came from outside the South altogether. The *Richmond Examiner*, contemplating the numbers of criminals who accosted their victims in the streets, observed in 1862 that "it can be said for the credit of Richmond that this class of thieves and robbers have no citizenship here, but belong to the foreign *lazaroni*, a far too numerous class the events of the war has thrown in our midst." The *Daily Dispatch* characterized "the shameful practices of drunkards, libertines, and profligates" as "not natural to the South," and regretted "the introduction here of these controlling elements of Northern society." As late as 1864, the *Richmond Sentinel* still claimed that new bands of criminals, presumably from outside the city, were making Richmond their "abiding place."[12]

If criminals constituted one problem to the city's image, nothing drew more scorn and hatred than speculators and extortionists. As inflation skyrocketed through the course of the war, high prices and shortages were often blamed, fairly or unfairly, on speculating and extortionist merchants and hucksters. Not just traitors to the cause, the press claimed that these people were men of bad principles generally; wartime practices merely allowed the public to see their "true" character. As early as 1861, the *Dispatch* considered it "a gross outrage" to call speculators "Southerners." These men, the *Dispatch* argued, lacked "that refined and discriminating sensibility which would regard with reprobation and abhorrence the levying of extravagant prices" upon articles of necessity. "Such men," the paper continued, "can have no hope of happiness in this world, or the world to come." Succinctly, the *Dispatch* claimed that speculators were "among us, but not of us." While the papers at least recognized that the people they termed "speculators" and "extortionists" were often native-born Southerners, they usually characterized them as people whose morals should be called into question rather than as businessmen trying to make a profit or as merchants simply caught up in wartime inflation.[13]

To the press, soldiers were, by virtue of their military service, without a doubt Confederates, and in explaining the presence of numerous soldiers that appeared in the city courts for drunkenness and public rowdiness, the press almost universally blamed the effects of alcohol and its distributors rather than the soldiers themselves. The *Enquirer* declared at one point that "no true soldier, no true officer, whatever his rank may be, will descend to the meanness of shirking duty to accomplish even the most tempting pleasure," but the blame for the behavior even of those who were legitimately off-duty was most often placed elsewhere than on the soldiers themselves. The *Dispatch* described naive soldiers, many of whom were from the country, as being "decoyed" into "dens of evil" by dissolute men. The *Examiner* argued that "the greatest injury results from the low Irish groggeries, where poisonous concoctions are dealt out to the soldiers," once again deflecting blame for the city's problems from the soldiers themselves onto, in this case, Irish immigrants. Brawls and public disturbances invariably could be traced back to the "overindulgence" of alcohol and the disreputable, unpatriotic people who dispensed it.[14]

While some newspapers, such as the *Whig* and *Examiner,* freely admitted that soldiers were at least partly responsible for the increase of disorder in the city, the other papers sometimes tried to preserve the otherwise good reputation of Confederate military personnel by hinting that many of the soldiers that the authorities arrested for drunkenness or rowdiness were not actually soldiers at all. Instead, they were men of the disreputable classes who managed to procure Confederate uniforms for nefarious purposes. The *Daily Dispatch* deplored the "frequent acts of violence reported as having been committed by parties dressed in 'soldier clothes,' whereby numbers of worthy men now engaged in the defense of their country are brought into contempt by no fault of their own," and warned citizens to beware of "imposters in soldiers' dress." The *Enquirer* on several occasions cast doubt on the true identity of men arrested "wearing the uniforms of soldiers," and an article in the *Sentinel* deplored the "false pretenses" of a man who was arrested while wearing "the uniform of a Confederate captain" that he certainly did not earn. Despite these efforts, however, the court records printed in the newspapers often belied such arguments, as numerous reports indicated that those "so-called" soldiers were often released back into the custody of their commanding officers.[15]

The Richmond press explained the Bread Riot of April 2, 1863, by discrediting its participants. A group of women, mostly from Richmond's working or artisan classes and many of whom had husbands or family members in the army, had taken to the streets after Governor John Letcher refused to grant their demands for food in the face of extreme shortages. They broke into numerous stores to take the provisions they saw as justly due to them. Joined by hundreds of others, both spectators and participants, the looting continued until authorities threatened to fire on the crowd, at which point it dispersed.[16]

In their coverage of the trials for those arrested during the riot, the press heaped blame on the individuals, men and women, who participated, and discredited the rioters' characters as much as their actions.[17] The *Richmond Sentinel,* while not immediately printing a story about the riot per se, hinted at it in an article about the poor just two days afterward. "It is a characteristic," the paper declared, "of virtuous distress to retreat from observation," clearly condemning the rioters simply on the basis of their disreputable behavior, even if they had been justified in their actions. The *Sentinel,* though, felt free to discuss the riot after five days' silence because it felt that the truth about the affair had been discerned. The *Sentinel* declared that the event "was no hunger riot." The rioters "simply plundered; milliner's goods, dry goods, fancy goods, &c., fully as much as more necessary articles" were taken. Furthermore, the *Sentinel* continued, "there was no distress among those persons," and "the very leader was independent, and herself an extortioner." Even the *Whig* and the *Examiner,* both bitter critics of the Davis administration that would logically have wanted to portray the rioters as honest people that government policies were starving, characterized the rioters as disreputable women, even prostitutes. The *Whig* printed a letter on April 6, 1863, that described the women as a mob of "courtezans and thieves." The *Examiner,* describing a scene in the courtroom where many accused rioters were being charged, claimed that more females "were clad in furs and silk than calico," hinting, like the *Whig,* that they were prostitutes, who were often dressed quite richly. These and other dissolute people who caused disorder and mayhem were not true Confederates; they were, as the *Sentinel* put it, *"ne plus ultra"* in "their utter want of decency."[18]

The press's reactions to criminals, speculators, unruly soldiers, and rioters reveals a strategic pattern: the papers tried to reconcile a chaotic, sometimes even lawless, wartime city with their professed claims of Southern respectability and morality by discrediting the morals of all troublemakers. Instead of probing the problems more deeply and revealing the real cracks and fissures in Confederate solidarity, the press attacked the character and respectability of those they felt had committed unpatriotic acts, whether those people were Northerners, foreigners, or even native-born white Southerners who lacked the proper moral sensibility to be "true" Confederates.

As conditions in Richmond worsened, the press worried not only about the immorality and disreputable behavior of those they claimed were outsiders, but also about how to keep respectable Confederate citizens fully supportive, in their behaviors and actions, of the war effort. The press insisted that patriotism could actually *increase* those qualities that helped make one respectable. In 1863, the *Richmond Sentinel* claimed that "those who are doing their duty to their country, and making sacrifices in its cause, are elevated by the consciousness of it, and feel a virtuous pride in maintaining such a character." A soldier, for example, by enlisting and defending his country, was "also being educated and developed in all the manly and generous elements of human character," while men who did not contribute to the war effort, either on the battlefield or off, were "shriveling and contracting into impotence and deformity." The soldier, the article concluded, "will be as much superior to [the other] in moral stature as a giant is to a dwarf." In response to a letter from a concerned parent that worried, as many people did during the war, about young men's exposure to bad morals in the course of army life, the *Sentinel* reassured readers that the good effects of patriotism on a soldier's character, no matter how young, would outweigh the chance of injury to it. "A boy may surely be a good patriot and a good boy at the same time," the *Sentinel* declared. "Nay, his patriotism should make him all the better."[19]

The press used women's nursing activities to illustrate how patriotism could elevate character. As women of all denominations revealed a "unity of motive" in caring for injured and sick soldiers, the press argued that they created bonds of understanding, respect, and charity for one another. "Whatever differences may exist in the peculiar tenets of the many," the *Enquirer* stated, "the amiable and unpretending Sister of Mercy, the earnest, bright-eyed Jewish girl, and the pleasant, gentle and energetic Protestant, mingle their labors with a freedom and geniality which would teach the most prejudiced Zealot a lesson that would never be forgotten." Patriotism worked to help create a more tolerant society by fostering a common purpose. While trying to show that people of all faiths supported the Confederacy, statements such as that of the *Enquirer* were sharply at odds with the numerous voices, public as well as private, that blamed many of the Confederacy's problems on religious and ethnic minorities. Anti-Semitic sentiments appeared frequently, especially as many Jewish residents were targeted unfairly as speculators, and many Irish Catholics bore criticism for operating illegal drinking establishments.[20]

Just as the press argued that respectable behavior went hand in hand with patriotism, so were immorality and unpatriotic behavior directly linked. The *Daily Dispatch*, deprecating men it saw lounging about Richmond rather than fighting, argued that "it may be accepted as a truth, that if able-bodied men are not willing to fight at this particular juncture they are not very good citizens, and their antecedents should be inquired into." The *Richmond Enquirer*, too, drew a link between a lack of patriotism and poor character. After praising the charitable contributions made to various causes during the war, the *Enquirer* asserted that "the stifling of the promptings of patriotism, in such a time as this, dry up every generous sentiment, and convert what ought to be a high-spirited, gallant citizen, into a selfish, sordid, abject thing, uncared for and uncaring." The *Sentinel* chimed in with similar sentiments, claiming that those who had failed to be patriotic, those who had "evaded the call of duty, and sheltered behind pretences, have daily become more effeminate spirited, and more diligent and shameless in finding cover from the exactions of public opinion and law." The *Sentinel* believed that people could reform themselves, however, and regain their respectability through patriotism. It warned that those people "who are found among the list of the selfish and money-grubbing, have no time to lose, if they would redeem themselves, and make a good character and good name."[21]

Shortly after the war began, the *Daily Dispatch,* in noting that social relations had already changed in the Confederate capital, observed that "the old landmarks of etiquette and social life have been wiped out by war." Over the course of the war, the *Dispatch* and Richmond's other newspapers would advocate new standards of social relations that ultimately led to a redefinition of social respectability in the wartime city. By 1864, these new definitions of Confederate respectability put forth by the press had become intimately linked with patriotism and personal sacrifice for the war effort. As wealth, leisure, food, and clothing supplies diminished, the papers began excluding those luxuries from their definitions of respectability. Instead, factors such as hard work, industriousness, usefulness, economy, thrift, and generosity—significantly, those qualities which could also best aid the war effort—marked those of truly admirable character. In doing so, they put forth a picture of Confederate respectability that virtually anyone, rich or poor, could aspire to, and one that more closely resembled a bourgeois individualism than an aristocratic honor culture. Indeed, as prices soared and income declined in wartime Richmond, the press tried hard to make even poverty inherently respectable, in order to both put a good face on the Confederacy's financial and provisioning problems and to try to maintain the allegiance of the common Confederate citizens. Ironically, the war drove the Confederate press to promote many of the same cultural values and behaviors, such as thrift, industry, and plainness, that had long been hallmarks of a "Yankee" character.[22]

Redefining the boundaries of what constituted appropriate white female behavior became an early objective of the press. White women were held up in Southern (and American) society as the standard-bearers of all that was virtuous, good, and unselfish. In newspapers, journals, and speeches, Southerners depicted women as possessing a higher degree of morality than men. In the press's eyes, women's support of the Confederacy gave weight to their claims that the Southern fight for independence was both right and moral, for women would not have supported it otherwise. The

Daily Dispatch claimed that "we have always regarded the enthusiastic and constant devotion of the Southern women to the Southern cause as a signal proof of the goodness of that cause, and of the moral strength it would command among the Southern people." The paper asked its readers how any man could refuse to defend "principles so universally espoused by the fairer sex." As the Civil War unfolded, these proper, moral women began stepping out of their antebellum roles as the conditions of the war demanded new efforts and behaviors of white female Confederates.[23]

During wartime, the Richmond press used patriotism to make women's assumption of masculine roles palatable to a culture steeped in the ideology of domesticity. That ideology assigned a certain realm of genteel duties to women, and another realm, which included the protection of and providing for one's family, to men. While working-class women sometimes could not afford the luxury of performing only "feminine actions," domesticity became a marker of respectability for women of the middle and upper classes. As the war drew many men away, however, women often were left alone at home, and in this situation the press lauded women who could take care of themselves. Women's use of firearms to protect themselves became quite acceptable, and even encouraged, in the press. After hearing of an incident in which a young lady of the "highest respectability" had to threaten an intruder to her home with a pistol, the *Whig* proclaimed that "every lady in the city should, in this crisis, follow her example, by keeping a pistol or gun within reach." Furthermore, the press applauded women for forming female "home guards" that drilled with rifles, and at times portrayed the occasional woman found to be a soldier as an "extraordinary" example of womanhood, although the participation of women in battle was a drastic step that the press could just as easily ridicule as being unfeminine. In 1862, the *Richmond Enquirer*, though, did praise a female soldier as "a woman of intelligence and good breeding." Because women performed these actions out of patriotism, for the good of the Confederacy, the press argued that they could be viewed as acceptable actions for respectable Southern ladies.[24]

Before the war, paid work was often seen as inappropriate for respectable women. Although this attitude was beginning to change during the 1850s, as the city grew and more white women needed jobs, the Civil War accelerated the change. The absence of male providers, the refugee status of many women in the city, and inflation combined to force many white women into paid work. None of papers indicated that the need to work cost any of these women their respectability. Instead, because their need often stemmed from other patriotic motives, such as giving the family breadwinner to the army, these women were held in all the more respect. The *Dispatch* ran an article as early as 1861 urging Richmonders who did not need jobs badly to leave them for women whose husbands went off to war. The paper expressed "profound regret that respectable ladies, whose husbands have gone to the war, and are compelled to support themselves and their little children by the needle, are unable to get work."[25]

The press's assertions that working women remained respectable often seemed less like simple observations and a celebration of Confederate citizens' sympathy for the women's plight than protestations that sought to change people's minds about those working women. The *Sentinel*, advocating a new, more orderly system for the Clothing Bureau to provide women with sewing work, reminded readers that "a large number of those who apply for work are ladies, and should be treated as such." The reminder, however, was occasioned by the treatment the women who applied to the Bureau received from other Richmonders. "We will say," admonished the *Sentinel*, "that the sneers of passers-by, who daily witness the throng of females on the pavement in front of the Clothing Bureau, are very uncalled for and humiliating." While the papers worked hard to refashion society's conceptions of respectable women to accord with wartime necessities, they met with resistance from other Richmonders who were not quite so sympathetic to new gender roles or the necessities of war-induced poverty.[26]

For many Confederate women, employment as nurses in the hospitals around Richmond represented another departure from their antebellum domestic roles. While women had long nursed family members within their own households, public nursing was something new, something that many women could not view as a respectable occupation for females. The Richmond press, however, from the very beginning of the war encouraged women of all classes to accept nursing positions, and never even hinted that women who did so were crossing the boundaries of respectability. Instead, the papers employed various tactics to portray women's nursing as an entirely respectable and laudable occupation for any Confederate woman. First, the press held up to the public exemplars of respectable womanhood who worked in public hospitals. In August 1861, for example, the *Dispatch* noted that a number of ladies, headed to Richmond and Culpeper to nurse Confederate soldiers, were "as well known for their unselfish devotion as personal worth." Second, the papers emphasized that in many cases, women who came to nurse the wounded in hospitals were members of churches. An article in the *Richmond Enquirer* observed that the women working in the hospitals as nurses were "of the different religious denominations" of the city. In the press's portrayals, churchgoing women thus lent an air of respectability to the nursing occupation.[27]

Just as the ill received the best possible care from mothers and wives, the press emphasized the benefit of respectable women to hospitals. A report on hospitals in the *Richmond Enquirer* stressed that decent women's "very presence is a rebuke to every impropriety," and that women of "good character" serving in hospitals added an element of cleanliness, neatness, and moral excellence that improved both the bodies and minds of ill soldiers. By stressing the respectability of nursing and the good that respectable female nurses could effect, the papers worked to solicit much-needed help for crowded hospitals and the scores of wounded and ill soldiers that poured into Richmond during the war. As the continued pleas for additional female nurses in the newspapers attested, though, even framing nursing in patriotic terms was not always sufficient to overcome some women's scruples about their proper roles, and concerns about the propriety of women working in hospitals never disappeared entirely.[28]

Another quite prominent marker of social standing to be flung aside during the war was wealth. Especially as the war continued into its third and fourth years, the press portrayed wealth as suspect, as true patriots supposedly gave all they had to the war effort, inflation made what money many people had worthless, and the only ones getting rich seemed to be immoral speculators. The *Sentinel* explained the new connections between wealth and social standing quite clearly in 1863. "There was a time," it concluded, "when wealth was in itself respectable. It was looked upon as the representative of long years of honest and useful toil, or the exercise of eminent talents, either in the possessor or his ancestors. . . . The time is at hand, however, when wealth will be held almost in odium. While the worthy men of the land have been in many cases reduced to poverty, the unpatriotic, the selfish, and the coarse, have risen to wealth. . . . Society will regulate itself. Mere wealth will go into insignificance." More specifically, wealth attained during the war was particularly scorned. An article in the *Religious Herald,* a Baptist newspaper published in Richmond, reprinted in the *Sentinel,* made this distinction clear. As the *Herald* explained, "when men speak of the wealth of others" after the war, "they will ask, how *old* is it? *When* was it amassed? And if the answer be, that they gathered it *during the war,* this fact will strip it of all respectability. . . . It will pass for robbery of the country at large," and "will be seen *as it is.* No disguise will cover it up; no apology extenuate it." Wealth would now be seen, as the press declared, as evidence of unpatriotic and disreputable actions.[29]

As supplies of all sorts became scarce during the war, the press tried to turn a lack of decent food and clothing, as with a lack of wealth, into not only a sign of patriotism, but a mark of respectability as well. A dwindling supply of resources constituted an extensive and contentious problem for the Confederacy, especially in overcrowded Richmond, and many papers tried their best to deflect anger over these mounting supply scarcities into a practice of new Confederate virtues—these deprivations, they argued, would only make the Confederate people stronger and more moral. The possession and use of luxury items received disdain from the press, who viewed the acquisition of such items as both unpatriotic, when money and goods could be put to better uses, and harmful to the good, wholesome character of true Confederates. Observing that smugglers who ran the blockades were bringing in what it saw as the unnecessary luxury items of silks, fancy clothing, and jewelry, also pointedly termed "Yankee notions," the *Richmond Examiner* stated its intent clearly. "It is our policy," the paper declared, "to discourage the consumption of these luxuries by our people. A happy and beautiful effect of this war should be to discard frivolity from the mind of our women to make them think less of silk dresses, hoop-skirts and other finery in the lots of Yankee importations . . . it will be a healthy self-denial; and the sooner our whole people, men and women, learn not to barter away self-respect and public interest for Yankee wares" the better. In an article entitled "Who Sets the Fashions?" the *Sentinel* described the new basis of social respect. "He is most in fashion and most patriotic who wears the oldest clothes," and "lives on the most frugal fare. . . . To eat but two meals a day is quite respectable. To eat only one is decidedly aristocratic." The *Enquirer* concurred with this assessment, declaring that "it is nearly as bad to grow fat as to get rich while this war is being waged."[30]

Shortly into the war, it became apparent to the press that in order for the Confederacy to achieve its independence, it would need the help of as many citizens as possible, not just to fight, but to work on the home front as well. The press, accordingly, portrayed work and industry not only as patriotic virtues, but as key elements of a respectable character. While industry and usefulness had long been seen as a part of a reputable character, the public glorification of work and labor was vastly increased during the Civil War. In 1862, the *Daily Dispatch* declared that all Confederates needed to work to help the cause, and instead of rich and poor classes, the new Confederate wartime society was divided into two different social groupings. Confederate society, the paper proclaimed, "must be divided into two classes—without respect to age, sex, or condition—the class who fight; and the class who assist by their labor and self-denial those who are offering their lives for the cause." Any idleness would become a marker of selfishness, frivolity, greed, or sloth. Industriousness could take many forms, and sometimes encompassed activities that would not necessarily have been considered respectable before the war. While the papers encouraged women to spin, weave, and sew to provide the army and civilians with cloth, these industrious tasks were not necessarily unladylike, and the *Dispatch* assured its readers that such industry would not "derogate from the dignity" of those who performed such labor. Field labor was less publicly accepted as work appropriate for women, but was praised as the epitome of industriousness during the war. Two German women received applause for their "patient industry" when they harvested two acres of oats by themselves because one woman's husband was in the army. Two sisters, in the absence of their brother, received similar applause for their field work.[31]

In 1863, the *Richmond Sentinel* went even farther and declared that useful work was the secret to personal happiness for all people, rich and poor, men or women, a well-timed opinion as the war necessitated ever-increasing efforts from Confederate citizens. "The most common error of men and women," the *Sentinel* declared, "is that of looking for happiness somewhere outside of useful work. It has never yet been found when thus sought; and never will be, while the world stands." Are the happiest people, the paper asked rhetorically, "the idlers, and pleasure-seekers, or the earnest workers?" The *Sentinel* concluded with the advice to "be ever engaged in useful work, if you would be happy." This "useful work," the press noted on many occasions, could come in a variety of forms that would aid the Confederacy. Critical of military appointments made for political reasons, the *Enquirer* felt that all appointments to army and government positions should be based on a candidate's industry, potential usefulness, and good character—the qualities that epitomized a respectable Confederate. The paper argued that "the very best common sense, practical business talent, the most indefatigable industry, as well as the most upright, impartial and considerate men, should be in the supply departments of the army." The *Dispatch* printed a letter that described nursing as a "path of usefulness" that had recently become "fashionable." The *Examiner*, too, contributed to the identification of useful occupations during the war. In one of its columns, that paper honored a man named James Durdin, a telegraph operator in North Carolina who stayed at his post to perform needed work even as the yellow fever broke out around him. He eventually died from the fever, and the *Examiner* proclaimed that "although he fell not on the tented field he was nobly performing his duty in the field of usefulness."

Useful work did not have to be highly visible to be highly acclaimed and respected.[32]

The Confederate cause needed the efforts of the poor as well as those of the rich, and with anger brewing among many of the poorer classes over such issues as conscription, substitution, and food shortages, the press recognized that they had to actively include the less wealthy portion of society in their definitions of Confederate citizens. Consequently, during the war, the press often sought to put a more respectable face on poverty than it had ever done before. The poor, the press began to argue, actually set the tone for what made a good Confederate citizen. As the *Sentinel* proclaimed, "the poor man consumes least and produces most; therefore, the poor man is the most useful citizen and best patriot." In the "millennium of poverty" that the war had ushered in, it was "the poor, that in this race of industry and frugality took the start, and yet maintain the lead." Furthermore, the actions of the poor should serve as a patriotic example to those who had more extensive pecuniary resources. The only sight more noble than that of a poor family engaged in honest and hard labor, the *Sentinel* asserted, was that of a "rich family following the fashion and example set by the poor." The actions of the poor, the paper argued, formed the very backbone of Confederate success.[33]

While the papers continued to heap scorn on what they saw as the idle, dissolute poor that constituted a burden on society, they extolled the characters and qualities of the honest, industrious poor of the city. The purpose of this praise seemed to be two-fold. First, the press used the poor as exemplars to the rest of society. The moral, hard-working poor set admirable examples of industry, sacrifice, and frugality that had become the marks of respectable Confederate patriots of all classes. Second, their praise of the poor aimed to make the lower classes of Confederate society part of the war effort and to give poor people a respectable place in the new society. An article in the *Sentinel* suggested both these themes when musing about the benefits of poverty on personal character and worth. "Poverty," it stated, "is the nurse of manly energy heaven climbing thoughts . . . and from whose countenance all the virtues gather strength. Look around you upon the distinguished men in every department of life who guide and control the times, and inquire what was their origin and what was their early fortune. Were they, as a general rule, rocked and dandled in the lap of wealth?" The answer was no. Poverty bred social virtue and character.[34]

Families who before the war existed comfortably on the salaries and wages of a male breadwinner now often fell into the ranks of the poor as men went off to war and prices of all items soared. Women, too, began to

enter the workforce in greater numbers simply to survive. These circumstances helped to elevate the character of work that the poor performed,
particularly when that work was linked to patriotism. The papers often
spoke of the benefits that the poor received from being given work rather
than charity. The *Dispatch* lauded the actions of a group of women who
provided sewing jobs to wives of soldiers, as the poor women's needs could
now be met "not by charity, but by the reward of labor, which is much better." The *Sentinel* similarly extolled the honesty and work ethic of the poor
who refused to ask for charity, but sought work instead, declaring that
those who did so retained their "self-reliance and manhood unimpaired."
Even plain labor was no sign of shame, but a method of retaining respectability in hard times.[35]

Work of almost any kind was portrayed as valuable and eminently respectable. While white working-class Richmonders had begun to demand
respect for their labors and occupations during the 1850s, lingering ideas
that manual work was for slaves still pervaded many people's attitudes
toward white working men. During the war, the press strove to make work
of all sorts respectable, even the jobs of poor workers, recognizing that the
war effort depended on the labor of all people, and that the Confederacy
could not afford to alienate any workers. In 1862, the *Daily Dispatch* reflected on the "Importance of Manufacturing Labor" by claiming that "no
statesman can underrate the value of mechanical labor to the State," or
diminish its dignity. As the Confederacy sought to establish itself as an
economically independent state, labor emerged as a decent, respectable
employment for white men much more fully than it had in the previous
decade. The *Enquirer* printed a letter from a clerk in which the author
argued for the respectability of lower-level government clerks. Disputing
a claim, reflective of continued prejudice against white men who worked
for wages, that they were merely "servants," the author asserted the clerks'
rights to the respect due any Southern citizen. He argued that clerks were
"part and parcel" of the "Southern people." They came from "the very
same states, cities, towns, villages, and plantations, that our fellow citizens come from, daily, to our offices, for transaction of business," and if
the "'Southern people' have a special catechism of good manners, we are
full as likely to have learned it in infancy" as anyone else. Hinting at the
former respectability of people now forced to take low paying jobs, the author claimed that in society, a clerk, "like every other, must take rank according to his personal qualifications" rather than the nature of his job.[36]

The *Sentinel* even ventured to say that some of the most arduous tasks
should be elevated in popular estimation and monetary remuneration be-

cause of their value to the war effort. The paper declared that it would "rejoice to see the wages of those increased whose toil is usually least requited." Speaking specifically about poor seamstresses, who were notoriously ill-paid, the *Sentinel* wished to "let no doleful 'Song of the Shirt' be sung in our land. Let the Government clothing agents, and let clothing dealers increase the wages of the seamstress. . . . We must be more thoughtful and more considerate in these things." Furthermore, sewing during wartime took on an added respectability as its value to the war effort became clearer. While women's voluntary sewing of uniforms and tents was welcomed, paying poor women to sew for the government not only provided the government with supplies of clothing for the army, but took care of poor women. The garment thus made, the *Sentinel* indicated, served two purposes: it clothed a poor soldier and "kindled a fire in some desolate hearth." It also preserved the respectability of the poor, as they could work for wages rather than accept outright charity. Work, aiding the poor, self-respect, and patriotism all went hand in hand.[37]

The poor not only worked hard for the Confederacy, they volunteered for the army. Few actions gained as much praise in the papers as that of a poor man's enlistment, even though he might be the sole support of a family that, with his departure, was left in serious financial straits. Such an action showed his true character and elevated him in the eyes of the press. The *Sentinel* argued that "a good soldier should need no other passport than his position, to every man's heart." The *Richmond Enquirer* went even further, declaring that by volunteering, soldiers had elevated their social standing forever. In dismissing the possibility that there could ever be a Confederate aristocracy, the *Enquirer* asserted that "he would be a bold man who should say to *our* soldiers, returning to their homes, that they are disfranchised and to call themselves hereafter the 'lower classes.'" Echoing the condemnations of wealthy merchants during the war, the *Sentinel* claimed that "the raggedest soldier in the army" was superior to the "richest money-grub in Richmond" in "all that entitles a man to respect, as a Christian is superior to a Hottentot." While the soldier's actions "have made a nobleman of him" in character, the "money-grub" had looked only "to sordid self, until he has become less than a man."[38]

Military service by a male family member imparted respectability to the soldier's family as well. Charitable organizations in the antebellum South were often picky about to whom they distributed their benevolence, and they tried to give aid to only the "deserving" poor—those that did their best to adhere to middle-class standards of respectability even while facing destitution. Having a family member in the army, however, gave many families automatic inclusion into the ranks of the respectable poor. Poverty became a circumstance of patriotism rather than the product of a character failing or lack of effort to secure work. The *Enquirer* felt that the families of poor soldiers should be elevated even above the rest of the honest poor, stating that sewing work "should be given only to the families of volunteers in the service, who are absolutely dependent upon their daily labor for support." The *Richmond Sentinel* similarly placed high on its charitable agenda the needs of soldiers' families. While widows and orphans demanded sympathy, the *Sentinel* declared, when "the wants of the families of our soldiers" were considered, "the promptings of charity are supported, if not indeed superseded, by the imperative demands of moral *justice.*" Not only deserving, these poor were elevated to a class of patriotic poor that Confederate society must help, no matter what their character or circumstances before the war.[39]

The idea that military service improved the character and social standing of poor men was echoed in the praise of army privates. While some papers tended to claim that a large portion of the privates in the army came from comfortable, and even wealthy, backgrounds, which made their patriotism that much more admirable, others recognized that many privates came from the poorer classes as well. The latter sometimes were seen as all the more patriotic because they gave up wages their families sorely needed to subsist on a private's pay. Whatever their origins, privates were universally praised for doing their duty without a promise of the rank, pay, or fame that officers might gather. And while the flash of an officer's uniform might catch the eyes of women, the press worked tirelessly to promote the army's privates. The *Dispatch* claimed that while people would honor a captain or general, "they love the private soldier," and it was that class of soldiers that stood "first in the heart of his countrymen." The *Examiner* and *Enquirer* even went so far as to propose that old ideas of military hierarchy, where privates did not normally garner much respect, be put aside in the new Confederacy. The army of the Confederacy, the *Examiner* claimed, embraced in its private soldiers "material even more respectable and respected than the body of commissioned officers," and the paper proposed a democratic plan whereby merit, rather than personal popularity or politics, won promotion.[40]

Many elements of the press's newly defined Confederate respectability mirrored the values and practices celebrated in nearly all societies during wartime, such as patriotism, sacrifice, and selflessness. In the Confederacy, though, the press's efforts to link those values to definitions of social respectability represent an important aspect of Confederate identity. White Southerners in the antebellum period had struggled to balance their devotion to an aristocratic culture of honor with new ideas of bourgeois domesticity and individualism. Under the concept of respectability, they had begun to fashion a society that still maintained a firmly entrenched slave system, but which was otherwise becoming a part of larger Anglo-American cultural trends stemming, in part, from the teachings of evangelical Christianity. The Civil War, in many ways, represented a culmination of those antebellum trends toward a culture of respectability. Faced with poverty, hardship, and new demands on individuals, Confederates emphasized the inner values of character, Christian morality, labor, and plainness. Rather than celebrating only the aristocratic and hierarchical nature of Southern society, the press used the language of simple respectability and moral worth in an attempt to draw Confederates from all backgrounds together in common cause, not as wealthy or poor, but as respectable Confederate citizens.

Notes

I would like to thank the editors, and especially Edward L. Ayers, for their valuable suggestions and assistance in preparing this essay.

1. *Daily Dispatch* (Richmond, Virginia), March 19, 1862.

2. Of Richmond's five major newspapers, the *Richmond Enquirer,* the *Richmond Daily Examiner,* and the *Richmond Daily Whig* were the oldest. The *Enquirer* and *Examiner* had both been Democratic newspapers before the war, and early supporters of secession. During the war, though, the papers would become quite different, as the *Enquirer* became a staunch supporter of President Jefferson Davis and his administration, while the *Examiner's* editor, John Moncure Daniel, became a harsh critic of Davis on almost every political move, a theme that dominated that paper's content. The *Whig,* formerly the paper of the Whig party while it existed, took a Unionist stance during the secession crisis, but eventually supported disunion. Like the *Examiner,* the *Whig* became critical of the Davis administration. The Richmond *Daily Dispatch,* founded in 1850 as the city's first penny daily, declined to affiliate itself with a particular political party and viewed itself as moderate in tone. After thoroughly debating the issue of secession in its columns, it, too, joined the ranks of the secessionist papers, and later became a firm supporter of the administration. The *Dispatch* retained the largest circulation of any newspaper in Richmond during the war. In 1863, the *Richmond Sentinel* joined the other papers. Formerly an Alexandria publication, Federal

occupation in northern Virginia had forced it to move to Richmond, where it worked tirelessly to encourage patriotism and the Confederate cause, including support for the administration. All the newspapers, despite their differing political viewpoints, remained fiercely dedicated to the Confederate war effort to the end. Emory M. Thomas, *The Confederate State of Richmond: A Biography of the Capital* (Baton Rouge: Louisiana State University Press, 1971), 16–19, 132–33; *Daily Dispatch*, March 13, 1862; *Richmond Sentinel*, March 11, 1863.

3. For economic growth and society in the antebellum city of Richmond, see David Goldfield, *Urban Growth in the Age of Sectionalism: Virginia, 1847–1861* (Baton Rouge: Louisiana State University Press, 1977); Marie Tyler-McGraw, *At the Falls: Richmond, Virginia, and Its People* (Chapel Hill: University of North Carolina Press, 1994), 103–31; and Gregg D. Kimball, *American City, Southern Place: A Cultural History of Antebellum Richmond* (Athens: University of Georgia Press, 2000). For population numbers, see Richard C. Wade, *Slavery in the Cities: The South, 1820–1860* (New York: Oxford University Press, 1964), 327.

4. For an overarching study of the hierarchical culture of honor in the South, see Bertram Wyatt-Brown, *Southern Honor: Ethics and Behavior in the Old South* (New York: Oxford University Press, 1982). For a study of how aristocracy in America as a whole was giving way to notions of democracy in the early nineteenth century, see Gordon Wood, *The Radicalism of the American Revolution* (New York: Vintage Books, 1991). Jeffrey Robert Young argues that Southern planters in the early nineteenth century practiced what he has termed "corporate individualism," which combined ideas of individualistic, market capitalism with hierarchical notions of an organic society. See Jeffrey Robert Young, *Domesticating Slavery: The Master Class in Georgia and South Carolina, 1670–1837* (Chapel Hill: University of North Carolina Press, 1999).

5. For the evangelical influence on Southern culture in the antebellum era, see Donald G. Mathews, *Religion in the Old South* (Chicago: University of Chicago Press, 1977). For a discussion of how religion influenced ideas of social respectability, see Beth Barton Schweiger, *The Gospel Working Up: Progress and the Pulpit in Nineteenth-Century Virginia* (New York: Oxford University Press, 2000), especially chapter 2.

6. Robert M. Saunders has argued that in Richmond hostility to the poor actually increased in the 1850s because of changing attitudes toward poverty. "By the 1850s," he writes, "with the erosion of a corporate concept of society and with the rise of religious and economic individualism, character failings of the poor were stressed as the chief cause of poverty. The poor were immoral, idle, drunken, and as such were responsible for their own depraved status" (Robert M. Saunders, "Modernization and the Political Process: Governmental Principles and Practices in Richmond, Virginia, from the Revolution to the Civil War," *Southern Studies* 24 [summer 1985]: 137). For the influence of religion on women's roles, see Mathews, *Religion in the Old South*, 109–24; for the growing emphasis on domesticity in Southern women's lives during the early nineteenth century, see

Cynthia A. Kierner, *Beyond the Household: Women's Place in the Early South, 1700–1835* (Ithaca: Cornell University Press, 1998), chapters 5 and 6; for examples of women's political roles in Southern society, see Elizabeth R. Varon, *We Mean to Be Counted: White Women and Politics in Antebellum Virginia* (Chapel Hill: University of North Carolina Press, 1998).

7. *Richmond Enquirer,* November 12, 1861. Unless otherwise noted, all citations refer to the semi-weekly edition of this paper; *Daily Dispatch,* June 19, 1861, May 3, 1861, October 25, 1861.

8. *Daily Dispatch,* April 16, 1861, May 4, 1861, March 21, 1862, October 30, 1861; *Richmond Daily Whig,* April 27, 1861; *Daily Dispatch,* May 6, 1861; *Richmond Enquirer,* September 30, 1862.

9. *Daily Dispatch,* October 16, 1861, October 27, 1861; *Richmond Daily Whig,* June 10, 1861.

10. *Daily Dispatch,* May 3, 1861, May 6, 1861, May 13, 1861.

11. Ibid., May 3, 1861; *Richmond Daily Whig,* April 20, 1861.

12. *Richmond Daily Examiner,* October 18, 1862; *Daily Dispatch,* February 5, 1862; *Richmond Sentinel,* February 29, 1864.

13. *Daily Dispatch,* November 13, 1861, July 3, 1861, May 6, 1862.

14. *Richmond Enquirer,* June 13, 1861; *Daily Dispatch,* February 18, 1862; *Richmond Daily Examiner,* October 21, 1862; *Richmond Sentinel,* June 4, 1863.

15. See, for example, *Richmond Daily Whig,* June 28, 1861, and *Richmond Daily Examiner,* October 14, 1862; *Daily Dispatch,* July 2, 1861, September 13, 1861; *Richmond Enquirer,* July 27, 1861, September 17, 1861; *Richmond Sentinel,* March 26, 1863.

16. Michael Chesson, "Harlots or Heroines? A New Look at the Richmond Bread Riot," *Virginia Magazine of History and Biography* 92, no. 2 (April 1984), 131–75.

17. E. Susan Barber makes a forceful argument that the press depicted the women of the Bread Riot as disreputable in order to discredit both them and their actions. E. Susan Barber, "Cartridge Makers and Myrmidon Viragoes: White Working-Class Women in Confederate Richmond," in *Negotiating Boundaries of Southern Womanhood: Dealing with the Powers That Be,* Southern Women Series, edited by Janet L. Coryell, Thomas H. Appleton Jr., Anastasia Sims, and Sandra Gioia Treadway (Columbia and London: University of Missouri Press, 2000), 199–214.

18. *Richmond Sentinel,* April 4, 1863, April 7, 1863; *Richmond Daily Whig,* April 6, 1863; *Richmond Daily Examiner,* April 6, 1863. For the press's portrayals of the rioters as prostitutes, see Barber, "Cartridge Makers and Myrmidon Viragoes," and Werner H. Steger, "'United to Support, But Not Combined to Injure': Free Workers and Immigrants in Richmond, Virginia, During the Era of Sectionalism, 1847–1865" (Ph.D. diss., The George Washington University, 1999), 293–94; *Richmond Sentinel,* November 20, 1863.

19. *Richmond Sentinel,* June 5, 1863, July 18, 1863.

20. *Richmond Enquirer,* June 6, 1862; for a discussion of Anti-Semitism in Richmond during the Civil War, see Eli N. Evans, *Judah P. Benjamin: The Jewish Con-*

federate (New York: Free Press, 1988), 198–210. In 1862, the *Richmond Examiner* directly linked the operations of "low Irish groceries" to the growing disorder in the city (*Richmond Daily Examiner,* October 21, 1862).

21. *Daily Dispatch,* March 19, 1862; *Richmond Enquirer,* March 19, 1862; *Richmond Sentinel,* June 5, 1863.

22. *Daily Dispatch,* June 8, 1861.

23. Drew Faust, *Mothers of Invention: Women of the Slaveholding South in the American Civil War* (New York: Vintage Books, 1996). For attitudes toward women in the antebellum period, see Varon, *We Mean to Be Counted; Daily Dispatch,* February 22, 1862, November 2, 1861.

24. *Richmond Daily Whig,* April 22, 1861. For examples of negative press attitudes toward female soldiers, see DeAnne Blanton and Lauren M. Cook, *They Fought Like Demons: Women Soldiers in the American Civil War* (Baton Rouge: Louisiana State University Press, 2002), 145–62; *Richmond Enquirer,* May 6, 1862. See also *Daily Dispatch,* June 1, 1861, for an even earlier approving account of women drilling and practicing with firearms, before any real threat was upon them. For examples of women stepping into another masculine role, tending crops, see the *Daily Dispatch,* August 7, 1861, January 7, 1862.

25. *Daily Dispatch,* July 26, 1861.

26. *Richmond Sentinel,* July 18, 1863.

27. See Faust, *Mothers of Invention,* 92–113; *Daily Dispatch,* August 1, 1861; *Richmond Enquirer,* July 27, 1861.

28. *Richmond Enquirer,* September 30, 1862.

29. *Richmond Sentinel,* June 5, 1863; *Religious Herald,* in the *Richmond Sentinel,* September 21, 1863. Many private citizens concurred with this assessment, and linked wealth with underhanded, dishonest, or simply disreputable dealings. John B. Jones, a clerk in the Confederate War Department, felt that those who distributed patronage and even "adroit clerks" could become very wealthy through underhanded practices. He angrily wrote that they "procure exemptions, discharges, and contracts for the speculators for heavy bribes, and invest the money immediately in real estate. . . . After the war the rascals and traitors will be rich, and ought to be marked and exposed" (John B. Jones, *A Rebel War Clerk's Diary at the Confederate States Capital,* vol. 1, edited by Howard Swiggett [New York: Old Hickory Bookshop, 1935], 332).

30. *Richmond Daily Examiner,* October 31, 1862; *Richmond Sentinel,* August 11, 1863; *Richmond Enquirer,* March 10, 1863.

31. *Daily Dispatch,* March 14, 1862, August 7, 1861, January 7, 1862.

32. *Richmond Sentinel,* September 12, 1863; *Richmond Enquirer,* April 22, 1862; *Daily Dispatch,* August 13, 1861; *Richmond Daily Examiner,* October 3, 1862.

33. Drew Gilpin Faust has argued that in order for Confederate nationalism to really work and unify the nation behind a common cause, it had to address the ideas and needs of both the more aristocratic leaders and the popular citizenry. Drew Gilpin Faust, *The Creation of Confederate Nationalism: Ideology and Iden-*

tity in the Civil War South (Baton Rouge: Louisiana State University Press, 1988), 15–17; *Richmond Sentinel,* August 11, 1863.

34. *Richmond Sentinel,* September 9, 1863.

35. *Daily Dispatch,* January 2, 1862; *Richmond Sentinel,* April 4, 1863.

36. Steger, "United to Support," provides an in-depth examination of the working class population in Richmond during the antebellum years. See especially chapter 2; *Daily Dispatch,* March 28, 1862; *Richmond Enquirer,* October 1, 1861.

37. *Richmond Sentinel,* April 4, 1863.

38. *Richmond Sentinel,* August 14, 1863; *Richmond Enquirer,* April 27, 1863; *Richmond Sentinel,* June 5, 1863.

39. *Richmond Enquirer,* March 28, 1862; *Richmond Sentinel,* February 20, 1864.

40. *Daily Dispatch,* November 5, 1861; *Richmond Daily Examiner,* August 22, 1862; also see the *Richmond Enquirer,* May 7, 1862.

The Slave Market in Civil War Virginia

Jaime Amanda Martinez

In January 1864, a young girl named Nelia remarked in a letter to her cousin Bettie that "Pa bought five negroes the other day (two men one woman and two children) he gave eleven thousand and eight hundred for them."[1] This quick sentence in the midst of Nelia's stories of holiday festivities and the approaching school year indicated that slave sales in Virginia were both important and commonplace occurrences, even in wartime. This sale was important enough to Nelia that she reported it to a disinterested party, in a letter filled with references to family and friends. The purchase was not so remarkable, however, that Nelia felt compelled to dwell on it or provide any details. Because Nelia's father purchased these slaves at the beginning of the calendar year, a traditional time for the hiring and sale of slaves, he may have been planning to increase his agricultural output in the coming year. None of these things were necessarily dependent on the Civil War.

Yet the war did affect slave sales, particularly in regard to price. The 1860 ledger of Richmond slave trader Silas Omohundro placed the price of a woman and two children near $1,600; the price for prime male field hands that year hovered around $1,500 each.[2] Based on this evidence, the value of Nelia's five new slaves jumped from $4,600 to $11,800, an increase of nearly 160 percent in four years. While it would have been impressive in peacetime, this rate of increase in slave property did not keep pace with wartime inflation in the Confederacy. Nelia's father likely believed, with some justification, that he had made a good deal; it is harder to know what motivated the unnamed seller, but he might have preferred ready cash, though depreciated, to the uncertainties of owning slave property during the war. The relative values of both slave property and Confederate currency, moreover, were tied intimately to the shifting prospects for Confederate victory over four years of war.

The few historians who have written extensively about the domestic slave trade have devoted very little time to slave trading during the Civil War itself. In part this is because the two poles of the antebellum trade, New Orleans, Louisiana, and Alexandria, Virginia, came under Union army control fairly early in the war, effectively halting the long-distance domestic slave trade. Yet intra-state and local slave sales in the seaboard states exceeded long-distance sales by nearly 30 percent in the decade before the Civil War, and there is no reason to believe that this local trade simply evaporated once the war began. Historian Bell Irvin Wiley examined evidence of wartime slave trading in newspapers from major Confederate cities such as Richmond, Charleston, and Augusta, concluding that "the general tendency from the beginning to the end of the conflict was toward an increase in the current prices of Negroes, a decrease in their real value, and a shrinkage in the volume of trade." Ervin Jordan's short treatment of slave sales and hiring in his examination of black Virginians during the Civil War modified Wiley's conclusions, suggesting that "runaways, Union incursions, and wartime vicissitudes did not seriously impair slavery's economic vitality until the end of 1863." Indeed, as Nelia's letter indicated, slaveholders in Virginia continued to purchase from the local slave market well into the war years.[3]

The existence of a local market for slave sales in Confederate Virginia paralleled an expanded wartime hiring market. In particular, Virginia's industrial employers and various Confederate government agencies played significant roles in the wartime slave hiring market, building on a foundation that existed well before the beginning of the war. Historian Frederic Bancroft indicated that at least eighteen Richmond establishments supplied slaves for the hiring market in 1860; in western Virginia counties, between 10 and 12 percent of slaves were hired out in the late 1850s.[4] This expansive antebellum hiring market, particularly for slaves with industrial skills, grew dramatically with the wartime industrial demands of the Confederacy. At the same time, the war strained the hiring market because both the manufacturers and the War Department sought only able-bodied male slaves, leaving a surplus of bondswomen and unproductive children with slaveholders, who faced dwindling resources.

In January 1865, Confederate War Department bureau head Robert Garlick Hill Kean observed Richmond slaveholders "selling their slaves very rapidly." He did not record whether anyone in Richmond actually bought all of these slaves. To Kean, attempts to unload slave property indicated a lack of confidence in the institution of slavery and, by extension, a lack of confidence in the prospects for Confederate victory.[5] It was certainly the case that the slave trade could only work if white Virginians remained confident about the safety of their peculiar institution. At the same time, many owners simply lacked the food and clothing necessary to care for slaves, and the white refugees flocking to the capital were probably unable to find productive work for so many servants. At any given moment, Virginians' ability to sell their slaves depended on local economic conditions as well as the political and military stability of their state. Although the local slave trade in Virginia faltered by early 1865, its ability to function throughout much of the war indicated an impressive confidence on the part of white Virginians in the economic, political, and military prospects of the Confederacy.

The stability of the slave sale and hiring markets often directly reflected the stability of Virginia's political and military affairs. Virginia's unsettled political situation during the secession winter kept slave prices fairly low, while secession itself prompted a renewed confidence in the value of slave property. The early demands of creating and maintaining an army in Virginia brought an expansion of the hiring market. Although Silas Omohundro's profits on slave sales in Richmond fell as General George B. McClellan's men neared the city in May 1862, they rose almost immediately following Confederate victories in the battles of the Seven Days in late June and early July. Moreover, owners benefited from the high prices paid for slave hires because Confederate Treasury notes held their value fairly well during the first year of the war. A gold dollar would cost $2.50 in Richmond by September 1, 1862, but this depreciation rate paled in comparison to that of later years.[6] Though fluctuating with military and political events, the market for slaves in Virginia generally remained stable from the outbreak of war until the fall of 1862, reflecting a high confidence in the vitality of slavery among Virginia's white citizens.

Price of male slaves

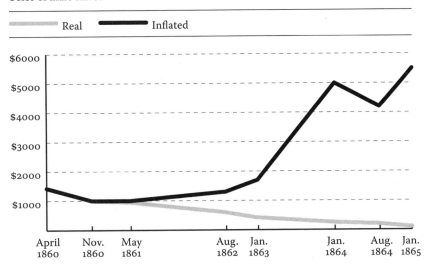

The political uncertainty of the winter of 1860–61 depressed prices in the slave markets. Although the editors of the Alexandria *Gazette* asserted that "we learn from the Richmond papers that the prices of negroes in that city have had an upward tendency ever since the inauguration of Lincoln," the records of Richmond slave trader Silas Omohundro tell a different story. On November 1, 1860, Omohundro purchased Packstal for $1,350, Jack for $1,300, and Susan for $900; he sold the three slaves in early 1861 for $1,075, $1,000, and $875, respectively. Omohundro's willingness to depart with these slaves at a loss of $600 indicates an eagerness to sell most likely related to the unsettled nature of political events.[7] Virginia's tenuous position within the Union was clearly not good for the Richmond slave-trading business.

By contrast, Virginia's decision to secede slightly improved Omohundro's fortunes. The six slaves he bought in April 1861 all sold at or above their purchase prices, although their sales did not approach the prices of January 1860. In addition, Omohundro's account ledger lists far fewer transactions for the years 1861 and 1862 than any previous years, while he recorded his first net losses in September 1861 and July 1862. Other Richmond traders advertised regularly in the newspapers seeking both to buy and sell slaves during these years, however, and may have maintained a more profitable business than Omohundro did. M. J. Farrington sought

150 slaves for sale in Arkansas and Mississippi, indicating a willingness to trade them for land he owned in the southwestern states. He promoted his land as "not exposed to acts of vicious characters, and where slave property cannot be interfered with by bad influences," an attractive proposition to Virginia planters in the summer of 1861. Although slave sales for the long-distance trade and in large lots fell dramatically after the first few months of war, traders still solicited slaves for sale within Virginia. Richmond auctioneers Dickinson, Hill & Co. ran their ads in papers across the state indicating that they would "attend particularly to the selling of Slaves at public and Private Sale."[8]

While prices for slave sales may have dropped slightly early in the war, many slave owners could take advantage of the war-related boom in the hiring market as industrial concerns in Virginia sought to increase production. William Weaver hired more than thirty slaves in January 1861 for work in his Rockbridge County Buffalo Forge, at an average price of $113.50. In August, James Boyd sought to employ immediately "25 ABLE BODIED NEGRO MEN, to work at Glenwood Furnace in Rockbridge County." From October 16, 1861, into the following January, the Virginia and Tennessee Railroad advertised in multiple papers, seeking to hire five hundred slaves for the coming year. James Cox sought an unspecified number of slave hands for his Clover Hill rock pits in December and promised to pay liberally for their hire. Masters and mistresses who hoped to hire out extra field hands saw expanded opportunities among regional industrialists.[9]

The Confederate army also became an active participant in the hiring market early in the war, as units and even individual officers from across the South sought the temporary services of Virginia slaves. Slaveholders in Gloucester, Middlesex, and Mathews counties began leasing male laborers to General John B. Magruder's officers for short-term work on fortifications as early as July 1861. The officers of the Nineteenth Georgia Regiment placed an advertisement for "TWO SERVANTS for the officer's mess of the 1st Company," while another unit sought "TWO HONEST AND trusty Negro Boys, to wait on officers in the army, free or slave. Liberal wages will be paid." This active hiring market in Virginia contrasts with the picture Wiley provided of hiring in the Lower South, where decreased cotton production limited the options of owners hoping to hire out their laborers. No doubt many Virginia slaveholders took advantage of the expanded options for hiring out their male slaves, particularly as white men departed for the front. Women left alone with their slaves for the first time may have welcomed the opportunity to relinquish day-to-day control over the most volatile element of their workforces.[10]

For those slaves sent into the hiring market, that market's expansion was clearly a mixed blessing. Industrial labor could offer enslaved men the ability to earn money through task systems providing overwork wages, particularly for those hired by William Weaver and Daniel Brady at Buffalo Forge. Some slaves also took advantage of the situation and ran away from hired positions. But the expanded hiring market also created difficult, if temporary, separations from friends and family. Charles Tibbs wrote to his master, Andrew Grinnan, lamenting his separation from his family:

> I was very sory to come away and leave my wife sick I would like to have stayed untill she got well but I lerned a few dayes ago that she was dead, and Dear Master I trust she has gone to a better plase than in this veil of sins and sorrow. I want you to give my love to Aunt Betsy and tell her to take good care of my little boy and I will pay her for it when I come I have bin sick ever since I have bin hear and I wold like to come home in the holidase if not before. . . .[11]

Hired slaves understandably took every opportunity to see and communicate with their loved ones during their terms of service.

Despite the burgeoning opportunities for hiring out slaves in the industrial sector as the war continued, the editors of the Lynchburg *Daily Republican* worried that prices in the hiring market would drop at the beginning of 1862. On New Year's Eve they reported, "we have been unable to observe much change in the prices obtained for cooks and house-servants from those of last year. Good cooks range from $60 to $75—house-servants about the same. Farm and factory hands have visibly declined from the former rates, with a prospect for those remaining over unhired, still further declining." Yet ads from industrial employers continued to appear in the *Republican* throughout the month of January, as they all sought to fill their workforces to meet expanding military demands. In Richmond, Joseph Anderson's agents hired more than one hundred slaves for the Tredegar Iron Works alone, paying an annual average of $102.87 for each worker in January 1862.[12]

If the slave hiring market may have stagnated in early 1862, it certainly grew rapidly the following summer. R. P. Richardson sought "20 Hands, for the balance of the year 1862, consisting of Men, Boys and Girls to work in tobacco factory or on farm near Danville, Va." On the same day, the Confederate War Department placed an urgent ad reading, "THE

PROMPT REPAIR OF THE injury done to the James River and Kanawha Canal by the late freshet being a matter of great public importance, the Government of the Confederate States wishes to employ 500 HANDS to work upon the Canal near Lynchburg, for which the highest prices will be paid in cash." Unlike Richardson, but like most industrial employers, the Confederacy's Engineer and Mining Bureaus preferred to hire adult male laborers.[13]

The Richmond market for slave sales also expanded in July 1862. Silas Omohundro sold eight male slaves between July 16 and August 16, 1862, at an average profit margin of $285. In fact, in December 1862 Omohundro listed his first net profit since the successful spring of 1860.[14] This resumption of sales, marked by high prices (although not quite as high as those of January 1860), was probably sparked by Confederate military successes outside Richmond in the summer of 1862. In fact, Omohundro's sales ledgers for the summer of 1862 provide the most obvious connection between the slave trade and the military fortunes of the Confederacy. While George McClellan's Army of the Potomac stood only miles from Richmond in May and June, Omohundro's sales stopped entirely, but those sales resumed almost immediately upon Robert E. Lee's victories in the Seven Days battles from June 25 to July 1, 1862. Confederate victory brought a return of business to the city of Richmond and especially a return of the potential for slave traders to make profitable sales.

Omohundro was not the only person to recognize this renewed potential for slave sales. The city press also noted the increase in slave sales in July: "at an auction sale on Franklin street a few days since a negro fellow, not specially likely, brought $1,500. A girl 19 years old, (ugly) $1,300; one 7 years old, $725; a man, (diseased) 58 years old, $150. These prices will serve to indicate both the appreciation and demand for this species of property." Even with Confederate currency likely worth half of its original value, these were reasonable, if slightly low, prices when compared to late antebellum slave sales. According to Wiley's compilation of sales figures, moreover, Omohundro seems to have received prices exceeding the national average of $1,100 in currency for an eighteen-year-old male during the third quarter of 1862, perhaps reflecting the high optimism of white Virginians in the months following Confederate victory in the Seven Days battles. The appreciation and demand for slave laborers only grew stronger as the Confederate government began impressing slaves, and as industrial employers proved particularly willing to pay well for hired laborers.[15]

The first year of the war, from secession through the summer of 1862, brought a remarkable confluence between slave prices and Virginia's political and military situation. Virginians continued to purchase slaves, and at good prices, but only when they felt confident in the success of their current government. The war in Virginia also brought an expanded hiring market, particularly for skilled slaves, as industrialists sought to expand their operations rapidly to meet the Confederacy's demands for war matériel. The high prices men like William Weaver and Joseph Anderson paid to hire skilled slaves most likely served to increase consumer confidence in the institution of slavery. Later stages of the war would see a continued—though sometimes less obvious—relationship between the slave market and political and military events.

In particular, the slave market in the fall of 1862 and early winter of 1863 reflected the political actions of both the United States and Confederate States governments, as well as state and local politicians. Most obviously, Virginians sought to answer Lincoln's Emancipation Proclamation by proclaiming their own continued confidence in the institution of slavery, often through the purchase of slaves. Equally important, the increasing labor demands of the Confederate war effort brought new municipal, state, and finally Confederate government purchases and requisitions of slaves for military and industrial use throughout 1863. With government requisition of slaves also came government regulation of individual slaves as well as numerous government provisions to maintain the safety and value of those slaves. Yet real prices for slaves failed to keep pace with an inflation rate that rose from 388 percent at the end of 1862 to 1,452 percent by the end of 1863.[16] The period of late 1862 and early 1863, then, saw an increased government presence in the institution of slavery as well as continued slave sales in Virginia.

State and local governing bodies sought to meet mounting wartime labor demands in the fall of 1862. On October 23, the Richmond City Council determined to "purchase as many negroes, as in the opinion of the Chairman of the committee and Superintendent of the Gas Works may be adviseable, to secure labor for the Gas Works" rather than imposing a citywide draft of slave labor. Earlier that month, the Virginia General Assembly enacted its first provision for the enrollment of slaves and empowered Governor John Letcher to impress slaves to work for the defense of the state. The governor requisitioned forty-five hundred slaves from fourteen Virginia counties in October 1862 and another 4,550 from twenty-six different counties in November. These impressment calls reduced by several hundred the number of able-bodied male slaves in larger counties such as Albemarle, Bedford, Campbell, Caroline, and Pittsylvania as the fall hiring season approached.[17]

Both industrial agents and private individuals worked actively to secure labor for the next year. The most common ads sought men for factory and forge work: "WANTED TO HIRE—100 able-bodied NEGRO MEN to work on the Western Railroad in Chatham county; for the remainder of the present and the ensuing year." Some slaveholders entered the hiring market more aggressively than in previous years because they needed to replace slaves lost to government requisitions. Other potential employers may have had alternative motives, as Jedediah Hotchkiss suggested to his wife. "I was in Staunton on Monday," wrote Hotchkiss, "trying to find a servant to come to the army, but it was of no avail, there are so many to go to Richmond & so many that want substitutes, to send to Richmond, for their servants that they want to have stay at home." The Petersburg *Daily Express* drew a particularly clear connection between slaveholders seeking to hire slaves to fill impressment quotas and draftees seeking white substitutes for Confederate army service by intermingling their ads in the same column of text.[18]

The slave market throughout Virginia proved particularly strong in the winter of 1862–63, and numerous editors commented on high prices for sales and hires.

> At the sale of Messrs. Dickinson, Hill & Co., yesterday, the following were the quotations: Likely young girls, one thousand two hundred and fifty dollars and one thousand four hundred dollars, house servants and body servants, one thousand four hundred dollars; cooks, washers and ironers, one thousand five hundred and ten dollars; likely boys, farm hands and plough boys, one thousand and forty dollars and one thousand three hundred and seventy dollars; likely boys, one thousand five hundred dollars and one thousand six hundred and ninety dollars; men, good farm hands, one thousand and twenty dollars and one thousand six hundred and sixty dollars.

Later in the same month, "At the sale of George F. Chambers, in Brunswick, Va., on the 16th instant, the following prices were obtained: Alexander, aged 21 years, $1,515; Henderson, aged 19, $1,476; Sena, aged 17, and young child, $1,725; total, $4,716. The slaves were all likely." With less fanfare from the press, the Tredegar Iron Works purchased a total of nineteen slaves in 1863 at an average price of nearly $1,700. Adjusted for roughly 400 percent inflation, Tredegar purchased these slaves at an average of $425 each, or less than one-third the price of a male laborer in 1860. Yet apparently neither editors nor readers took the time to calculate these high prices in real terms, taking them instead as proof of the continuing vitality of the institution of slavery, proof that was particularly important in December 1862.[19]

Editors were anxious to record high prices for slave sales in January 1863 to highlight the futility of Lincoln's impending Emancipation Proclamation. This was a well-advertised goal for the editor of the Lynchburg *Daily Republican*, who asserted,

> one thing is manifest, that ought to teach Lincoln and his advisers wisdom, if they are capable of being taught. Negroes are selling in the South almost double as high as ever heretofore, and are going up higher and higher every day.—No longer than yesterday, they sold on the block of this city, for twenty two hundred dollars, from which it is manifest that our people hold Lincoln's threats in supreme contempt. The Yankees can and may steal a large number of our slaves, as they have done wherever an opportunity has presented itself, but they can never get possession of them in any other way.

As the paper also reported, the previous day Lynchburg auctioneer B. Akers had sold a total of 116 slaves, at an average price of over $1,000. In this sale, "the highest price obtained was for a negro man, 21 years old, an ordinary field hand, but very likely, who brought $2925, the lowest for a woman, 46 years old, $120—Abraham's proclamation has made negro property go up like a sky rocket." On the same page, six different items advertised the availability of at least thirty-two slaves for impending sales, as local slaveholders sought to take advantage of this spike in prices.[20]

The high prices for slaves continued into January, as did the *Republican*'s desire to record each record-breaking sale. On January 5, "Messes J.B. Hargrove & Co, Auctioneers, sold, Saturday, twelve negroes, at an average of $1,020 each," while ten days later the paper reported, "Messrs Hargrove & Co. sold seven yesterday at auction for $9,280, an average of $1,326 each. If old Mr Abe is to be believed, these gentlemen are now engaged in an illicit trade, that of selling free negroes into slavery, and we suggest that a special term of the Circuit Court be held for their trial." The Lynchburg paper even reported slave prices in other towns, perhaps for purposes of comparison. "The ancient town of Charlottesville is but little behind Lynchburg in the prices paid for negroes. A negro girl, 18 years old, was sold there a few days since for $2,500. Ordinary men sold for from $2,300 to $2,400, a girl 8 years old brought, at the same sale, $1,600. Hurrah for Abe and his proclamation!"[21]

Once again, it is worth attempting to adjust these prices for an inflation rate of nearly 400 percent in January 1863. The eighteen-year-old girl, for example, sold for the equivalent of $625 in gold, the men at roughly $575, and the child $400. A comparison to Omohundro's 1860 ledger suggests that the price of male slaves in Virginia may have depreciated faster than that of women and children. If so, this could represent a more persistent fear that male slaves could run away most easily, or the reality that male slaves were subject to Confederate impressment while female slaves were not. By comparison, Wiley's average figures for Charleston, South Carolina, show twenty-year-old men selling at $1,450 in currency, or the equivalent of $410 in gold. Wiley suggests that food production needs in South Carolina had not reached a high enough level by early 1863 to employ all the surplus slaves who were no longer growing cotton, which may be one explanation for the price differential between Charlottesville and Charleston. Meanwhile, though disregarding currency depreciation, Virginia editors turned the purchase of slaves into a supremely political act expressing widespread public confidence in the Confederate war effort.[22]

With less explicitly avowed political intent, the editor of the *Staunton Spectator* published similar information about the market for slaves. "Just at the very time when Lincoln declares that they are emancipated," he argued, "they command higher prices than ever before. Could anything demonstrate more satisfactorily the futility of his infamous proclamation? The people of the South never felt that the institution of slavery was ever safer than at the present time." This confidence on the part of Virginians was crucial to sustaining the high prices of the wartime slave market. Whatever political message the newspaper editors hoped to send, they could not have done so if citizens had not been willing to spend their money on more slaves, and citizens would not have purchased more slaves if they expected the Union army to be able to enforce the Emancipation Proclamation. In January 1863, their confidence in future Confederate military success was so strong that they were willing to pay the following prices:

> A man aged 25 years, and defective, $1,500; man aged 21 years, $2,305; man aged 45 years, $2,000; woman and child $1,500; girl, aged 14 years, $1,500; man, aged 60 years, $1,615; man, defective, aged 35 years, $1,225; boy aged 13 years, $2,410; boy 12 years old, $1,605; woman 25 years old, $2,050; woman 45 years, $1,700; man, defective, 85 years old, $1,015. Amounting to $21,865.

These high prices reflected the understandably high expectations of Virginia's civilians following the Union army debacle at Fredericksburg in December 1862.[23]

Increasing prices: gold vs. slaves

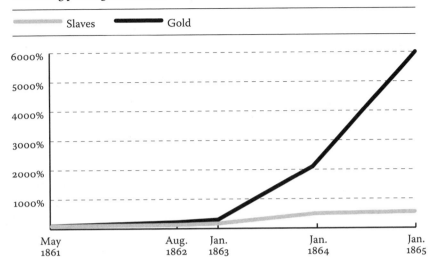

Slaves   Gold

Of course, the high prices recorded for slave sales in Virginia in the winter of 1862–63 paralleled increased prices for all commodities. As William Blair reports in *Virginia's Private War,* the price of dietary staples increased threefold in Lynchburg. "Family flour that had cost $7.50 per barrel in 1860 went from a low of $10 per barrel to $30. Bacon soared from a low of 35 cents per pound to $1.10 per pound." On January 17, 1863, Confederate clerk John B. Jones lamented similarly high prices in Richmond, asking, "Shall we starve? Yesterday beef was sold for 40 cts. per pound; to-day it is 60 cts. Lard is $1.00. Butter $2.00." This increase was due in part to a sharp decline in the relative purchasing power of Confederate Treasury notes during the winter months: while a single gold dollar was worth $2.50 in notes in September 1862 and $3.00 in February 1863, by mid-March a gold dollar would have cost a full $5.00 in Treasury notes, had anyone been willing to sell it. Yet as long as merchants were willing to accept Treasury notes, however depreciated, slave sales continued, and those willing to sell saw their high profits recorded in the local newspapers.[24]

Newspaper editors were not the only people to recognize the high profits slave sales brought in early 1863. Ex-slave Virginia Shepherd remembered that in 1863, "when there was so much talk about freeing the slaves," the sheriff took her family to a slave jail at the request of her master. There they waited with "hundreds of other mothers and their children sleeping on the floor at night just waiting their turn to be sold South. Each day some were sold off."[25] Shepherd's experiences highlighted the fears of some Confederate masters, who responded to the Emancipation Proclamation by attempting to sell their slaves rather than losing their investments. But these nervous masters would not have been able to sell their slaves unless someone else, more confident in the continued viability of slavery and probably farther from the reach of Union troops, had wished to buy them. The traders who purchased these families, perhaps in hopes of reviving the long-distance domestic slave trade, certainly did not foresee an imminent end to the institution of slavery.

The slave hiring market experienced similarly high rates in December 1862 and January 1863, particularly for those slaves with industrial skills. J. R. Anderson & Co. spent considerably more on hiring in January 1863 than they had the previous year, with average annual prices ranging from $190.86 for the sixty-four slaves at Grace Furnace to $227.59 for the fifty-four slaves at Rebecca Furnace.[26] In addition, agents at each furnace had to feed and clothe all hired slaves while commodity prices continued to rise.

Owners hoped to take advantage of high prices and eagerly sought the most remunerative positions for their slaves. The *Examiner* reported with some anger the high prices of slave hires for the coming year, "stimulated by the spirit of extortion, which has come to pervade all transactions, in which money is concerned, the 'negro,' in commercial parlance, may be quoted as 'stiff' and 'holding firm' above former quotations considerably." These slaves commanded high prices despite the fact that "the number of negroes hiring in Richmond and vicinity is greater than at any former season, from the fact that hundreds have been sent here by their owners from the counties to prevent their falling into the possession of the enemy." Thus, the war created an expanded supply of slave labor in Richmond, which somehow the local population managed to employ even at inflated prices. J. R. Bryan of Carysbrook reported to his cousin Andrew Grinnan, "Negroes hire very high even here, in Richd. they bring unheard of prices. I wanted to consult you about Hannah, if you want her why have you not mentioned it. She can be hired for a high price in Richmond—I think I will sell Katy. Hannah has given satisfaction to Mrs Brooke, but of course she cannot stay there at the present rate." For slaves, the high prices of the hiring and sale markets in January 1863 meant a greater potential for dislocation and the disruption of family ties, as they faced sale or hiring away from a familiar household.[27]

Potential hirers also faced new demands on slaves' time and labor. Augusta County minister Francis McFarland had hired a slave named Jefferson for an annual sum of $110 between 1860 and 1862, and another named Moses on a short-term basis during the same years. As January 1863 approached, however, he made arrangements instead to hire Moses at the lower rate of $100, "with the reserve that if he goes to work for the Govt. a reduction must be made, or if he returns unfit for service." Government impressment of slaves had thus begun to reduce the available pool of male slave labor as early as January 1863, although McFarland was still able to find sufficient labor for threshing and harvesting through short-term hiring from other local farmers.[28]

Despite these much-vaunted high prices for slave sales and hires in January 1863, cracks began to appear in the stability of the slave market. As early as May 1863, F. F. Mayo reported to a friend "that Negroes now have declined in price in Richmond & Lynchburg and will no doubt come down very much in a short time." Although prices were still increasing in general, the demand for male laborers, especially those with industrial experience, vastly exceeded the demand for women, children, and house servants. This marked a particular difficulty for the Richmond slave market, where domestic workers had dominated the ranks of hired slaves throughout the antebellum years. It probably also meant that enslaved men hired into industrial firms like the Tredegar Iron Works had fewer opportunities to bring their wives and families to the city with them. Granvill Clark implored his owner, William Cabell, "to let my wife Nancy to Remain as she is until I come up and see you You have done one Peice of Kindness for when I was up there Before and sorry to troble you again and I am in hope that you will Let my Wife Be hire out here in Richmond." Cabell's reply has not been preserved, but he was probably influenced more by economic realities than anything else when he considered whether or not to leave Nancy in Richmond. Cabell could not have taken advantage of the high rates offered by iron manufacturers to find a place for Nancy; while the Confederate Medical Department as well as individual units hired female slaves, these opportunities were limited in comparison to those available for male slaves in the Engineer or Nitre and Mining Bureaus.[29]

The market for able-bodied male slaves became even more crowded with potential employers in March 1863, after the close of the traditional hiring season. The Virginia General Assembly, recognizing that the Confederate War Department, Engineer Bureau, and Mining Bureau had not been able to fill all of their labor needs through hiring, issued another call for 2,832 slaves. At the same time, state legislators responded to the concerns of their constituents by exempting "agricultural counties where slave impressment would materially affect production." Also in March 1863, the Confederate Congress took steps toward centralizing slave impressment but worked through the Virginia General Assembly to make a fourth requisition by counties in August, this time for 4,230 slaves. With each round of impressments, slaveholders became more concerned that the Confederacy's demand for military laborers would deprive them of agricultural laborers.[30]

Slaveholders also worried that slaves they had leased to the Confederate War Department would sustain serious injuries or run away while working on fortifications. These fears echoed in the regular proposals Confederate congressmen made regarding government compensation for owners of injured, killed, or runaway slaves. Due to the persistence of these congressmen, acts providing for impressment of slaves regularly included clauses specifying that "in the event of the loss of any slaves while so employed, by the act of the enemy, or by escape to the enemy, or by death inflicted by the enemy, or by disease contracted while in any service required of such slaves, then the owners of the same shall be entitled to receive the full value of such slaves, to be ascertained by agreement, or by appraisement." Savvy slaveholders such as Joseph Anderson took care to have their slaves appraised and recorded their values before sending men to work on Confederate fortifications. The pervasive motions to ensure government compensation represented, on some level, a continued confidence in the economic profitability of slavery on the part of slaveholders and their congressional representatives.[31]

This confidence certainly seemed warranted, from all observable conditions, in late 1863. Although one interpretation of the flurry of slave sales in January 1863 would be that Virginia's slaveholders doubted the continued existence of the institution and thus sought to get money quickly, the fact remains that these men and women could not have sold their slaves—especially at staggeringly inflated prices—unless somebody else had wanted to buy them. The presence of a local and even a limited long-distance market for slaves in 1863 represented white Virginians' material as well as rhetorical observance of the futility of the Emancipation Proclamation. This second stage of the war was also remarkable for the growing importance of the state and Confederate governments in the slave market, as impressers if not as purchasers of slaves. Despite some cracks in Virginia's hiring market, particularly along gender lines, the slave market showed impressive stability at the close of 1863, reflecting the continued confidence of Virginians in the success of their new government.

The strains and cracks in the slave market continued to grow, albeit slowly, from the last months of 1863 to Lee's surrender in April 1865. Many of these strains simply reflected the dwindling economic resources of many Virginians, as they reacted to scarcity, inflation, and new issues of paper currency. Other cracks continued the hiring trends of early 1863, as government and industrial agents sought male laborers in a hiring market flooded by women, children, and domestic servants. Despite these strains, however, confidence in the slave market never collapsed completely, and some Virginians continued to purchase slaves until the very end of the war.

In the winter of 1863–64, Francis McFarland reported increased difficulty in finding male slaves to hire, as government impressments took more slaves from the Shenandoah Valley. After nearly a week of searching for an available slave, McFarland made arrangements to hire Zeke for "$300, which sum I am to pay & cloathe him." Perhaps sensing his power in a tight hiring market, Zeke originally objected to his new situation because he was "unwilling to live so far from his wife," though McFarland eventually persuaded Zeke to come home with him. Hiring female slaves was significantly less difficult, as McFarland arranged to again hire Rhoda, who had been with the family for several years, for only fifty dollars. Indeed, McFarland's experiences closely paralleled the strains within the broader hiring market for slaves in Virginia.[32]

The hiring season of December 1863 and January 1864 began well, according to the press. "Notwithstanding the precarious situation in which alarmists would make the people believe the 'peculiar institution' has fallen, negroes sold higher yesterday by three or four hundred dollars than they did last week. Likely negro women brought four thousand four hundred dollars, and there was a general advance in all descriptions offered." As in January 1863, there was a clear propaganda element to news items touting high slave prices, as editors both reflected and sought to shape consumer behavior. Certainly, slaveholders looking to sell or hire took heart in news items like this one, as well as in advertisements like that of Joseph R. Anderson, who "wish[ed] to hire for the year 1864, ONE THOUSAND NEGROES, to be employed at the Tredegar Iron Works, Richmond, and at our Blast furnaces in the counties of Rockbridge, Botetourt and Allegheny, and Collieries in Goochland and Henrico, for which we are willing to pay the market prices." Anderson eventually paid an average of $417.10 for the slaves he hired at Mt. Torry furnace, with rates in Richmond most likely exceeding this average in January 1864.[33]

Anderson even expressed a willingness to hire families, since he could use women and older children on the farms that fed his furnace hands. He also reassured owners that "our furnaces and other works are located in healthy sections of the country, remote from the enemy's line, offering unusual inducements to the owners of negroes to send them to us." Anderson was probably unique among industrial employers in taking families, since the size of his operation allowed him to find employment for women and children. More common was the response of forge manager Jonathan Fry to William Cabell: "in the Bond, there are four children named, what are they for. I never gave a bond for children before." Most Richmond industrialists simply had no use for slave families.[34]

Despite Anderson's call for one thousand laborers, the slave hiring market seemed less healthy in the winter of 1863–64 than it had been the previous year. This was in part due to increased numbers of potential hirees, particularly among domestic servants, as owners sought to decrease their own expenses or earn extra income in difficult wartime economic conditions. As one Lynchburg paper reported, "the offices of Agents are filling with all classes and sexes of darkies, and the streets are thronged with them. The prevailing idea is that the hiring rates will rule higher than the past year, notwithstanding the advance in the prices of food and clothing, but as yet, we have heard of no contracts, to enable us to specify the probable prices." Editors expressed their concern that in this year's hiring market, the number of potential hirers was "not so numerous as servants seeking masters and mistresses."[35]

The Richmond press also commented on high asking prices in the slave hiring market in December 1863, and proposed that more households would do without extra help. Rather than pay annual hiring rates "in some cases equal to what they would have sold for three years ago," some Richmond families might even forego domestic servants altogether. The editor facetiously proposed that "young ladies, and middle aged ones too, will now have an opportunity of becoming acquainted with that unknown locality, the kitchen; and also, of perfecting themselves in an accomplishment of which the great majority are utterly ignorant—the art of cooking."[36] By late 1863, it was becoming harder for the market to sustain the high monetary expectations of slave owners, as those looking to hire also frequently suffered from a lack of money and supplies.

Virginia's newspapers in January 1864 reported a strange phenomenon, as editors frequently reiterated the decreasing profitability of slave hiring while advertisements from manufacturers seeking laborers continued to appear. This disparity underscored the existence of a hiring market saturated by domestic servants at a time when the Confederacy needed to increase dramatically its industrial output. Thus, an ad hoping to place three house servants appeared sandwiched between Anderson's ad seeking six hundred furnace workers and two hundred coal miners and the Piedmont Railroad's ad for two hundred slave laborers. The Confederate Engineer Bureau began advertising its intent to hire one thousand laborers in mid-December 1863. Meanwhile, the Lynchburg firm Hargrove & Co. became increasingly insistent about hiring out their remaining slaves, reporting, "we still have for hire a variety of Servants, and we are very anxious to get them off. Thos who want to hire, had better do so at once, as we shall be forced to raise the hires, if we have to keep them until Meal, Meat and Wood get cheaper, which we suppose will be the case when vegetation puts forth and labor is in demand."[37]

Hargrove & Co.'s eagerness to divest themselves of remaining slave property was perfectly natural given the high prices that William Blair reports foodstuffs demanded in Lynchburg that winter: "by December [1863], the price [of flour] catapulted from $80 to $100 and then hit an astronomical $250 to $275 per barrel the following spring. Bacon, corn, and butter increased as dramatically." Richmond slave traders and owners likely faced similar difficulties. Citing the Richmond newspapers, John B. Jones recorded on December 10, 1863, that "Wheat may be quoted at $15 to $18 per bushel, according to quality. Corn is bringing from $14 to $15 per bushel." Jones also lamented the inability of the Confederate government to curb inflation by stabilizing the value of Confederate currency. Any difficulties owners faced in hiring out their slaves in early 1864 likely reflected scarcity of goods and specie rather than decreasing confidence among white Virginians in the long-term stability of slavery as an institution.[38]

The editor of the Lynchburg *Daily Republican* blamed the problems of the hiring market on grasping slaveholders, who had sought to make too large of a profit in January 1864. As potential employers decided to do without hired slaves, the editor exulted, "the tables are completely turned on the owners of negroes, and instead of asking $500 and $600 each for them, they are begging people to take them, and in some instances we have heard of, are offering to pay them to do so. We hope this will be a lesson to these people in the future and teach them not to extortion on what they believe to be the necessities of the people."[39] He thus sought to turn widespread animosity toward extortion and profiteering in the Confederacy against those who had offered slaves in the hiring market, telling a morality tale that he hoped would bring about a reduction in prices.

Some masters did indeed offer slaves to others at little or no cost, preferring simply to place the responsibility of feeding and clothing them on another party. In January 1864, John D. Brockenbrough rented out his slave Charles to Luke W. Davis for $25 plus clothing and board; Cyrus Clark paid only $20 to hire Mous. H. D. Taliaferro reported to Andrew Grinnan from Richmond that "McCorys tells me that he has some excellent servants that he is willing to hire for their food & clothing but cant put them off his hands." Finally, William Mitchell actually agreed to pay Samuel Blair $640 for boarding Philada and her two children for the year 1864, provided "said Blair binds himself to treat the above named Slaves humanely & furnish them with the usual clothing." Those able to provide food and clothing to hired slaves—and often their dependents—without extreme hardship had an available source of extremely cheap labor. In some cases, they could increase the size of their workforce and receive pay in addition.[40]

While the hiring market seemed to disappear outside of industrial and government agents, those seeking to purchase slaves saw prices continue to increase. Nelia's father's purchase, reported earlier, was not the only substantial transaction in slave property in early 1864. On January 14, Lynchburg citizens read that "a negro man was sold in Petersburg Tuesday for $5,000. On the same day a negro woman brought $4,925. People seem to have faith yet in their 'right of property in slaves,' notwithstanding Abe's proclamation." Robert Grinnan told his brother Andrew of his attempts to purchase slaves in Richmond. "I was three times to the Caryshod Jail to find the proprietor & at the auction rooms to hunt him up to enquire after the slaves advertised—Their master ran off from Loudon Co. to the Yankees They have been sequestered and sold—their present owner offers them for sale at $4000." In addition to the firm's numerous hires, the Tredegar Iron Works purchased five skilled slaves, three of whom cost over $4,000 each. Adjusted for 1,452 percent inflation at the end of 1863, male slaves brought around $275 in January 1864.[41]

Contrary to Jordan's argument, this evidence suggests that slave sales may have exceeded hiring from 1864 onward. Perhaps the market for slave sales continued in the face of decreasing slave hires because those with the resources to feed and clothe extra laborers preferred to own them. Certainly, those men who paid upwards of $4,000 for each slave in January 1864 must have felt secure in the future of the institution of slavery and, by extension, Confederate independence. If they had expected the war to end in just over a year, most rational businessmen would have chosen the more economical route of hiring a slave for $300 to $500 annually.

As growing numbers of Virginians found themselves in close proximity to Union soldiers, slave sales slowly continued into the fall of 1864. Robert Grinnan attributed any decline in slave sales and particularly slave prices to Confederate monetary policy rather than a lack of confidence in the institution of slavery, reporting that since not all citizens had access to newly issued currency, "two negro boys sold at $3000—that would have brought $4500—there are many trades made in the old issue privately." In 1892, Mrs. R. A. Morris compiled a list of her former slaves from her husband's records, noting that he sold a slave named John for $4,500 sometime after October 1864. The executors for Silas Omohundro's estate sold thirteen slaves through two Richmond traders in July 1864, netting $43,435, before expenses, for Omohundro's heirs. Ironically, Omohundro's heirs were the children of his recognized slave mistress, all of whom he freed in his will, so that a woman and several children formerly held in slavery themselves received the profits of the sale of other black men and women. And J. W. Harper of Dinwiddie, without explanation, sought in July "to purchase fifty NEGROES between the ages of 4 and 12 (four and twelve)." Overall, however, slave sales seem to have fallen off in Virginia by mid-1864. This was particularly the case in Petersburg as Union forces approached in June; one ex-slave remembered, "just before the shelling of Petersburg dey were selling niggers for little nothin' hardly." Newspaper editors stopped printing frequent notices of local sales and instead turned to more frequent discussions of high sale prices in North Carolina.[42]

North Carolinians were able to maintain a more active slave trade than Virginians due to their isolation from the Union and Confederate armies. Moreover, as John Inscoe has demonstrated, the mountainous regions of the state experienced rapid growth in slave population during the war years, as lowcountry masters sent or brought their slaves to the upcountry to minimize their property losses. During the war years, slavery actually increased its stability and economic vitality in western North Carolina, since the region developed railroad and mining concerns that benefited from these new influxes of slave labor. A similar phenomenon occurred in some areas of Virginia; for example, the enslaved population of the southwestern tier of counties in Virginia more than doubled between 1860 and

1863. Not only did these southwestern counties remain isolated from the Union army, but they also contained valuable salt resources that claimed the labor of many Virginia slaves. These counties most likely experienced rapid growth because Tidewater planters sought both security and employment for their slaves in relatively isolated areas. The military fortunes of the Confederacy, it seems, determined the best locations as well as the best times for slave sales.[43]

Even taking into account regional variations throughout Virginia, however, the slave hiring season of December 1864–January 1865 experienced the same contradictions between domestic and industrial labor that had plagued the previous year's business, complicated by the continuing downward spiral of Virginia's economy. William Mitchell paid a total of $5,240 to local slaveholders who agreed to board and clothe three slave women and their eight children for the ensuing year, while he received over $500 for the hire of a young enslaved man. Editors expected difficulties in the hiring market since so few Virginians had extra cash on hand, or extra food to feed hired slaves. The price for able-bodied male slaves seemed secure at $500 per year, since "the government price, $500 for laborers, seems to be the figure which this class of servants will command, but, with this exception, owners and hirers have been unable to agree on satisfactory terms. It is generally conceded, however, that there will be but little difference in the general hiring prices from those which prevailed last year." The government's ability to put a price cap on slaves by hiring hundreds of men at a fixed rate should have pleased potential employers, given the previous year's fulminations over price-gouging in the slave hiring market.[44]

Yet the editor of the Richmond *Examiner* was more vicious on the subject of slave hiring than usual in January 1865, reserving particular ire for those slaves allowed to hire out themselves. Such slaves' "original masters care nothing for them, so they are fed and clothed and their hire forthcoming in money upon the arrival of every quarter day—Whether they live honestly, or by traffick, speculation or stealth, it don't concern their owners." Thus, the semi-independent slaves that had formed a key part of the Richmond labor market for decades were supposedly left to prey on innocent white citizens who had little or no food to begin with. The *Examiner*'s editor, while expecting the government to solve this problem by outlawing the practice of slaves hiring their own time, also seemed angry that the Confederate government acted as "the monopolist of the market for male negroes."[45]

Such contradictory positions abounded as editors tried to make sense of the hiring market in early 1865. The Lynchburg *Daily Republican's* editor proposed that citizens forego hiring slaves, remarking that in a time when food and clothing were scarce commodities, "few servants are worth more than they can eat, steal and wear, let alone a large sum payable to their owners for the privilege of doing so." But only two days later the paper complained that government hiring agents had monopolized all available black male labor "by pledging the government to insure the life of the slave, and to give the owner credit in any future impressments." They feared that Confederate hiring practices would leave the surrounding countryside without the labor necessary for the upcoming agricultural year. Indeed, the Confederate Senate had already responded to such concerns in late 1864, providing exemptions for Virginia counties or individuals that had "lost one third of its male slaves between the ages of eighteen and fifty-five years." Again, much of the problem stemmed from a surplus of domestic servants, especially women and children, and a shortage of male slaves fit for industrial or military labor.[46]

Yet the difficulties of the hiring market in January 1865 did not seem to represent any widespread expectation that slavery would disappear in the near future, despite Robert Kean's gloomy predictions. Indeed, the Lynchburg paper believed the opposite sentiment prevailed: "a large number of negroes were sold yesterday by Hargrove & Co and Dunnington & Myler. The prices ranged from $5000 to $8500, and showed a very healthy state of the market for this species of property." A few days later, "eleven negroes, comprising nine boys and girls, were sold yesterday by Myler & Williams at the high average of $5,500." Ex-slave Amarci Adams remembered that her owners "kept sellin' slaves until dey only hab two men ter work on de farm an' me ter do all de housewuk," right up until the fall of Richmond. The Virginians who purchased these slaves at very high prices clearly did not anticipate the surrender of the Confederate armies in just a few short months.[47]

Virginia's slaveholders also risked great expense to secure the return of runaway slaves. Advertisements appearing in December 1864 promised $500, $1,000, and even $2,000 for the return of young, able-bodied male slaves, who simultaneously were the most valuable to slaveowners while constituting the vast majority of runaways. Once again, the willingness of Virginia's slaveholders to expend large sums of money to purchase or regain slave property indicates their firm confidence in the future of slavery and, by extension, Confederate victory. This confidence clearly supports the arguments of historians such as William Blair, Gary Gallagher, and George Rable, who have maintained that while Confederate citizens frequently expressed dissatisfaction with their government, they remained firmly committed to their war for independence until the Confederate armies surrendered.[48]

Slave sales late in the war involved mostly women and children, as the enslaved male population of areas close to the two armies had diminished due to impressments and flight. Francis McFarland sold his widowed daughter's slave, Julia, to a Captain Roberts for $4,000 in December 1864. Julia's reaction to the impending sale, as recorded by McFarland, was most extraordinary:

> This morning, when I was dressing, Mrs McFarland & Mary Lou rushed into my room & Julia following them in an insane rage with an axe. I seized the poker & ran out & Rhoda & Liz were holding Julia & trying to get the axe from her which she was holding up over her head & trying to get at us. Rhoda cried to me to get out of the way, which I did & locked the door believing I could not contend with her & the axe. They got the axe from her & took her to the kitchen. I sent for Mr McPheeters & he & Capt. Roberts came & tied her & I sent her in the Waggon [sic] to Staunton and Mr McPheeters had her put in Jail.[49]

Julia's actions may have given local farmers a reason to reconsider any impending slave sales but probably failed to have statewide repercussions. Rather, slave sales in Virginia diminished toward the end of the war due to a lack of supplies and money.

Slaves even became a part of Virginia's informal barter economy, an arrangement that lasted until surprisingly late in the war. Thomas S. Bocock, Speaker of the Confederate House of Representatives and a resident of Appomattox County, reported one such trade in April 1865. With a surprising ability to ignore the obvious, Bocock "bought of Col. Thomas H. Flood in April, after Lee's surrender . . . Lydia + nine children, Martha + four + Sarah mother of Lydia and Martha, for whom I agreed to give him Seven Bushels + a half of corn already furnished him on loan + to deliver fourteen barrels in addition. After bargain concluded I threw in voluntarily seventy four bushels of wheat to satisfy him." The absence of men in this parcel sale underscored the uneven nature of the hiring market in Confederate Virginia. It is not clear what motivated Bocock to make such a trade, but he clearly began to regret it soon after and by May asserted "I do not think that the wheat is due."[50] Flood certainly had no reason to regret the trade, since by April 1865 corn was of considerably more value than sixteen slave women and children, who shortly thereafter received official notice of their freedom.

It is impossible to estimate with any confidence the number of slave sales that took place in Virginia over the course of the Civil War based on fragmentary newspaper notices and personal papers. Silas and R. H. Omohundro's business certainly shrank during the war years; the two brothers closed accounts in July 1863 after making a few good sales early in the year. Executors for Silas's estate, however, managed to sell his remaining inventory and personal servants in just a few short weeks after his death during the summer of 1864, so clearly a Richmond market for slaves still existed. The Lynchburg firm Hargrove & Co. took a more active role in the hiring market during the war years than they previously had, and by January 1864 their ads took on a note of urgency that suggested dwindling sales, but Hargrove remained in the slave trading business until the end of the war.

The prices Hargrove and Omohundro received for slaves never kept pace with inflation in the Confederacy, since by January 1865 Confederate Treasury notes had depreciated to the point that one gold dollar was the equivalent of sixty dollars in paper currency, and this depreciation only continued during the remaining months of the war. This figure, amounting to 6,000 percent inflation, was high enough but still significantly lower than the 9,000 percent that historians usually quote. The Confederate government's revaluation of paper currency in mid-1864 accounts for the discrepancy. Essentially seeking to curb inflation by increasing the dollar's purchasing power through government proclamation, this attempt was spectacularly unsuccessful. The reissue, however, allowed Confederate leaders to report a lower official inflation rate than actually existed. If slave prices had kept pace with (conservatively) 6,000 percent inflation, a single field hand would have cost upwards of $84,000 in Confederate currency by the end of the war. Charging such high prices would clearly have put traders out of business.[51]

The fact that slave traders remained in business, and that Omohundro retained some personal property to bequeath to his slave mistress and their children, indicated sufficient confidence to maintain a reasonably viable slave market until nearly the end of the war. The limited evidence available from the perspective of Virginia's enslaved population suggests that this market brought frequent separations from family and friends in an atmosphere already made chaotic and potentially frightening by the proximity of Confederate and Union armies. In his detailed study of New Orleans's slave jails, Walter Johnson suggested that slaves themselves retained some power—although limited—in a marketplace designed to fulfill slaveowners' ideals of mastery as well as their economic needs.[52] In general, however, it seems that the inflated prices of the wartime slave marketplace eliminated or at least severely limited the ability of Virginia's slaves to exert any control over their futures.

Although the Virginians selling their slaves may have feared the impending death of the institution, those who purchased likely did not, and these purchasers also contributed to the newspaper effort to proclaim the vitality of slavery throughout the course of the war. Moreover, the difficulties owners faced in hiring out domestic servants from as early as 1863 seem to undermine Ervin Jordan's contention that in 1864 and 1865, as "inflation and war made slaves increasingly unaffordable for many Virginians, more of them took to hiring slaves rather than buying them." Rather than this simple schema of decreasing sales and an increasingly profitable hiring market, the war created a gender-based hiring market that had the potential to both strengthen and undermine the sense of community among white Virginians.[53]

Before the Civil War, the hiring market had tied many nonslaveholders firmly into the economy of slavery and all political measures designed to strengthen the institution. Hiring field hands or domestic workers from their neighbors had created ties across the socioeconomic divisions of planters, small slaveholders, and nonslaveholders and rural and urban dwellers.[54] As the hiring market for domestic workers faltered with the war, however, slave-based economic and social ties—particularly those between rural and urban areas—diminished. Impressment and government hiring had the double effect of destroying the most concrete ties between the owners and leasers of male laborers while creating a new link between slave owners and the Confederacy. Through their slaves as through their loved ones in the army, Virginians maintained direct connections to their government.

This connection is perhaps only tangentially related to the maintenance of white confidence in the wartime slave market. But the relationship of the Confederate government to the institution of slavery in Virginia is a question that merits further study. Politics clearly interacted with economics and military successes and failures to determine the value of slaves at any given point during the war. Furthermore, while not disputing Wiley's argument that slave property and sales became decreasingly valuable over the course of the Civil War, the fact that sales continued at all suggests that white Virginians expected to succeed in their bid for independent nationhood. Until the very end of the Civil War, white Virginians continued to believe in the economic and social vitality of the institution of slavery, and whenever possible they participated in a sales and hiring market fully dependent on their level of confidence in Confederate independence.

Notes

I would like to thank Donna Tolson, Geospacial and Statistical Data Center, and Jama Coartney, Digital Media Services, both of the University of Virginia, for their assistance in creating and formatting the graphs accompanying this essay.

1. Letter from Nelia to Bettie, January 10, 1864, Letters from the Edgehill School for Girls, Albert and Shirley Small Special Collections Library, University of Virginia, Charlottesville, Va. (hereafter cited as UVA), mss 38–421.

2. Accounts of Silas and R. H. Omohundro's slave trade, 1857–1864, pp. 23–24, UVA, mss 4122.

3. The classic work on the domestic slave trade, Frederic Bancroft's *Slave-Trading in the Old South* (Baltimore: J. H. Furst Company, 1931), emphasizes Virginia's role as the "mother of slaves" in the antebellum long-distance trade and thus ends with the beginning of the war. Phillip Troutman's recent dissertation, "Slave Trade and Sentiment in Antebellum Virginia" (Ph.D. diss., University of Virginia, 2000), likewise concentrates on the antebellum years. Walter Johnson's *Soul by Soul: Life Inside the Antebellum Slave Market* (Cambridge, Mass.: Harvard University Press, 1999), is really about the New Orleans market and pays little attention to its Virginia side. Michael Tadman, *Speculators and Slaves: Masters, Traders, and Slaves in the Old South* (Madison: University of Wisconsin Press, 1989), 120; Bell Irvin Wiley, *Southern Negroes, 1861–1865* (New Haven: Yale University Press, 1938), 97; Ervin L. Jordan, *Black Confederates and Afro-Yankees in Civil War Virginia* (Charlottesville: University Press of Virginia, 1995), 45.

4. Bancroft, *Slave-Trading in the Old South*, 147–50.

5. Robert Garlick Hill Kean, *Inside the Confederate Government*, ed. Edward Younger (Baton Rouge: Louisiana State University Press, 1993), 186.

6. Confederate Inflation Chart, Official Publication #13 (Richmond: Richmond Civil War Centennial Committee, 1963).

7. Alexandria *Gazette*, March 14, 1861, quoted in Jordan, *Black Confederates and Afro-Yankees*, 335 n. 45; Accounts of Silas and R. H. Omohundro's slave trade, 1857–1864, 24–25.

8. Accounts of Silas and R. H. Omohundro, 24–27; Richmond *Examiner*, November 2, 1861, page 3, column 2; Lynchburg *Daily Republican*, August 16, 1861, page 1, column 1.

9. Charles B. Dew, *Bond of Iron: Master and Slave at Buffalo Forge* (New York: W. W. Norton, 1994), 292; Lynchburg *Daily Republican*, August 7, 1861, page 2, column 5; Petersburg *Daily Express*, November 9, 1861, page 3, column 7, Novem-

ber 25, 1861, December 28, 1861, January 3, 1862; also Lynchburg *Daily Republican,* November 12, 1861, December 30, 1861; Petersburg *Daily Express,* December 28, 1861, page 3, column 6.

10. 260A: Headquarters of the Confederate Army of the Peninsula to the Confederate Commander at Gloucester Point, Virginia, in *Freedom: A Documentary History of Emancipation, 1861–1867,* series 1, vol. 1, *The Destruction of Slavery,* ed. Ira Berlin et al. (Cambridge, U.K.: Cambridge University Press, 1985), 686; Lynchburg *Daily Republican,* August 26, 1861, page 2, column 4; Petersburg *Daily Express,* November 25, 1861, page 3, column 7; Wiley, *Southern Negroes,* 94–95.

11. Charles Tibbs to Andrew Grinnan, April 10, 1861, Grinnan Family Papers, UVA, mss 49.

12. Lynchburg *Daily Republican,* December 31, 1861, page 3, column 1; List of Negroes hired January 1862, pp. 239–40, Tredegar Iron Works records, Library of Virginia, Richmond, Va. (hereafter cited as LVA), acc #23881.

13. Petersburg *Daily Express,* July 1, 1862, page 1, column 1.

14. Accounts of Silas and R. H. Omohundro, 26–30.

15. Richmond *Daily Dispatch,* July 24, 1862, page 1, column 6; Wiley, *Southern Negroes,* 89.

16. Don Paarlberg, *An Analysis and History of Inflation* (Westport, Conn.: Praeger, 1993), 51.

17. Louis H. Manarin, ed., *Richmond at War: The Minutes of the City Council, 1861–1865* (Chapel Hill: University of North Carolina Press, 1966), 231; James H. Brewer, *The Confederate Negro: Virginia's Craftsmen and Military Laborers, 1861–1865* (Durham, N.C.: Duke University Press, 1969), 8, 142–43.

18. Petersburg *Daily Express,* November 5, 1862, page 1, column 1; Jedediah Hotchkiss to Sara A. Hotchkiss, January 2, 1863, *The Valley of the Shadow: Two Communities in the American Civil War,* http://valley.vcdh.virginia.edu, accessed March 20, 2003; Petersburg *Daily Express,* July 2, 1862, page 1, column 1, July 3, 1862, page 1, column 1.

19. Richmond *Examiner,* December 11, 1862, page 1, column 2, December 23, 1862, page 1, column 3; Brewer, *The Confederate Negro,* 64; Accounts of Silas and R. H. Omohundro, 24–25.

20. Lynchburg *Daily Republican,* December 31, 1862, page 3, column 2.

21. Ibid., January 5, 1863, page 3, column 1, January 14, 1863, page 3, column 2, January 9, 1863, page 3, column 1.

22. Accounts of Silas and R. H. Omohundro, 24–25; Wiley, *Southern Negroes,* 89.

23. *Staunton Spectator,* January 6, 1863, page 2, column 2.

24. William A. Blair, *Virginia's Private War: Feeding Body and Soul in the Confederacy, 1861–1865* (New York: Oxford University Press, 1998), 69; John B. Jones, *A Rebel War Clerk's Diary at the Confederate States Capital,* 2 vols. (Philadelphia: J. B. Lippincott & Co., 1866), 1:240; Confederate Inflation Chart.

25. Mrs. Virginia Hayes Shepherd in *Weevils in the Wheat: Interviews with Virginia Ex-Slaves,* edited by Charles L. Perdue, Thomas E. Barden, and Robert K. Phillips (Charlottesville: University Press of Virginia, 1999), 256.

26. List of Negroes and Rations at Catawba Furnace and others, 1863, Tredegar Iron Works records, LVA, acc #23881.

27. Richmond *Examiner,* January 2, 1863, page 1, column 2; J. R. Bryan to A. G. Grinnan, January 1, 1863, Grinnan Family Papers, UVA, mss 49.

28. Diary of Francis McFarland, January 2, 1863 (see also December 24, 1860, January 13, 1862, January 16, 1862, December 29–30, 1862); for short-term hiring, see January 12–14, 1863, January 23, 1863, July 15, 1863, Francis McFarland Papers, UVA, mss 318.

29. F. F. Mayo to Col. Joel McPherson, May 4, 1863, LVA, acc #39591; Gregg D. Kimball, *American City, Southern Place: A Cultural History of Antebellum Richmond* (Athens: University of Georgia Press, 2000), 114; Granvill Clark to Wm D. Cabell, September 18, 1863, Cabell Family Papers, UVA, mss 278; Brewer, *The Confederate Negro,* 95.

30. Brewer, *The Confederate Negro,* 144, 8–9, 147.

31. See, for example, motions submitted to the House of Representatives on August 26, 1862, August 28, 1862, and February 1, 1864, and submitted to the Senate on March 12, 1863, March 23, 1863, November 9, 1864, December 7, 1864, and December 12, 1864 (*Journal of the Congress of the Confederate States of America, 1861–1865,* vols. 3–6 [Washington, D.C.: Government Printing Office, 1904–1905]). A bill to be entitled An Act to increase the efficiency of the army by the employment of free negroes and slaves in certain capacities, February 1, 1864, *Southern Historical Society Papers* 50 (Richmond: Southern Historical Society, 1953): 359; List of Negros Sent to Work on the Fortifications at Drewrys Bluff, October 7, 1864, Tredegar Inspection of Ordnance and Use of Slaves, 1845–1864, LVA, acc #26393.

32. Diary of Francis McFarland, December 31, 1863, January 6–7 1864, January, 12, 1864.

33. Richmond *Examiner,* November 18, 1863, page 1, column 2; November 20, 1863, page 1, column 4; List of Negroes and Rations at Catawba Furnace and others, 1864.

34. Richmond *Examiner,* November 20, 1863, page 1, column 4; Jno. J. Fry to W. D. Cabell, December 5, 1863, Cabell Family Papers, UVA, mss 278.

35. Lynchburg *Daily Republican,* December 31, 1863, page 2, column 4; Richmond *Examiner,* January 2, 1864, page 1, column 2.

36. Richmond *Sentinel,* December 31, 1863, page 2, column 2.

37. Richmond *Examiner,* January 5, 1864, page 1, column 2; Richmond *Daily Enquirer,* January 3, 1864, page 1, column 1; Lynchburg *Daily Republican,* January 18, 1864, page 2, column 4. A previous ad on January 12, 1864, page 2, column 4, asserted that the company would charge modest rates to those willing to feed and clothe the slaves they had on hand.

38. Blair, *Virginia's Private War,* 94; Jones, *A Rebel War Clerk's Diary,* 2:113–14.

39. Lynchburg *Daily Republican,* January 30, 1864, page 2, column 5.

40. Miscellaneous notes in Brockenbrough-Lamb Papers, UVA, mss 10987-a (box 5); H. D. Taliaferro to A. G. Grinnan, February 18, 1864, Grinnan Family Pa-

pers, UVA, mss 49; Wm T. Mitchell Slave Papers & Contracts, 1862–1875, Southside Virginia Family Papers, UVA, mss 550.

41. Lynchburg *Daily Republican,* January 14, 1864, page 2, column 3; Robt Grinnan to A. G. Grinnan, January 13, 1864, Grinnan Family Papers, UVA, mss 49; Brewer, *The Confederate Negro,* 64; Paarlberg, *A History and Analysis of Inflation,* 51.

42. Rt Grinnan to A. G. Grinnan, April 13, 1864, Grinnan Family Papers, UVA, mss 49; List of Former Slaves, December 10, 1892, and Book of Slave Births, etc., 1853–1865, Morris Family Papers, UVA, mss 38–79; Silas Omohundro Business Records, 1851–1877, LVA, acc #29642; Troutman, "Slave Trade and Sentiment in Antebellum Virginia," 102–6; Petersburg *Daily Express,* July 23, 1864, page 2, column 6; Mrs. Fannie Berry in *Weevils in the Wheat,* 39.

43. John C. Inscoe, "Mountain Masters as Confederate Opportunists: The Profitability of Slavery in Western North Carolina, 1861–1865," in *Slavery and Abolition* 16 (April 1995): 97; Troutman, "Geographies of Family and Market: Virginia's Domestic Slave Trade in the Nineteenth Century," http://fisher.lib.virginia.edu/slavetrade/mapsframe.html, accessed April 10, 2003; Ella Lonn, *Salt as a Factor in the Confederacy* (New York: Walter Neale, 1933), 123.

44. Wm T. Mitchell Slave Papers & Contracts, Southside Virginia Family Papers, UVA, mss 550; Lynchburg *Daily Republican,* December 28, 1864, page 1, column 3.

45. Richmond *Examiner,* January 2, 1865, page 1, column 4.

46. Lynchburg *Daily Republican,* January 6, 1865, page 2, column 4, January 8, 1865, page 1, column 3. Blair estimated that ninety thousand able-bodied male slaves remained in Virginia by the last year of the war, so the concerns of editors that government impressments would leave them without necessary agricultural labor were reasonable even though the situation was not quite so dire as they reported (see *Virginia's Private War,* 122); An act to regulate the impressment of slaves in the State of Virginia, December 9, 1864, *Southern Historical Society Papers* 51 (Richmond: Southern Historical Society, 1958): 441.

47. Lynchburg *Daily Republican,* January 5, 1865, page 1, columns 4–5, January 12, 1865, page 1, columns 4–5; Mrs. Amarci Adams in *Weevils in the Wheat,* 3.

48. Richmond *Examiner,* December 13, 1864, page 2, column 4. Arguments for strong Confederate nationalism are evident in Blair, *Virginia's Private War;* Gary Gallagher, *The Confederate War* (Cambridge, Mass.: Harvard University Press, 1997); and George Rable, *The Confederate Republic* (Chapel Hill: University of North Carolina Press, 1994).

49. Diary of Francis McFarland, December 20–21, 1864.

50. Memoranda Book of Thomas S. Bocock, 1861 January–1866 December, Bocock Family Papers, UVA, mss 10612.

51. Confederate Inflation Chart; Paarlberg, *An Analysis and History of Inflation,* 51.

52. Johnson, *Soul by Soul,* especially chapter 3, "Making a World Out of Slaves."

53. Jordan, *Black Confederates and Afro-Yankees,* 45.

54. Keith C. Barton has argued convincingly in "'Good Cooks and Washers': Slave Hiring, Domestic Labor, and the Market in Bourbon County, Kentucky," *Journal of American History* 84 (September 1997): 436–60, that hiring practices conformed to the economic needs of large slaveholders rather than their desire to maintain social capital among their neighbors, but this does not negate the fact that hiring created ties between slaveholders and nonslaveholders that might not otherwise have existed.

Race, Religion, and Rebellion

Black and White Baptists in Albemarle County,
Virginia, during the Civil War

Andrew Witmer

The reminiscences of Horace Tonsler, born into slavery in Albemarle County, Virginia, in 1857, offer a revealing glimpse into the structure of race relations in central Virginia churches during the Civil War period. "When we git to de church," Tonsler recalled, "de white folks would go inside, an' de slaves would sit round under de trees outside. Den de preacher git de white folks to singin' an' shoutin', an' he start to walkin' up an' down de pulpit an' ev'y once in a while he lean out de winder an' shout somepin' out to us black folks."[1] Relegated to the periphery, the slaves took full advantage of their situation. Tonsler described how from time to time an older member of the black congregation would rise from his place and quietly begin shadow-preaching, waving his arms and contorting his face in imitation of the white minister, to the endless amusement of his fellow slaves. The satirical aspects of these performances were scrupulously concealed from those inside the church, and the practice slowly grew into something more serious. According to Tonsler, whites became accustomed to the arrangement and eventually allowed their slaves to preach and pray for themselves under the shade trees surrounding the church.

Whites and blacks performed many such tacit negotiations in churches across the South, but Tonsler's account indicates that beneath the veneer of peaceful coexistence, the two congregations were deeply distrustful of one another. White leaders carefully regulated their black members, requiring them to worship quietly within sight of the church. Black members preferred to be left alone to worship in their own manner and looked warily upon white intervention. Tonsler recalled that the black preacher was so far superior to his white counterpart that white boys would come late to church in order to remain outside and listen to him. The white boys' unwelcome presence forced the minister to choose his words with special care. "Preacher always got quiet when dey come," Tonsler remembered. "Couldn't trust dem white boys. Dey go back home an' tell dey fathers dat de slaves plannin' to run away."[2]

The patterns of ecclesiastical race relations established during the antebellum years—particularly the circumscribed flexibility that permitted varying degrees of black autonomy—provided much of the distinctive flavor of Southern religious life and thus formed the crucial context for understanding the dramatic changes in Albemarle County churches during the Civil War. While it is clear in retrospect that the war permanently altered Southern race relations, it was not so obvious at the time that this would be the result, and even those who anticipated serious changes did so within the framework of the system they had always known. As the war raged on, the same sorts of competing concerns that divided whites and blacks in Horace Tonsler's Albemarle congregation persisted and multiplied in Baptist churches across the county, creating racially distinctive expectations of the war's implications for church life. Many black Baptists pushed for greater autonomy within their racially mixed churches, while many whites, confident of Confederate victory and a return to the relatively malleable racial system of the antebellum years, proved remarkably receptive to limited increases in black ecclesiastical autonomy. Other whites emphasized the need to tighten rather than relax systems of racial control within Baptist congregations.

Such patterns can be discerned only by looking more carefully into the life of the institutional church in the antebellum and wartime South.[3] In a religious historiography that understandably prizes expressions of extra-institutional black religious life, the church—where black strategies of autonomy and self-determination are often less immediately obvious—is sometimes undervalued. A number of historians have shown, however, that such strategies did exist within the church, and careful attention to the texture of interracial church life reveals a host of other important dynamics as well. This essay examines some of those dynamics in the experiences of several interracial Virginia congregations, revealing the nature and limits of religious constraint, white and black expectations about how the war would reshape religious life, and the motives of white leaders who permitted and even welcomed increased black religious autonomy during the war. For a variety of reasons, hundreds of thousands of slaves and free blacks joined Southern churches. In such settings—most often alongside white people—they worshipped, prayed, experienced the delights and frustrations of communal life, suffered racial discrimination, and made some of their most lasting contributions to the common religious culture of the South. Until we understand the complex patterns, compromises, and negotiations of interracial church life, our understanding of the Southern religious experience before, during, and after the Civil War will remain incomplete.

On the eve of the Civil War, few local whites could have imagined life in Albemarle County without slavery.[4] The institution undergirded every aspect of social life and played a central role in Albemarle's economic prosperity, helping to make it the fourth richest county in Virginia. In 1860, slaves constituted just over half the county's total population. Many worked on the farms covering the central Virginia countryside, growing tobacco, wheat, Indian corn, and oats, and caring for livestock. Most of the county's wealthiest citizens in 1860 were slave-holding farmers, though some were merchants, attorneys, and university professors. Albemarle's major industry was the milling of local cereal crops. Residents also produced hats, carriages, cotton and woolen goods, tobacco products, and farm implements. They marketed their goods in Charlottesville, the county seat and home of Thomas Jefferson's University of Virginia. Charlottesville was also the county's largest town, with 1,890 inhabitants by the middle of the nineteenth century. More than half of the town's residents were African Americans, and 128 members of the black community were free. During the antebellum period, Albemarle's social and economic life was shaped by the arrival of new technologies. The Virginia Central Railroad steamed into the county on newly laid tracks during the late 1840s, and Charlottesville received its first telegram from the nearby town of Lynchburg in 1860. At the Oyster Depot on Main Street, Thomas H. Duke gave local residents their most vivid taste of modern progress by selling fresh seafood shipped in daily from the coast.

Baptist churches in antebellum Albemarle County were deeply, and for the most part unapologetically, complicit in the Southern slaveholding system, but there were nevertheless opportunities in Southern society and in many Baptist churches for black members to exercise limited control over their own religious lives.[5] Free and enslaved African Americans joined Baptist churches in large numbers, due to the relative autonomy offered to black members, the appeal of Baptist doctrines and worship styles, and the fact that while white Baptists shared the racial prejudices of their countrymen, they possessed a more egalitarian ethos and a better record on race relations than most other Southern denominations.[6] Baptist churches in Albemarle County were financially and ecclesiastically autonomous, but most were members of the Albemarle Baptist Association (ABA), an advisory body that also included churches from several nearby counties.[7] During the 1850s, many ABA churches experienced dramatic growth, with black membership in the association rising by 50 percent and white membership by 64 percent.[8] By the end of the decade, there were thousands of black members, accounting for 52 percent of ABA membership.[9] Percentages varied widely from church to church, with African Americans forming a large majority of some congregations.[10]

Free and enslaved African Americans in antebellum Albemarle County enjoyed significant freedom over which church they attended and even whether they would attend church at all. Most Baptist ministers urged masters to encourage but not force their slaves to participate in public worship. A. B. Brown, who pastored First Baptist Church of Charlottesville during the late 1850s, argued that "The negro is, and it is well for him that he is politically a slave, but it is wrong—it is inexpedient to force him to the family altar, the church or the baptistry." Evidence that this concern for freedom of conscience was more than merely theoretical can be found in the repeated advice of denominational leaders before the war that local Baptist churches strive to make their services more attractive to slaves. According to one associational report, slaves "should be distinctly and frequently assured that the preaching is addressed to them equally with the whites, and Pastors should see that, as a matter of fact, this be so. They should endeavor to say much that is calculated to interest the colored people and should often look at them while preaching." A second report recommended that Baptist churches attract black members by holding special services in which they could participate more freely. Clearly, such recommendations were based on the assumption that African Americans would attend services only when they desired to do so.[11]

Another indication of the genuine (though circumscribed) freedom of conscience accorded to at least some African Americans is the existence of masters and slaves who worshipped in different churches. Cross-referencing the membership records of Baptist and Episcopal churches in antebellum Albemarle County reveals numerous cases in which the slaves of Episcopalian masters worshipped in Baptist churches, suggesting that some masters permitted their slaves to embrace religious traditions quite different from their own. At Christ Church Episcopal, the rector himself,

Reverend Richard K. Meade, owned at least four slaves who worshiped at First Baptist Church; Rebecca, Margaret, and Lina were received for baptism in 1861, and the church refused to restore Casey to fellowship that same year.[12] Dr. R. B. Nelson, who joined Christ Church in 1857 and later served as a vestryman, also owned slaves who worshiped at First Baptist Church.[13] George Omohundro owned a slave named Charlotte, a member of Chestnut Grove Baptist Church.[14] Finally, some wealthy Episcopalians, such as Alexander Rives, owned slaves who worshiped at several different Albemarle churches, including First Baptist Church and Ballenger's Creek Baptist Church.[15] Some of Rives's slaves seem to have participated alternately in both his and their own religious communities. Virginia, for example, was baptized into the membership of First Baptist Church but was married and later buried at Christ Church.[16] Rives's own body servant, Paul Lewis, joined First Baptist Church in 1855 but was married in a ceremony at Christ Church in 1857.[17]

Further evidence that Albemarle County blacks enjoyed at least limited freedom to choose where they would worship comes from an 1852 letter written by the white Baptist pastor James Fife. After criticizing those ministers who allowed black members to lead prayers in religious services, Fife discussed what seemed to him to be the negative consequences: "Giving them liberty to pray is giving them other liberties such as exhorting, exercising authority over the others all which they will do, leave or no leave, if you once break the ground and ask them to pray they are off without ballast and from henceforth you cannot stop them. They become from this time self important and learn the other members that they can do without going to the white peoples meeting and from henceforth if there were 400 coloured members in a church you will scarcely see fifty at meeting at the Lord's supper."[18] As in other places in the antebellum South, slaves in Albemarle County were generally free to choose where they would worship. James Fife's concern was preventing them from fully exercising this freedom.

Still, with devout masters sometimes impressing upon them the importance of the spiritual life, few Albemarle slaves enjoyed unhindered freedom of conscience in religious matters. One possible, though far from conclusive, sign of religious constraint is the frequent mass baptism of slaves belonging to a single master. While it is certainly possible that Susan, Annie, Jack, Godfrey, Richmond, and Joe, all slaves of Willis Garth, sought baptism of their own accord or under one another's influence in October 1851, one must also consider the possibility that Garth had in some way made his wishes known to all six. Such a possibility seems even greater in the case of the thirteen slaves belonging to Dr. Cook who were baptized in 1861 and the thirteen slaves belonging to Colonel Durrelt who were baptized into Chestnut Grove Baptist Church in September 1862.[19]

It would be a serious mistake to think of Albemarle County's antebellum Baptist churches as islands of egalitarianism and equality in the midst of a hierarchical and racist society. There were no such islands. The thousands of African Americans who joined Baptist churches entered tightly knit and highly ordered religious communities in which racial and gender hierarchies were scrupulously enforced. In most church membership rolls from the period, these distinctions were reflected in separate lists of white males, white females, black males, and black females. Church minutes invariably appended the names of masters when referring to enslaved members. Racial hierarchies were also evident in the segregated seating arrangements, which relegated both free and enslaved blacks to balconies or back pews, and in some instances, as in Horace Tonsler's congregation, denied them even these inferior accommodations.

But while certain sorts of discrimination were nearly universal, the experience of black Baptists also varied significantly from church to church. At First Baptist Church in Charlottesville, black congregants met separately for worship services and, to some extent, controlled the discipline of their own members. Other congregations frequently refused to permit even this partial measure of independence. In most Baptist churches, one or two white leaders assumed the task of supervising black members, sometimes as part of an official standing committee and in other cases on an ad hoc basis. This supervisory role was filled at First Baptist Church by a succession of white elders who served as pastors of the black congregation. During the mid-1850s, the position was occupied by William P. Farish, a prominent member of the church who in 1860 was the wealthiest resident of Albemarle County, possessing assets valued at over $300,000, including 131 slaves.[20] Farish owned several slaves who worshipped at First Baptist Church, as did his successor, the most important white minister to the church's black members, John T. Randolph.[21] One Baptist pastor, in fact, believed that white slaveholding congregations would never fully accept preachers who did not themselves own slaves, perhaps suspecting them of abolitionist sympathies.[22]

The role of spiritual overseer was usually filled at Mountain Plain Baptist Church by Colonel John Jones, who frequently investigated accusations of immorality against black members of the church. On one occasion, Jones accused his own slave, Adam, of disorderly conduct. Adam came before the congregation at its next meeting, confessed his guilt, and was immediately excluded from fellowship. The efforts and activities of Jones, who owned at least six other enslaved members of the congregation, reveal the important place of church discipline in the lives of white and black Baptists.[23]

Virginia Baptists in the era of the Civil War took church discipline seriously, and their church minutes are sprinkled liberally with accounts of investigations into charges of dancing, drunkenness, adultery, and a host of other sins. Those found guilty of these offenses were excluded from fellowship if they failed to repent, and sometimes even if they did. Final control over all discipline meted out by the church was reserved for its white male members, though in some churches black male members exercised partial control over the discipline of the African American portion of the congregation. The decision to rebuke or exclude a member for misconduct was decided by vote at the monthly business meeting of the church. Such decisions were typically guided by the report of a committee of white males assigned to investigate charges brought forward at an earlier meeting. As the central administrative event in the life of the local church, monthly meetings were almost entirely dominated by white men. While white women frequently attended meetings, they were mentioned only irregularly in church minutes and never in a speaking or voting capacity. Just as black members were typically not allowed to speak for themselves, but were forced to rely upon the services of white male spokesmen, the women of Baptist churches were spoken for when necessary by white male representatives.[24]

The church minutes of First Baptist Church in Charlottesville provide a detailed and sustained account of the workings of church discipline in a typical Baptist church. In most cases, the reports of disciplinary investigations and exclusions include both the gender and race of the offending parties, allowing for statistical analysis of the sorts of members who were most frequently subjected to church discipline. The results of such an analysis of the 104 disciplinary investigations and exclusions listed in the minutes of First Baptist Church between 1854 and 1863 demonstrate that church discipline was not, at least in any obvious way, primarily a tool for racial or gender control. Instead, the practice, controlled by white men, was directed most frequently against themselves.[25]

Gender was clearly a key factor in the incidence of church discipline. Black and white males were cited in 76 percent of the total cases of disciplinary action taken by the church between 1854 and 1863, while black and white females comprised only 21 percent.[26] This means that men were approximately three and a half times more likely to encounter in some form the disciplinary arm of the church. One's racial identity also affected the likelihood that one would undergo investigation or exclusion from fellowship in the church. White members were involved in 62 percent of disciplinary proceedings and black members in only 38 percent. This disparity is seen to be even more significant when one considers that black members comprised on average about 62 percent of total church membership during the 1850s.[27]

By far the single most likely group in the church to receive disciplinary attention were white males, who were cited in 55 percent of all such cases. They were followed by black males, at 21 percent, and black females at 15 percent of total cases. White females were investigated or excluded from membership only six times (6 percent of total cases) in the ten-year period under consideration.[28] The most dramatic disparity in incidence of discipline, then, was between white males and white females. While 52 percent of white church members admitted to First Baptist Church between 1839 and 1866 were women, white men were almost ten times more likely to be investigated or excluded from membership between 1854 and 1863.[29]

If it vigorously disciplined errant members, First Baptist also frequently restored repentant members to fellowship in the church. Since restoration, unlike discipline, was a process that typically originated with the individual rather than the leadership of the church, the incidence of restoration suggests the relative importance of membership to the various populations under study. In other words, not all excluded congregants requested restoration, and the fact that some groups did so with greater frequency than others may provide evidence of how relatively significant church membership was for them. Of the forty-nine recorded cases of restoration to fellowship between 1854 and 1863, 71 percent involved black members and 29 percent involved white members. This disparity cannot be explained solely in terms of the greater percentage of black church members, since that percentage probably averaged 62 percent during this period.[30] Black males were most likely to seek restoration to fellowship, comprising 43 percent of all cases. They were followed by white males at 24 percent and black females at 22 percent. Only one white woman (2 percent of total cases) was restored to fellowship during this period.[31]

In evaluating these findings, it is important, but difficult, to determine the degree of control held by the African American men of First Baptist Church over the discipline of the church's black members during the 1850s and early 1860s. Several sources seem to point to a relatively high degree of black disciplinary autonomy during this period. In 1859, John Hart, a prominent white member of the church, claimed in a report to the Albe-marle Baptist Association that "the colored brethren have the discipline among themselves mainly in their own hands. They feel the responsibilities thus placed on them, and are the more watchful and better christians for it." Unfortunately, neither the black members of the church nor their white supervisors seem to have kept records of their disciplinary actions. Much can be learned, however, from the minutes of the business meetings conducted by the white members of the church. These records show that, at least on the face of things, disciplinary action against African American church members only rarely originated with the white congregation. Instead, black members, supervised by their white overseers, typically met in separate session, voted on matters of discipline or admission to membership, and reported their decisions through a white liaison to the white business meeting, where their decisions were almost invariably approved and entered without alteration in the church minutes. What is still unclear, and will likely remain so, is precisely how much influence white leaders such as John Hart exerted over the supposedly independent disciplinary actions taken by black members.[32]

One possible indication of this sort of control is a resolution passed in 1855 by the white congregation thanking William P. Farish for "preaching to the colored brethren and *presiding over their business meetings.*" Additional clues can be located in the record of tensions between free and enslaved black members of the church shortly after the black congregation won greater independence for itself in 1863. In 1864, a small faction consisting mainly of free blacks sparked controversy by announcing their desire to form a wholly independent church. This group complained that the black congregation had not been granted as much independence in 1863 as it deserved. They protested, in the words of a report on the matter prepared for the white congregation, that their pastor, John T. Randolph, had unfairly and "uniformly made discriminations against the free persons and those who acted with them, and in favor of the slaves, *who in the main quietly acquiesced in the plan of organization as all that they desire.*" In the opinion of these free blacks, enslaved members of the congregation were either unable or unwilling to disagree with their white leaders.[33]

In some Albemarle Baptist churches where there were not enough white or black members to warrant racially distinct congregations, white male members assumed direct responsibility for the discipline of all other members of the church. Under such circumstances, black men sometimes participated in the disciplinary work of the church in an advisory capacity. At a meeting of the Chestnut Grove Baptist Church in 1858, for example, a slave named Adam accused a female slave named Mary of adultery. After Mary refused to appear at the next church meeting and publicly repent, she was excluded from membership.[34] Adam went on to become one of three enslaved deacons appointed by the white members of the church in September 1861 and directed by them to "supervise the conduct of the colored members of this church & to report any disorderly conduct among them." Similarly, the members of Ballenger's Creek Baptist Church determined in 1857 to "ask several of the coloured members to meet at the Church on the next regular meeting day and give the clerk all the information they could of the state and standing of all the coloured members." Even in those churches where white congregations directly disciplined their black members, disciplinary action sometimes proved ineffectual. The members of Mountain Plain Baptist Church voted in 1852 to exclude a slave who had been cited three times to appear before the church but had failed to do so and "treated the citations with indifference."[35]

At least two conclusions about the racial aspects of discipline and restoration at First Baptist Church of Charlottesville seem warranted. First, between 1854 and 1863, white male members of the church do not appear to have abused their disciplinary powers in an effort to extend their social control over free and enslaved blacks. In his examination of similar cases in antebellum Georgia, Clarence Mohr has argued that the reason for such restraint was the religious freedom enjoyed by most slaves: "Unlike labor, a slave's religious faith could not be obtained through coercion, and the bondsman's freedom to accept or reject Christianity acted as a check upon the natural tendency of church discipline to reinforce other methods of slave control."[36] This explanation seems equally persuasive for churches in Albemarle County, where most of the evidence indicates that free and enslaved blacks were free to choose whether and where they would worship.

The second conclusion is that retaining church membership was, on the whole, more important for disciplined blacks than whites. Black church members constituted only 38 percent of disciplinary actions—usually initiated by other members—but 71 percent of restorations, initiated by individuals themselves. More specifically, black male members were cited in 22 cases of discipline (21 percent of total cases) and 21 cases of restoration (43 percent of total cases), while white males were named in 57 cases of discipline (55 percent of total cases) and only 12 cases of restoration (24 percent of total cases). In the absence of contemporary testimony, it is impossible to explain this difference with certainty. It seems likely, however, that the importance of church membership for black Baptists was rooted in the hope and joy offered by Christian experience, the sustaining sense of community fostered by fellowship with others of similar religious beliefs, the unique opportunity to participate in a socially respected institution, and the danger of angering devout masters by not seeking restoration as quickly as possible.[37]

The hierarchical system of race relations within Baptist churches in antebellum Albemarle County allowed varying degrees of black religious autonomy. Most African Americans were generally free to choose whether or not they would attend church and which congregation they would join, freedoms which rested, sometimes tenuously, on whites' commitment to freedom of conscience. These circumstances were not uncommon in Virginia before the war. As some residents of Albemarle County may have known, their state contained at least twenty-five antebellum African American churches with some degree of autonomy, including the four largest black churches in the South.[38] This ubiquitous but unstable blend of racial hierarchy and circumscribed flexibility was eventually shattered by the momentous changes precipitated by the Civil War.

With the onset of war in 1861, Baptist church life in Albemarle County suffered many of the shocks and setbacks experienced throughout the South, prompting members of the ABA to complain that the war had "greatly paralyzed the progress of Christianity in every direction and in every branch."[39] Perhaps the most immediate result of the war was a decrease in church attendance among whites. A laconic note in the minutes of Chestnut Grove Baptist Church, for example, reported in June 1861 that "This being muster day at Earlysville, but few members were in attendance."[40] Many churches also found it more difficult to attract and retain capable pastoral leadership. The number of churches without pastors, a statistic first introduced into ABA records in 1860, increased from two in that year to eight in 1865. One year after Appomattox the number had returned to two.[41] The management of church finances became more difficult because of the severe wartime inflation of Confederate currency, a problem particularly evident in the continual readjustment of pastors' salaries. The Baptist Church of Christ at Spring Hill, for example, paid John Fox an annual salary of $125 in 1862. The following year, the church raised the sum to $300. By 1864, members had offered $340 and Fox had agreed to continue as pastor "with the hope the church would make the sum five hundred dollars."[42] Financial difficulties continued to plague the church during the next year, finally forcing its members to release their sexton and divide his work among themselves.[43] Such problems were common among ABA churches. One reason for A. B. Brown's resignation as pastor of First Baptist Church in Charlottesville late in 1861 was the reduction of his already small salary.[44] First Baptist's financial position had grown even worse by late 1863, despite the contribution by black members of $50 and "two Loads of wood to the winter's supply."[45] Chestnut Grove Baptist also struggled financially but attempted to avoid the loss of its pastor by doubling his salary from $300 to $600 in April 1863 and continuing to discuss further increases during the following months.[46]

In spite of these hardships, white Albemarle County Christians from all denominations participated enthusiastically in the Confederate war effort. In an early 1861 letter, John Cowper Granbery, a young Methodist minister at the University of Virginia who later served as a chaplain in the Army of Northern Virginia, eloquently described the war fever that gripped his community: "We breakfasted, dined, supped on war. We read, talked, thought, dreamed of nothing else." While Granbery was concerned about the injury which he believed the war would inflict upon educational and religious work, he nevertheless believed that armed conflict was necessary and said so, with some qualifications, in his sermons: "I preach to my congregation against vengeful feelings in the war, while of course I inculcate a defense of our rights at all hazards."[47] Not to be outdone in their ardent support for the war, the members of First Baptist Church, like some other local congregations, donated their church bell to the Confederate War Department in 1862 for the manufacturing of cannon. And on a less exalted but equally picturesque note, the church loaned its spittoons to a military hospital for use by wounded soldiers. Rarely were Christian voices raised in protest against the aims or prosecution of the war.[48]

Military conflict in Albemarle County during the Civil War was restricted to a minor skirmish in early 1864 and the brief occupation of Charlottesville in early 1865, events which infuriated many of the county's residents. Sarah Strickler, a nineteen-year-old student at the Albemarle Female Institute in Charlottesville, became so angry with one Union soldier that she publicly insulted him on March 4, 1865. Strickler described the incident in her diary, venting her irritation in decidedly unladylike fantasies: "Oh! if I was only a boy, to fight them—it chafes me so sorely to have to submit to their insolence. Why was I not born a boy? In spirit I am all a man. The sound of clashing arms & whistling bullets would be the sweetest musick to my ear now." Several days later, after Union forces had departed, Strickler attended a service at First Baptist Church in which several denominations united to observe a day of fasting. One assumes that she had by then recovered the veneer of religious respectability expected of young women.[49]

While Albemarle County was safe behind Confederate lines for most of the war, many of its citizens nevertheless came in contact with the war's consequences on a daily basis through the hundreds of wounded Confederate soldiers convalescing in hospitals, churches, and homes in Charlottesville and nearby towns. Many other Virginians, of course, found themselves closer to armed conflict and regularly experienced its disruptions. George White, who served with the home guard while pastoring a Presbyterian church in Virginia, later recalled wearing a belt of pistols into the pulpit and "laying them off when preaching on the pulpit floor." James B. Taylor, a prominent figure in statewide Baptist circles, complained in an 1862 diary entry that the war had wreaked havoc on an annual Baptist conference: "Never has such a meeting occurred. Instead of hundreds gathered together as usual, but a few, perhaps not more than thirty-five, were here. How anxiously may all pray that this war may pass away! When, oh when, shall the people of God resume their accustomed labors for the spread of the gospel?"[50]

The Civil War permanently altered the lives of Albemarle County churches and their parishioners, although it did not always do so in the ways that they might have expected. The war did not, for example, cause an immediate decline in the membership statistics of ABA churches. To the contrary, black membership in these churches grew by 17 percent between 1860 and 1865, while white membership grew by 14 percent and the association added three churches to its ranks.[51] It is difficult to interpret these statistics without reliable information on the number of white males who retained membership in ABA churches while serving in the Confederate army. At least one conclusion seems warranted, however—the increase in black membership likely seemed particularly dramatic, since far fewer blacks than white males were absent from the community.

The wartime changes which so distressed white Baptists seem to have made church membership more, not less, attractive to the black residents of Albemarle County. The case of Chestnut Grove Baptist Church conforms closely to an overall pattern in which black membership increased dramatically as white male church members departed for the war. In 1861, seventy-two African Americans were baptized into the church in August alone, raising black membership by at least 118 percent since 1860.[52] Significantly, this increase took place only four months after an unspecified number of white males from Chestnut Grove Baptist joined a Confederate volunteer company raised in nearby Earlysville.[53] One year later, African Americans were continuing to join the church in large numbers and almost half of the white male members of the congregation had enlisted in the war effort.[54] At Chestnut Grove and other churches across Albemarle County, an inverse relationship appears to have existed between the number of paternalistic white males in a church and the attractiveness of that church to black members of the community.

White church members who remained on the home front often struggled over how best to deal with the sudden wartime influx of black converts. Heightened concern over the regulation of enslaved blacks was evident at Chestnut Grove as early as June 1861, when the church began to preserve records of letters from white masters granting permission for their slaves to become members, a practice which does not seem to have been common before that time.[55] This concern clearly came from both inside and outside the church, for in August a proposal to organize a special monthly service for black members was "so violently opposed by a portion of the community and a *few of the members of this church* that it had to be abandoned."[56]

There are indications that Baptists in Albemarle County had encountered at least scattered opposition from other whites to their antebellum efforts to minister to slaves. One Baptist leader counseled in 1859, for example, that white members who conducted religious services for slaves should continue to do so even when it exposed them to the "taunts and jeerings of ungodly men." Careful religious instruction, he claimed, made slaves more industrious and reliable, and not (as some whites had claimed since the 1831 Nat Turner rebellion) more idle and vicious.[57] What was novel about the controversy at Chestnut Grove, then, was not the presence of dissension but the fact that divisions were now appearing within the church itself. The heated debate over how best to deal with the growing black membership of the church expanded during the following months. In September a supporter of the defeated plan for special services successfully proposed the appointment of three African American deacons to help oversee the discipline of the church's black members, representing a more inclusive approach to regulation.[58] One month later, a member who had voted against the earlier plan for special services successfully introduced a resolution requiring slaves to receive written permission from their masters before being allowed to join with other churches.[59]

What appears to have developed at Chestnut Grove during the early years of the war was a running conflict between two factions of white male members, both of which advocated their own approach to a new wartime situation in which black members very likely constituted a majority of the church membership.[60] Both factions recognized the need for increased attention to the activities of the church's black members, but one side proposed a more inclusive form of regulation involving special religious services and cooperation with carefully selected black leaders, while the other hoped to extend white authority in more direct ways. This division probably continued throughout the war, exacerbated by the influx of black members and the departure of white soldiers. Even after 1865 one can discern traces of its presence in the quarrel between white members who still wished to contribute in some way to the religious welfare of the freedmen and those who wanted nothing to do with their former slaves. Church minutes indicate that an 1866 proposal to organize a Sunday school for the benefit of local freedmen met with "violent opposition" both in the broader community and among the white members of Chestnut Grove Baptist Church. The project was consequently abandoned.[61] Whites successfully maintained control over the black members of their church during the war, even as they argued over how best to wield their power. For at least some white church members, augmenting black religious autonomy and participation in church discipline seemed to be the most effective way to deal with the flood of new converts.

The wartime experience of First Baptist Church in Charlottesville was marked by disruption in the disciplinary life of the church, serious financial strain, and, preeminently, the successful effort of its free and enslaved African American members to form a partially independent black congregation. In the absence of contemporary explanations for the timing of the drive for independence or for white acquiescence in that effort, we are left to search for clues within the broader history of religion and race relations in the antebellum and wartime South. The account that emerges illuminates the hopes, fears, and expectations raised by the Civil War in members of both races. While Confederate defeats and Union promises of emancipation bolstered African Americans in their quest for ecclesiastical autonomy, it remained necessary for them to move cautiously. The willingness of many white male church members to allow this movement to occur was rooted in a long history of reflection on the racial organization of churches and may indicate white confidence in the long-term stability of the antebellum racial system.

First Baptist Church of Charlottesville, like Chestnut Grove Baptist, experienced a rapid increase in its black membership during the opening years of the Civil War. The church reported to the Albemarle Baptist Association in 1861 that there had been little spiritual interest among whites but a great deal of religious excitement among blacks, resulting in

220 baptisms. Church records show that in one three-month period 119 enslaved and 13 free blacks were baptized into membership. In 1862, the church again reported that its ministry to African Americans had been very successful, even as "so many other interests have seemed to fail." The consequences of this success were dramatically different than at Chestnut Grove, and do not appear to have involved the same sorts of divisions between white members of the church. Increases in black membership were much less alarming at First Baptist, where whites had been a minority even before the war began. In 1860, African Americans constituted 60 percent of the total church membership and, as shown above, met separately for worship and exercised a significant measure of control over their own church discipline.[62]

The first evidence of new black initiative at First Baptist Church came in early 1861 and was linked directly to the pastoral needs created by the increasing size of the black congregation. On April 29, at the request of a number of free and enslaved blacks, John T. Randolph, a white member of the church who had served as a deacon since 1854 and as an intermediary between the white and black congregations since 1858, was licensed to preach the gospel. The procedure did little more than formalize an earlier arrangement—Randolph had been preaching to the black congregation for some time—but it is an important early example of the carefully circumscribed efforts of African Americans to shape their religious environment and of the possibility that whites would respond positively to those cautious efforts.[63]

During the following two years, the members of First Baptist experienced serious wartime disruptions in the life of their church. Reverend A. B. Brown resigned as pastor in October 1861, in part because of the congregation's inability to offer him an adequate salary, and the church was subsequently forced to rely upon the services of a string of temporary preachers.[64] There were no recorded church meetings during August, September, November, and December of 1862, a disheartening period in which the church continued to search fruitlessly for a new pastor. Church discipline, an activity that lay at the very heart of communal life, was also curtailed by the war. Disciplinary action against white and black members had been distributed unevenly across the years between 1854 and 1860.[65] After 1861, disciplinary actions and restorations fell precipitously. Between 1861 and 1863, only one black and four white members were investigated or excluded from fellowship. Seven black members were restored to fellowship in 1861, but none were restored in 1862 or 1863, and only one white member was restored during these years. The Civil War had thrown this crucial aspect of communal life into deep disarray. And all this time, perhaps not coincidentally, African American membership was growing rapidly.

On March 16, 1863, in the most important and certainly the most dramatic action it would take during the entire war, the black congregation of First Baptist Church announced its wish to separate from the white church and form an independent African church.[66] After some discussion during the following months over the details of the separation, black members accepted a plan from the white congregation in June that was strikingly similar to their original proposal. The final agreement allowed black members to choose their own deacons, select their pastor from among the white members of the church, make their own decisions on all matters of membership and discipline, and meet separately in the basement of the white church until they could find their own place of worship.[67] While these new powers represented an important step in the direction of ecclesiastical autonomy and may well have been interpreted by black members as a foretaste of the political freedoms that the war promised to deliver, this was clearly not what the white church had in mind. White members stated pointedly that the new organizational structure "would not place the colored brethren beyond the care and control of this church."[68] One must ask, then, why African American church members timed their push for increased independence as they did and what their white counterparts were thinking when they acquiesced.

Daniel Stowell has argued that the formation of independent black congregations during the Civil War was an important manifestation of the powerful African American desire for liberation and freedom. For slaves, the decision to leave a white church could eloquently express a deeper desire: "The primary action of many black Christians during the latter half of the war was to leave the biracial churches of antebellum times as an exercise of personal freedom and as an expression of religious independence. For some this action took on symbolic importance similar to that of leaving their place of bondage."[69] Given these considerations, it seems appropriate to note that the decision of the black members of First Baptist to press for more freedom within their church was made only two months after the announcement of the Emancipation Proclamation and in the wake of Confederate military reversals at Antietam. Whatever the power of the parallels between ecclesiastical and political freedom, there were other reasons for their decision to press for greater independence as well, including the influence of those black church members who had been part of independent black congregations in other locations. Church minutes indicate that at least two such individuals joined the church during the late 1850s, and it seems almost certain that they would have described their experiences with these more desirable arrangements.[70] Additionally, black members of the church submitted their request for greater autonomy in the midst of what was clearly a difficult period in the life of First Baptist, when white leaders had few viable alternatives for dealing with the church's burgeoning black membership.

Still, the decision of white church members, reached without apparent dissension or controversy, to allow African Americans to move in the direction of greater religious freedom just as the broader Charlottesville community was limiting the independence of its slaves must strike one, at least initially, as a bit curious. On June 13, 1863, only two weeks before the final plan for partial ecclesiastical independence was approved by the black members of First Baptist, the town of Charlottesville passed an ordinance establishing a nightly slave patrol and imposing a curfew on slaves without written passes from their masters.[71] That Confederate churches would choose to extend rather than restrict the freedom of their black members under such circumstances was by no means a foregone conclusion. To cite only one counter-example, authorities in Georgia responded to fears of a slave insurrection in 1861 with a broad array of tightened regulations that included slave patrols, severe travel restrictions, and the suspension of separate worship services for blacks in some white churches.[72]

There are at least two possible explanations for why the white members of First Baptist did not choose a similar path. The first is that their authority or their will had been weakened by the same Confederate military defeats and Union promises which so emboldened their black counterparts. The main problems with this explanation are that morale in Virginia was high in the spring and early summer of 1863, and that there is not the slightest indication in the church records that white members understood themselves to be pressured into unwelcome or undesirable decisions. To the contrary, white leaders made it clear that decisions about church life would be made on their own terms and timetable. The more persuasive explanation is that their willingness to allow black members to move toward greater ecclesiastical independence was grounded in conceptions and practices regarding church life that were well established before and during the war.[73] Far from being a sign of weakness or despair, the creation of a separate black church was an indication of white confidence in eventual Confederate military victory and the maintenance of the antebellum racial order.[74]

White Baptists, after all, had been familiar with the concept of independent black churches during the antebellum period. For at least two decades before the war, many urban churches in Virginia had practiced segregated worship and even permitted their black congregations to control most of their own affairs.[75] Thus, the formation of what soon became known as the African Church of Charlottesville was within the accepted bounds of traditional Baptist practice. As we have seen, moreover, white members of First Baptist granted considerable independence to their black congregation during the antebellum period and do not seem to have wielded their disciplinary powers as a tool for social control. In light of this antebellum experience, what is most noteworthy about the establishment of the African Church is not its formation but its creation during a time of war. That the white members of First Baptist chose to extend rather than curtail their antebellum ecclesiastical policies after 1861 is an indication of their expectations for a successful war and the eventual reestablishment of the antebellum social order.

It is also possible, especially in light of the antebellum views of ABA leaders on the need to make slavery a more humane and morally respectable institution, that some members of First Baptist Church viewed the creation of an independent black church as a way to atone for earlier failures in the religious mission to the slaves.[76] By 1863, a limited number of Southern Christians had come to believe that any and all Confederate military reversals were signs of God's judgment on the South. One writer claimed that "God is now chastening the country for its sins in connection with slavery."[77] As noted earlier, however, Confederate morale was high in Virginia in June 1863, in the wake of Lee's victory at Chancellorsville. Additionally, even those who believed that God was chastising the South did not necessarily suffer from demoralization. As Daniel Stowell has pointed out, many white Southerners believed that God was punishing the South as He would punish a beloved son whom He continued to cherish and uphold.[78]

Nevertheless, those church leaders who proclaimed God's judgment made it clear that He required serious changes in the way that slavery was practiced in the South. Rooted in the antebellum demands of religious leaders for a purified slave system, a wartime reform movement swept across the Confederacy. Clarence Mohr has described how advocates of reform in Georgia won attention by claiming that military defeats were signs of God's imminent wrath, avoidable only if Southerners changed their ways.[79] One of these changes involved granting greater personal and institutional autonomy to African Americans.[80] This was precisely the approach taken by the white members of First Baptist Church of Charlottesville during the summer of 1863. Still, even if fear of divine judgment partially motivated some whites, it was a fear that prompted them to ameliorate rather than to repudiate the antebellum racial order. They were not rejecting slavery, only becoming better slaveholders.

The remaining years of the war saw a continuation of the cautious efforts by the black members of the African Church to secure their total ecclesiastical independence, a process that may have been influenced by Union incursions into Albemarle County in 1864 and 1865. In the absence of personal testimonies, the extent to which black church members were affected by these displays of Union strength remains unclear, but in July 1864, several months after the first skirmish in Albemarle, several free black members acted with unprecedented boldness. Complaining that the African church had never been allowed enough independence and that its white pastor, John Randolph, routinely and unfairly sided with enslaved blacks over free blacks, these men threatened to start a new church. The matter ended, however, after the white congregation forbade them to do so and the men retreated, claiming that they had not realized that their plan was improper.[81]

The presence of the Union army also appears to have increased the concerns of the white members of First Baptist over the low number of white males still active in the life of the church. In early 1864, around the time of the first Union incursion, the church decided that attendance for white males would be taken at each business meeting and that persistent and unexplained absences would thenceforward constitute grounds for church discipline. A similar measure was enacted shortly after the town was occupied by Union forces in 1865.[82] While the personal reactions of white church members are more difficult to trace, one wonders whether the assertiveness of blacks after local Union raids finally began to open the eyes of Baptist leaders like William Farish to the falseness of the religious paternalism they had been promoting for so many years. A pious man who frequently preached to the black members of his church, Farish nevertheless saw many of his own slaves run off to the Union army when it occupied the town of Charlottesville in early 1865.[83]

Even after the war ended, members of the African Church continued to meet in the basement of First Baptist Church, occasionally requesting help in adjudicating their membership disputes.[84] In another important way, the association between the two churches remained powerful. James Fife, a Baptist leader who had earlier criticized the idea of establishing a separate congregation for black members of the church, agreed to serve as pastor of the new congregation in 1865 and early 1866.[85] Later that year, the church moved nearer to complete autonomy when it called its first black pastor, William Gibbons. Philena Carkin, a Northern schoolteacher who worked for many years among the freedmen of Charlottesville, later wrote with deep respect of Gibbons's character and with disdain for his evangelical doctrines and temperament: "His preaching while in Charlottesville was of the type in vogue at that time, not only among the negroes, but to a great extent among the white people as well—the vociferous and excitable kind, with its terrible denunciation of sinners (meaning those outside the church fold) its arraignment of all wickedness (such as dancing, card playing and similar evils) its word painting of the joys of heaven, and its vivid depiction of the torments of hell."[86]

The Civil War permanently altered race relations in Albemarle County churches, allowing for a mass exodus of black members from white churches, an exodus that took place so swiftly as to provide eloquent testimony of black dissatisfaction with the antebellum order. Many churches began to lose their black members during the war itself—sometimes, as in Charlottesville, with the sanction of white masters, and at other times when enslaved members stole away to the Union army. In August 1862, for example, Chestnut Grove Baptist Church excluded two black members who had "absconded and gone to the Yankees." In the immediate aftermath of the war, some churches noticed black members leaving the neighborhood and quietly dropped their names from the membership rolls.[87]

Those African Americans who left white churches frequently did so in order to join black congregations in which they could elect their own pastors, worship in their own manner, and make their own membership decisions. Many of the freedmen who remained in Albemarle County after 1865 joined the African Baptist Church or pursued their own plans for religious autonomy.[88] In 1866, Pine Grove Baptist Church awarded preaching licenses to two of its black members and provided letters of dismission to members who wished to join the "African church."[89] The white members of Mountain Plain Baptist Church resolved in May 1866 that "the coloured members of this church be advised to have themselves organized into a separate church and that the Pastor & Deacons be a committee to confer with them upon the subject."[90]

Associational statistics confirm the picture of a massive black exodus from white churches. Between 1864 and 1867, black membership in ABA churches decreased by 35 percent.[91] These changes were part of a broader exodus taking place throughout the state—while approximately fifty thousand black Baptists were members of white churches in Virginia in 1865, three years later at least thirty-nine thousand of them had left to join black churches.[92] Whites reacted in a variety of ways to the departure of African Americans from their churches. For many, the new realities of the postwar period took a great deal of adjustment, a situation evident in the minute book of Mountain Plain Baptist Church, where the clerk noted that among those baptized on October 29, 1865, was "Lizzy Woods Free." He then caught his mistake and scratched out the word "Free." The description was no longer meaningful now that it applied equally to all remaining black members of the church. In the midst of potentially difficult deliberations over the use of their church building by former black members, the white members of First Baptist Church in Charlottesville reminded themselves in 1866 that "If we believe the members of the African church to be Christians, it is our bounden duty to deal with them in a spirit of harmony and brotherly love, as brethren of the church of Christ."[93]

Unfortunately, such exhortations spoke more to the good intentions of a few than to any concrete postwar reality. Most interracial relationships withered as whites and blacks withdrew from one another in the months and years after the war. When three members of First Baptist Church in Charlottesville compiled a new membership roll in 1891, meant to cover the years between 1831 and 1891, they entered only the names of former white church members in the new book.[94] In doing so, they silently erased the memory of the hundreds of free and enslaved blacks who had prayed, worshipped, and served in their church between its founding and 1863.

Notes

I wish to thank Gary Gallagher, Edward Ayers, Andrew Torget, and George Rable for reading and commenting insightfully on this essay; Charles Irons for his encouragement and advice; and the staffs of the Albemarle Charlottesville Historical Society, Virginia Baptist Historical Society, and Special Collections Department at the University of Virginia for their expert assistance. I am also grateful to the Jefferson Scholars Foundation and the Institute for Advanced Studies in Culture, both at the University of Virginia, for their generous intellectual and financial support.

1. Charles L. Perdue Jr., Thomas E. Barden, and Robert K. Phillips, eds., *Weevils in the Wheat: Interviews with Virginia Ex-Slaves* (Bloomington: Indiana University Press, 1980), 287, quoted from *Negro in Virginia*, published version, 107–8. The date of the interview and name of the interviewer are listed as unknown. It seems reasonable to assume that Tonsler was describing church life during the Civil War, since on the one hand he was only four years old when the war began and on the other he refers repeatedly to the presence of slaves at church services.

2. Ibid. While Tonsler dismissed these reports as mere prevarications, one wonders whether his preacher was not more likely to dwell upon the biblical themes of freedom and liberation when no whites were present. For a helpful discussion

of the ways in which slaves understood and emphasized these biblical ideas, see Albert J. Raboteau, *Canaan Land: A Religious History of African Americans* (Oxford: Oxford University Press, 2001), chapter 3. Raboteau's discussion centers on a topic not examined in this essay: the secretive religious gatherings of slaves in "hush harbors" outside of the institutional church that flourished during the antebellum years.

3. This essay addresses gaps in several historiographies. Historians of the Civil War have long been aware of the significance of religion among Union and Confederate soldiers and civilians, but are only now beginning to examine in any depth the religious dimensions of the war in the armies and on the home front. For one insightful collection of essays on this theme, see Randall M. Miller, Harry S. Stout, and Charles Reagan Wilson, *Religion and the American Civil War* (Oxford: Oxford University Press, 1998). Even this volume, however, does not deal adequately with the key question of African American religious life and how it was altered by the war. Historians who do examine the development of African American Christianity have typically focused on the antebellum period or postwar years, with relatively little to say about the war itself. For examples of such studies, see Mechal Sobel, *Trabelin' On: The Slave Journey to an Afro-Baptist Faith* (Westport, Conn.: Greenwood Press, 1979); Janet Duitsman Cornelius, *Slave Missions and the Black Church in the Antebellum South* (Columbia: University of South Carolina Press, 1999); William E. Montgomery, *Under Their Own Vine and Fig Tree: The African-American Church in the South, 1865–1900* (Baton Rouge: Louisiana State University Press, 1993); Albert J. Raboteau, *Canaan Land: A Religious History of African Americans* (Oxford: Oxford University Press, 2001); and Albert J. Raboteau, *Slave Religion: The "Invisible Institution" in the Antebellum South* (Oxford: Oxford University Press, 1978). Finally, when historians have examined religious change during the war, most have understandably done so from the perspective of African Americans seeking to secure greater ecclesiastical independence. The result has been a neglect of what changes in church life during the war might tell us about white experiences and expectations and Confederate morale.

4. The description of Albemarle County in this paragraph is drawn from John Hammond Moore, *Albemarle: Jefferson's County, 1727–1976* (Charlottesville: University Press of Virginia, 1976), chapters 9 and 10. Population figures are calculated from census data printed on pages 115 and 159.

5. For an excellent study of the relationship between black and white evangelical Christians in antebellum Virginia, see Charles F. Irons, "'The Chief Cornerstone': The Spiritual Foundations of Virginia's Slave Society, 1776–1861" (Ph.D. diss., University of Virginia, 2003).

6. On the attractiveness of both the Baptist and Methodist denominations among slaves, see Raboteau, *Canaan Land*, 18–20; Raboteau, *Slave Religion*, chapters 3 and 4; Sobel, *Trabelin' On*, part 2; and Montgomery, *Under Their Own Vine and Fig Tree*, chapter 1.

7. In 1852, the ABA contained a total of twenty-nine churches and 5,368 members. See the *Minutes of the Sixty-First Anniversary of the Albemarle Baptist Association* (Charlottesville: James Alexander, Printer, 1852), 8–9.

8. Computed from figures in the minutes of the ABA between 1850 and 1860. The number of churches in the association rose from twenty-six to forty during these years.

9. Computed from figures in the *Minutes of the Sixty-Ninth Anniversary of the Albemarle Baptist Association* (Charlottesville: James Alexander, Printer, 1860), 7.

10. In 1860, for example, blacks constituted nearly 87 percent (258 out of 298) of the membership of Ballenger's Creek Baptist Church and just under 95 percent (163 of 172) of the membership of Limestone Baptist Church. For these numbers, see Ballenger's Creek Baptist Church, Church Minutes, Special Collections, University of Virginia Library, Charlottesville, Virginia (hereafter cited as BCBC), August 1860, and *Minutes of the Sixty-Ninth Anniversary of the Albemarle Baptist Association*, 6.

11. *Minutes of the Sixty-Ninth Anniversary of the Albemarle Baptist Association*, 22; *Minutes of the Sixty-Seventh Anniversary of the Albemarle Baptist Association* (Charlottesville: James Alexander, Printer, 1858), 16; *Minutes of the Sixty-Eighth Anniversary of the Albemarle Baptist Association* (Charlottesville: James Alexander, Printer, 1859), 20. John Hart argued here that separate services could and should be designed to interest and attract blacks.

12. First Baptist Church, Charlottesville, Church Minutes, Special Collections, University of Virginia Library, Charlottesville, Virginia (hereafter cited as FBCC), March 18, 1861, April 14, 1861.

13. The record of Nelson's membership is found in Christ Church Episcopal, Parish Register 1836–1868, Special Collections, University of Virginia Library, Charlottesville, Virginia (hereafter cited as CCE), 170. References to his slaves are made in FBCC, March 22, 1858, March 18, 1861.

14. George Omohundro baptized his son at Christ Church in 1864. See CCE, 118–19. For the reference to Charlotte, see Chestnut Grove Baptist Church, Church Minutes, Microfilm, Special Collections, University of Virginia Library, Charlottesville, Virginia (hereafter cited as CGBC), Membership Roll.

15. For evidence of Rives's long membership at Christ Church, see "Pew Holders in the Episcopal Church Charlottesville," in Christ Church Episcopal Treasurer's Records 1853–79, Special Collections, University of Virginia Library, Charlottesville, Virginia. For references to Rives's slaves, who were subject to church discipline just like the slaves of less wealthy and prominent men, see FBCC, October 19, 1857, February 24, 1858, July 16, 1860; BCBC, May 15, 1858, November 20, 1858, December 18, 1858.

16. FBCC, June 4, 1855, July 1, 1855; CCE, 204–5, 222–23.

17. FBCC, June 4, 1855, July 1, 1855; CCE, 202–3. For more on Rives and Lewis, see Philena Carkin, "Reminiscences of My Life and Work among the Freedmen of Charlottesville, Virginia, from March 1st 1866 to July 1st 1875. Vol. 1," part of the Philena Carkin Papers, 1866–1875, Accession #11123, Special Collections, University of Virginia Library, Charlottesville, Virginia, 32.

18. James Fife to Martin Baskett Shepherd, February 30, 1852, Papers of Martin Baskett Shepherd, Special Collections, University of Virginia Library, Charlottesville, Virginia.

19. FBCC, October 5, 1851; FBCC, June 9, 1861; CGBC, Membership Roll.

20. Moore, *Albemarle: Jefferson's County*, 152. For one of many references to Farish in church records, see FBCC, September 19, 1855. The entry praises Farish for his pastoral work among the black members of the congregation.

21. For references to slaves owned by Farish, see FBCC, October 21, 1854, January 17, 1859. For references to slaves owned by Randolph, see FBCC, March, 1858.

22. James Fife to Martin Baskett Shepherd, February 30, 1852, Papers of Martin Baskett Shepherd, Special Collections, University of Virginia Library, Charlottesville, Virginia.

23. See Mountain Plain Baptist Church, Church Minutes, Microfilm, Special Collections, University of Virginia Library, Charlottesville, Virginia (hereafter cited as MPBC), January 17, 1852, September 7, 1853, January 7, 1854, and August 25, 1860, for a record of Jones's disciplinary activities. Adam's case is noted in MPBC, May 15, 1853, May 18, 1853. Adam was restored to fellowship in 1858 on the motion of another church member and the testimony of his master. See MPBC, Membership Roll, for a record of enslaved church members belonging to Jones.

24. The church minutes from March 9, 1862, reported that "Quite a number of Brethren and Sisters were present." See FBCC, March 9, 1862. The minutes for another meeting noted that "a few of the sisters" were present. See FBCC, December 25, 1863. On January 17, 1859, William H. Crank reported for the women of the church on the disbursement of over $800 that they had collected. See FBCC, January 17, 1859.

25. Data compiled from FBCC, 1854–1863. The suggestion that church discipline might be used to exercise racial or gender control rather than strictly enforced without regard to considerations other than the guilt or innocence of the accused would probably have dismayed and offended Virginia Baptists. The possibility I have considered here is not that church leaders would fabricate offenses but that they would perhaps be more apt to ignore or exercise leniency toward the sins of white men while prosecuting the offenses of white women or African Americans of either gender with greater zeal and tenacity. For historical works that suggest that this was in fact the case, see Cornelius, *Slave Missions and the Black Church in the Antebellum South*, 38, and Randy Sparks, *On Jordan's Stormy Banks: Evangelicalism in Mississippi, 1773–1876* (Athens: University of Georgia Press, 1994), 151. My own findings dispute this interpretation and are more consistent with the view found in Sobel, *Trabelin' On*, 207–8. The case of First Baptist Church contradicts Janet Duitsman Cornelius's generalization that "Biracial churches disciplined black church members, women and men, much more frequently than whites." See *Slave Missions and the Black Church in the Antebellum Church*, 38. The size of the sample on which Cornelius based her generalization is unclear.

26. Gender was not listed in three of the cases (about 3 percent of the total sample).

27. I have based my calculations on statistics listed in the ABA records. The general trend was an increase in black membership but a gradual decrease in per-

centage of total membership due to even greater increases in white membership. Statistics for black membership during the 1850s are as follows: 1852: 70 percent (383 out of 549); 1853: 67 percent (400 out of 599); 1858: 58 percent (436 out of 752); 1859: 58 percent (466 out of 806); 1860: 60 percent (496 out of 828). The average of these figures is 62 percent.

28. The three cases in which gender was not listed again constitute 3 percent of the total.

29. The membership figures are drawn from a review of the membership rolls conducted by the church in February 1866. See FBCC, February 1866.

30. See note 27.

31. Gender was not indicated in four cases of restoration, accounting for 8 percent of the total.

32. *Minutes of the Sixty-Eighth Anniversary of the Albemarle Baptist Association*, 19–20; I have found only one case in which the white congregation failed to approve a disciplinary action taken by the church's black members. See FBCC, March 18, 1861. My description of the disciplinary system is based in part on a note made in 1858 that two slaves were excluded from membership in the church by vote of the "colored brethren." See FBCC, March 1858.

33. FBCC, September 19, 1855, emphasis added; FBCC, July 22, 1864, emphasis added.

34. CGBC, 4th Sunday in February 1858, 4th Sunday in March 1858.

35. CGBC, September 1861; BCBC, August 15, 1857; MPBC, March 21, 1852.

36. Clarence Mohr, *On the Threshold of Freedom: Masters and Slaves in Civil War Georgia* (Baton Rouge: Louisiana State University Press, 2001, first published in 1986), 244. This conclusion appears to have been based on a rather impressionistic reading of church records. Mohr states that "valid generalizations must await large scale statistical research in manuscript records" (see 356–57 n. 32). To my knowledge, such a study has not yet been attempted.

37. Given the well-known importance of extra-institutional Christian gatherings for slaves, it is worth noting that although such gatherings could satisfy the first two needs mentioned here, formal church membership was required if slaves wished to satisfy the other two.

38. Sobel, *Trabelin' On*, 215, 291–309.

39. *Minutes of the Seventieth Anniversary of the Albemarle Baptist Association* (Charlottesville: James Alexander, Printer, 1861), 12.

40. CGBC, 4th Saturday in June 1861.

41. See the 1860, 1865, and 1866 ABA minutes.

42. Baptist Church of Christ at Spring Hill, Church Minutes, Virginia Baptist Historical Society, Richmond, Virginia (hereafter cited as BCCSH), July 13, 1862, June 13, 1863, 2nd Saturday in June 1864.

43. BCCSH, July 1865.

44. FBCC, October 7, 1861.

45. FBCC, December 25, 1863.

46. CGBC, 4th Saturday in April 1863, November 1863.

47. John Cowper Granbery to Ella Winston, May 14, 1861, Special Collections, University of Virginia Library, Charlottesville, Virginia; John Cowper Granbery to Ella Winston, May 3, 1861, Special Collections, University of Virginia Library, Charlottesville, Virginia.

48. FBCC, April 6, 1862; FBCC, February 26, 1864; the single protest I have found is William Carr Thurman, *Non-resistance; or, The spirit of Christianity restored* (Charlottesville: Published by the author, 1864).

49. On the fighting in Albemarle County, see Moore, *Albemarle: Jefferson's County,* 205–10; for the quotation, see Anne Freundenberg, "Sheridan's Raid: An Account By Sarah A.G. Strickler," *The Magazine of the Albemarle County Historical Society* (Civil War Issue) 22 (1963–1964): 61; for details about the church service, see Strickler's March 10 diary entry, reprinted in Freundenberg, "Sheridan's Raid," 64.

50. For information on war hospitals, see Moore, *Albemarle: Jefferson's County,* 202–5; transcript of the papers of the Reverend George W. White (location of original papers unknown), Special Collections, University of Virginia Library, Charlottesville, Virginia, 41; George B. Taylor, *Life and Times of James B. Taylor* (Philadelphia: The Bible and Publication Society, 1872), 262. The entry was made on May 30, 1862.

51. Calculated from figures in the 1860 and 1865 ABA minutes.

52. CGBC, 2nd Sunday in August 1861. Black membership in 1860 was thirty-three. See *Minutes of the Sixty-Ninth Anniversary of the Albemarle Baptist Association,* 4.

53. CGBC, 4th Saturday in April 1861.

54. CGBC, 4th Saturday in July 1862.

55. See, for example, CGBC, June 1861, 2nd Sunday in August 1861, 2nd Sunday in July 1862.

56. CGBC, 2nd Sunday in August 1861, emphasis in original.

57. *Minutes of the Sixty-Eighth Anniversary of the Albemarle Baptist Association,* 20–21.

58. CGBC, August 1861, September 1861.

59. CGBC, August 1861, October 26, 1861.

60. Associational records show thirty-three black members and ninety-nine white members in 1860. Given the steady departure of white males for the war, the addition of seventy-two black members in 1861 would alone have been enough to form a black majority. For membership statistics, see the *Minutes of the Sixty-Ninth Anniversary of the Albemarle Baptist Association,* 4.

61. CGBC, June 1866, July 1866, July 1867.

62. *Minutes of the Seventieth Anniversary of the Albemarle Baptist Association,* 18; statistics on new black members compiled from FBCC, April 29, 1861, June 9, 1861; *Minutes of the Seventy-First Anniversary of the Albemarle Baptist Association* (Charlottesville: James Alexander, Printer, 1862), 20; membership percentage computed from *Minutes of the Sixty-Ninth Anniversary of the Albemarle Baptist Association,* 4. There were 496 black and 332 white members.

63. For Randolph's election as deacon, service as a liaison, and receipt of a preaching license, see FBCC, December 18, 1854, February 1858, and April 29, 1861, respectively. For the request of the black congregation, see FBCC, March 18, 1861. For further evidence of Randolph's earlier work among the black members of the congregation, see *Minutes of the Sixty-Eighth Anniversary of the Albemarle Baptist Association,* 19–20.

64. FBCC, October 7, 1861.

65. FBCC, 1854–1860. The peak year for disciplinary actions against white members was 1858 (19 cases), while 1855 and 1859 (8 cases) were the two leading years for African American members. The breakdown by year for black members was: 4 in 1854, 8 in 1855, 4 in 1856, 4 in 1857, 7 in 1858, 8 in 1859, and 4 in 1860; and for white members: 5 in 1854, 2 in 1855, 10 in 1856, 13 in 1857, 19 in 1858, 4 in 1859, and 7 in 1860. The temporal distribution of restorations was even more uneven, with peaks for both white and black members in 1855 (9 and 13 cases, respectively), and disproportionate numbers of black restorations also occurring in 1859 and 1861. FBCC, 1854–1861. Black restorations: 1 in 1854, 13 in 1855, 0 in 1856, 1 in 1857, 4 in 1858, 8 in 1859, 1 in 1860, and 7 in 1861. White restorations: 0 in 1854, 9 in 1855, 0 in 1856, 0 in 1857, 2 in 1858, 0 in 1859, 2 in 1860, and 0 in 1861.

66. FBCC, March 16, 1863.

67. FBCC, April 20, 1863, May 22, 1863, June 26, 1863.

68. FBCC, June 26, 1863.

69. Daniel Stowell, *Rebuilding Zion: The Religious Reconstruction of the South, 1863–1877* (New York: Oxford University Press, 1998), 70–71.

70. FBCC, March 22, 1858, August 22, 1859.

71. Moore, *Albemarle: Jefferson's County,* 127.

72. Mohr, *On the Threshold of Freedom,* 52.

73. Charles F. Irons has argued persuasively that white congregants at First Baptist believed that allowing greater black autonomy would win more souls and that they saw the move as "an extension of the antebellum ministry to the quarters." See Irons, "The Chief Cornerstone," 266.

74. This conclusion—that many white Virginians were confident of ultimate Confederate victory during much of the war and were thus operating from a position of strength rather than suffering from a paralyzing demoralization or "loss of will"—runs counter to the dominant position in the historiography of the Civil War. For a forceful and convincing critique of the dominant historiographical position, see Gary Gallagher, *The Confederate War* (Cambridge, Mass.: Harvard University Press, 1997).

75. Beth Barton Schweiger, *The Gospel Working Up: Progress and the Pulpit in Nineteenth-Century Virginia* (Oxford: Oxford University Press, 2000), 116; Sobel, *Trabelin' On,* chapter 7.

76. On the antebellum campaign to evangelize slaves and clean up the worst abuses of the institution of slavery, see Mitchell Snay, *Gospel of Disunion: Religion and Separatism in the Antebellum South* (Cambridge: Cambridge University Press, 1993), 89–90; and Mohr, *On the Threshold of Freedom,* 235–46.

77. Quoted in Stowell, *Rebuilding Zion,* 37. The quotation is from *Scriptural Views of National Trials* (Greensboro, N.C.: Sterling, Campbell, & Albright, 1863), by the North Carolina Presbyterian minister Calvin H. Wiley.

78. Ibid., 37–40.

79. Mohr, *On the Threshold of Freedom,* 247–71.

80. Ibid., 267.

81. FBCC, June 24, 1864, July 22, 1864, August 21, 1864.

82. FBCC, February 26, 1864, April 3, 1864, March 24, 1865.

83. See the 1865 letter from Judge Egbert Watson to Mrs. Henry Smith quoted in John R. Brown, "Sheridan's Occupation of Charlottesville," *The Magazine of the Albemarle County Historical Society* (Civil War Issue) 22 (1963–64): 42.

84. FBCC, June 23, 1865, September 22, 1865, November 24, 1865.

85. See James Fife to Martin Baskett Shepherd, February 30, 1852, Papers of Martin Baskett Shepherd, Special Collections, University of Virginia Library, Charlottesville, Virginia; FBCC, December 22, 1865, January 6, 1866; and *Minutes of the Seventy-Fourth Anniversary of the Albemarle Baptist Association* (Charlottesville: James Alexander, Printer, 1865), 4.

86. Philena Carkin, "Reminiscences of My Life and Work Among the Freedmen of Charlottesville, Virginia, from March 1st 1866 to July 1st 1875. Vol. 1," part of the Philena Carkin Papers, 1866–1875, Accession #11123, Special Collections, University of Virginia Library, Charlottesville, Virginia, 52. Carkin claimed that Gibbons was pastor of the black church when she arrived in Charlottesville in 1866.

87. For a discussion of the scope and meaning of the black exodus from white churches throughout the state of Virginia, see the epilogue of Irons, "The Chief Cornerstone"; CGBC, 4th Saturday in August 1862, July 1866.

88. See, for example, the notice of a former slave named Julius who left his church to join the Charlottesville church in CGBC, 4th Saturday in July 1865.

89. Pine Grove Baptist Church, Church Minutes, Virginia Baptist Historical Society, Richmond, Virginia, April 1866, July 1866, August 1866.

90. MPBC, May 19, 1866.

91. This figure was calculated from data in the ABA minutes for the relevant years.

92. Schweiger, *The Gospel Working Up,* 113.

93. MPBC, October 29, 1865; FBCC, January 6, 1866.

94. First Baptist Church, Charlottesville, Membership Roll 1831–1891, Special Collections, University of Virginia Library, Charlottesville, Virginia, compiled by M. C. Thomas, J. C. Matthews, and Lew Wood.

"The Right to Love and to Mourn"

The Origins of Virginia's Ladies' Memorial Associations, 1865–1867

Caroline E. Janney

Less than a month after Robert E. Lee surrendered at Appomattox, the first Ladies' Memorial Association in Virginia organized to eulogize and praise the fallen South.[1] The spring of 1865 had brought peace to the state, but the scars of war remained quite visible in the quaint town of Winchester. Graves of Southern soldiers had been scattered across the lower Shenandoah Valley, and with each passing month residents uncovered more bodies as farming activities resumed. One Winchester woman, Mary Dunbar Williams, was greatly disturbed by the lack of proper burials for the Confederate soldiers who had so ardently defended the town. In May of 1865, Williams visited her sister-in-law, Eleanor Williams Boyd, and told her of a farmer who had been preparing his land for corn when he plowed up two Confederate soldiers. The two women decided that they should call a meeting of all the women who had worked together during the war, with the objective of forming a memorial organization to gather all the dead within a radius of twelve to fifteen miles and place them within one graveyard. Additionally, they agreed it was imperative that the entire town assemble each year to place flowers and evergreens on the graves. Throughout the South in 1865 and 1866, Southern women followed in the path of those in Winchester and began honoring the Confederate dead by forming their own Ladies' Memorial Associations.[2]

In the antebellum period death and mourning had been the province of women and ministers. Funerals were usually private affairs situated firmly within the domestic sphere.[3] But the astronomical number of casualties brought on by the war necessitated that strangers perform many of the sentimental and personal rituals associated with death. While the Federal government hired troops and the Sanitary Commission to provide proper burials for Northern soldiers, the Confederacy lacked such resources to care for its dead. Elite and middle-class Southern women never relinquished their role as caregivers to the dead, but embraced the cause of caring for their fallen soldiers as an extension of their antebellum and wartime duties. In the months and years following Lee's surrender at Appomattox, women in several communities across Virginia, including Richmond, Fredericksburg, Lynchburg, Petersburg, and Winchester, organized Ladies' Memorial Associations (LMAs) to provide proper burials honoring the South and its dead. LMAs, however, did much more than provide suitable resting places for their fallen menfolk; Southern men and women realized that these "ladies" might deploy gender in the interest of Confederate politics, laying the foundation for the Lost Cause.[4]

Recent years have seen the publication of numerous books and articles on Confederate memory and the Lost Cause.[5] The authors of these books have explored the cultural, political, and social dimensions of the Lost Cause, the racial promptings and implications of the movement, and the significance of Confederate identity in contemporary America.[6] But in all these debates, historians have largely overlooked the role of women and gender in Confederate memorialization. At most, historians have tended to see women as peripheral to the movement until the 1890s and early 1900s, when the United Daughters of the Confederacy became active. In fact, Gaines M. Foster claims that most white Southerners were hesitant to celebrate the Confederate past in the years between 1865 and the mid-1880s because he fails to recognize the significance of women's role. W. Fitzhugh Brundage, too, suggests that the 1860s and 1870s were marked by "little organized interest in the past"—even among women—ignoring the importance of LMAs.[7] By examining the roles of Virginia's LMAs, however, we discover that not only were white women the first to organize community efforts to honor the Confederacy in a region still occupied by Northern soldiers, but also that "memorial" work itself was intensely political and should not be cast aside as insignificant.

Many of the same women who had sewn battle flags, volunteered in hospitals, and snubbed Yankee soldiers during the war turned to the LMAs so that they might continue to display their Confederate patriotism through memorial activities. Such work allowed them to create an extensive network of like-minded women throughout the South much earlier and with much greater coordination than historians have previously argued. But equally important, white Southerners recognized the potential social and political ramifications of females memorializing the defeated Confederacy, repeatedly justifying the women's right to pay tribute to their kinsmen by emphasizing the supposedly nonpolitical nature of such "mourning" ceremonies. Middle- and upper-class women of the LMAs thus served in the forefront of the postwar battle over Confederate memory, simultaneously allowing men to skirt the issue of treason and laying the foundation for the Lost Cause. The women of the LMAs, and not the Confederate veterans or the United Daughters of the Confederacy, were responsible for remaking military defeat into a political, social, and cultural victory for the white South.[8]

In the wake of defeat, Virginia's Confederate women not only mourned their lost loved ones, but also agonized over the destruction of their homeland. "Although no State of the South had been exempt from the scourge," wrote Sallie Brock Putnam in 1867, "Virginia had borne the brunt of the war." In her memoir she detailed the destruction of the once grand state. "Wherever the foot of the invader had been pressed, it left its mark in desolation. Along the Potomac River scarcely a dwelling remained to indicate that the fair region had once been the abode of one of the happiest, most refined and intelligent communities in our country, but charred monuments of destruction betokened the work of the incendiary and the despoiler."[9] After visiting Richmond's ruins, Lucy Fletcher noted that from the south end of Capitol Square to the river, from 8th Street to 18th, scarcely one building was standing. "All was in ruins and desolation," she exclaimed.[10] Smoke billowed from the city's burnt business district, where brick chimneys remained the last remnants of the city's antebellum industrial strength. Already bursting at the seams with refugees and government officials, the city witnessed a deluge of more refugees, veterans, freedmen, and the Union army at the war's end.

Like those in the state's capital, many of Petersburg's warehouses and railroads had been destroyed in the final days of war, and the city's white residents had lost $3.5 million in slave property. In Winchester, two hundred businesses had been destroyed, including the Lutheran School House, the Catholic Church, the Quaker Meeting House, the Reformed Church, part of the old Market House, and numerous homes.[11] Fredericksburg's population had fallen from an antebellum high of five thousand to between six hundred and eight hundred people, primarily women and children. A traveler describing the destruction of the city noted that only a few trees remained on the hills and not a fence or inhabitable house could be found between the city and Hamilton's Crossing. Bridges and depots had been burned, while rifle pits and entrenchments marred the landscape for miles around the city.[12] Lynchburg's once prosperous tobacco industry lay in ruins and not a single bank was left, as all had gone into liquidation.[13] All told, the war had shattered the commonwealth's economy, causing nearly $457 million in losses, including slaves.[14] Virginia's status as a Southern industrial stronghold and national capital had been swept away in a mere four years.

Surrounded by the chaos of destruction, Virginia's ex-Confederates, like most white Southerners, were exhausted from four years of battle and not inclined to continue fighting. While a few fiery souls, such as Colonel Thomas T. Munford, attempted to keep his troops in the field following Lee's surrender, most soldiers and citizens agreed that the Confederacy had tried its hardest but was unable to overcome the superior manpower and military strength of the well-supplied Union army.[15] Virginia's white residents laid down their guns, accepted defeat, abandoned secession, and acknowledged the abolition of slavery, although they remained loyal to old political values and the principle of white supremacy. Many expressed their indignation that slavery had ended.

Restoring and rebuilding the defeated South became the primary objective for most ex-Confederates. While the state's warehouses, shops, mills, and factories lay in shambles, farmers and businessmen alike believed they could rebuild the prosperity of their beloved Virginia. A correspondent from the *New York Tribune* traveling through the commonwealth reported that a captain in Lee's late army had been seen plowing a small garden with his war horse, his slaves and other personal property having been lost. The *Richmond Times* believed that every Southern man should follow this captain's example, arguing that labor was the "true way" to restore the South to order and prosperity. Though ten thousand Union soldiers guarded Richmond and attempted to control its inhabitants, the white population turned its thoughts to "peaceful pursuits, returning to their homes, cultivating their crops, rebuilding their fences, and setting about earning a subsistence for their families."[16] Rather than publicly lamenting their lost cause, most of the state's political and business leaders focused on reviving the shattered economy.[17]

If white men felt it best to get on with reorganizing businesses and replanting the barren landscape, many of Virginia's middle- and upper-class white women exhibited a more mixed reaction to the South's defeat.

Emmy Wellford of Richmond begged her brother Phil to seek parole. "You are in danger of being captured where you are," she warned, "and I so see no other plan open to you but to come in."[18] When Elizabeth Munford's husband, George, wrote her in April expressing his reluctance to take the oath of loyalty to the Union, she responded with a practical plea. While the oath was "a bitter pill to all," she insisted that it "is rendered absolutely necessary, unless you leave your families to starve, for I supposed not a dozen families in Richmond have a dollar in any thing but Confederate money." Lest her husband think she was a sellout, she added, "I hope you all do not think we have lost all our patriotism because we preach caution."[19]

Perhaps it was this tension between loyalty to the South and practical matters of reconstruction that led numerous Virginian women to feel obligated to properly memorialize and honor the fallen Confederacy. No doubt both elite and poor women faced the daunting task of rebuilding their homes and social order. They encountered tremendous adjustments in running and managing households without slaves and the provisions they had enjoyed prior to the war. For many, public activities took a back seat to more pressing concerns of poverty and domestic relations. Historians, however, have underestimated the number of women involved in efforts to enshrine the Lost Cause, suggesting that only a handful had the energy, resources, and inclination to engage in memorial activities.[20] Evidence from Virginia suggests that a solid core of dedicated women emerged as early as 1865 and 1866 to serve as guardians of the sacred past.

Many of these women perceived themselves as Southern "Ladies," from whom society still expected a certain amount of decorum and dedication to the fallen Confederacy.[21] Historian Suzanne Lebsock has pointed out that the notion of the devoted Confederate woman was fixed in the public imagination as early as 1862. According to this mythos, Southern women had willingly sacrificed their men and comfort, enduring four relentless years of battles and privations with their faith in God and the cause intact.[22] This image did not fade with the war's end, even as women faced the harsh difficulties of widowhood and poverty. Rather, the notion seemed to intensify. Only a year after the surrender a Lynchburg paper remarked on the works of its "noble Ladies": "Who will ever forget their self-sacrificing and unwearied labors for those who were putting on the panoply of war to go out to battle for rights held dear to their hearts?" the editor wrote. "The end has come; the ashes of desolation are on their hearth-stories . . . but their beautiful deeds live, bright and fresh, in faithful memories, uneffaced by time, undiminished by defeat." No doubt this veneration of

Southern white women compelled many of them to continue the devotion they had shown during the war, as is evident in the postwar activities of Lynchburg's women, who continued to provide aid and food for soldiers returning from Northern prisons.[23]

As had been the case during the war, many of these elite women remained the staunchest supporters of the defeated Confederacy and the fiercest opponents of the Federal government. Some women tried to deny the collapse of the Confederacy. Mary Cabell of Lynchburg conceded that "my brain refuses to grasp the idea of this great calamity," even though "it is written on my brain in letters of fire."[24] After hearing "fearful rumors" of Lee's surrender, Judith Brokenbrough McGuire of Richmond proclaimed that she had "not yet give[n] up all hope," as General Johnston was still in the field.[25] Another Richmond woman likewise commented that though she had heard "rumors of Lee's surrender," and had seen an official account of it in Yankee papers, she had "as yet seen none of our people who *know* anything of it."[26] As William Blair has pointed out, slaveholding women were often the most virulent in expressing their opinions regarding emancipation. Sarah Strickler Fife of Albemarle County raged about having to live without slavery. "I truly believe that African slavery is right. I love it & all the South loves it. It suits us, & I do not see how we can do without it."[27]

Not only did many upper-class women grieve for their lost cause, but they fumed about the Yankee invaders—and a few openly turned cold shoulders on Union officers, as they had done during the war. In Richmond, Lucy Fletcher observed the "capital square lined with blue coats," and resented that these were "the people who for 4 years have been slaying our brethren, and desolating our land, burning and ravaging our homes insulting and robbing our defenceless women and grey haired men."[28] As Federal troops flooded the streets of the former capital, Confederate women who appeared in public at all did so in mourning dress. Mrs. Charles Ellis noted that the "young Ladies have scrupulously avoided the acquaintance or recognition of any of the Enemy and for the first two or three weeks when they went on the streets wore veils 2 or 8 fold."[29] Believing that gender behavior was indicative of "civilization," white Northerners quickly pointed out that these Southern white women were lacking in proper Victorian manners. According to Northern men, Southern women displayed an intense attachment to the Confederacy and hostility to the Federal government, beyond that of Southern men.[30] Consciously or not, Southern white women fulfilled this reputation with their devotion to the

Confederate dead. What better way to show disdain for U.S. officers and reverence for Southern soldiers than to memorialize the Confederacy?

During the summer of 1865, the Winchester Ladies' Memorial Association (WLMA) met frequently at the residence of Mrs. Boyd. But they were not alone in their desire to commemorate the Confederacy. Sometime that summer or fall, the citizens of Winchester held a meeting and appointed a committee to cooperate with the WLMA, during which the citizens wrote an appeal to the people of the South for aid. The appeal described the destruction in the Valley and noted that "the dead were generally buried where they fell, and their rude graves are fast disappearing beneath the feet of men and beasts—free, from the want of enclosure, to go where they will." The citizens of Winchester explained that their resources had been greatly reduced by the war. "We are therefore induced to appeal to you for aid in this matter, encouraged by the belief that you will feel it a privilege as well as duty to pay this tribute of respect to the memory of those who fell in your cause." Because every Southern state was represented among the fallen, the Winchester residents believed that all states should feel obliged to aid the town's efforts.[31]

Despite the South's poverty, donations for Winchester's cemetery fund began to pour in from across the former Confederacy.[32] By the spring of 1866, Winchester had received $14,000 in contributions ($1,200 from Alabama alone) and the WLMA, in conjunction with the Stonewall Monumental Association, was able to purchase five acres for a Confederate cemetery to be named after General Thomas Jonathan Jackson. Mrs. Williams and Mrs. Boyd then organized a public meeting at which they assigned a group of men to begin collecting the remains of the dead and reinter them prior to the coming summer heat.[33] By late spring the men had collected the dead from a radius of fifteen miles around Stonewall cemetery and buried them in individual graves. Under the direction of the WLMA, the committee collected and buried 2,489 Confederate soldiers' bodies in the five-acre cemetery within a year.[34]

The work of Winchester's women, along with other cities' Memorial Day celebrations, reflected a ripple effect of activism throughout both the state and region.[35] As early as June 9, 1865, Nora Fontaine Maury Davidson, who had established a school for young women in Petersburg, led her students to Blandford Cemetery, where they decorated the graves of both Union and Confederate dead with flowers and flags.[36] By the following spring, newspaper editors across the region were publishing accounts of women's memorial efforts and suggesting that their local women pursue similar activities. One "fair daughter of Virginia," from Orange County, wrote to local newspapers encouraging women of the state to set aside the second Wednesday of May 1866 as "a day to be consecrated by floral offerings and decorations to the memory of our lost heroes." She encouraged Virginia's women to "follow the good example set us by our Southern sisters, and consecrate the sacred memory of our fallen heroes."[37]

Apparently her letter and like sentiment across the South prompted church leaders, municipal officials, and elite women to organize memorial groups, as a wave of Ladies' Memorial Associations emerged across the state. On April 19, 1866, 107 Richmond women representing the city's eastern churches gathered to organize the Oakwood Memorial Association (OMA). At least forty women in Lynchburg met on April 26 after an appeal from former members of the Ladies' Relief Hospital, and yet another group of Richmond women responded to a call from Hollywood Cemetery president Thomas Elliot to form the Hollywood Memorial Association on May 3.[38] On May 6, 1866, 278 of Petersburg's most prominent women met at Library Hall to organize a Ladies' Memorial Association, and on May 10 the women of Fredericksburg called their first meeting.[39] Within a matter of two weeks, several of the most influential and active Ladies' Memorial Associations in the state, not to mention the South, had formed from a variety of sources.

But women were not the only impetus behind such organizations. In fact, while the Ladies of Petersburg, Winchester, and Lynchburg and the Oakwood women of Richmond appear to have met of their own fruition, it was men at both Fredericksburg and Richmond's Hollywood Cemetery that spurred the development of their respective LMAs. In 1866, the staff at Hollywood had been unable to maintain the grounds and prevent thefts, especially of flowers and memorial wreathes. Simultaneously, city residents became angered when they learned that the Federal government had appropriated land and funds to care for the graves of Union soldiers without providing any provisions for the Confederate dead. An article in the *Richmond Examiner* exclaimed that the U.S. government was wrong to see the Confederate soldier as less heroic because he had failed, and urged the city's churchwomen to honor the neglected Confederates. The cemetery's president, Colonel Thomas A. Ellis, likewise was in distress regarding the financial situation of Hollywood Cemetery, and he published an appeal for donations. His notice led to an anonymous letter to the paper suggesting that Ellis request the aid of Richmond's Ladies. Ellis subsequently issued a call in the papers inviting all interested citizens to meet in St. Paul's Church on May 3, 1866. Richmond's women responded en masse, and by mid-May the Hollywood Memorial Association (HMA) claimed over one hundred active members.[40]

While financial motives and competition from the Oakwood Memorial Association inspired the women of the HMA, Fredericksburg's clergy provided the impetus for their city's LMA when they called a meeting on May 10, 1866, to make arrangements for their Confederate dead.[41] On that Thursday, the city's stores and businesses closed to commemorate the death of General Thomas "Stonewall" Jackson, while women, children, and old men gathered at the Episcopal Church to mourn the Confederacy. Following an address by Major J. Horace Lacy, the Ladies in attendance, including young Lizzie Alsop, agreed to organize a Ladies' Memorial Association for the purpose of taking care of the numerous Confederate graves that dotted the landscape as well as the city cemetery. Immediately the Ladies elected officers and appointed several men to serve on committees to aid their endeavors. As they would continue to do well into the future, after the meeting ended a large number of Ladies formed a procession to the city cemetery, where they decorated Confederate graves with flowers and evergreens.[42] Thus, while Richmond, Winchester, and Petersburg all celebrated organized Memorial Days as early as 1866, Fredericksburg's women had laid the foundation for future Memorial Days with their impromptu and reserved tribute to the Confederate dead.

As the editor of the *Lynchburg Daily Virginian* noted, white Southerners believed that memorial activities were "a fitting work" for Ladies.[43] Most obviously, this work appeared to be a natural extension of women's wartime activities. As they had done for soldiers' relief societies, hospitals, and churches since 1861, these women continued to employ their money-raising skills. In order to finance reburials and cemetery beautification projects, the LMAs collected membership dues, solicited donations from Southerners near and far, held lecture series, performed tableaux, and sponsored teas. One of the largest and most elaborate fund-raising ventures was the gala bazaar sponsored by the HMA in the spring of 1867. War mementos and other donated articles filled two floors of a Richmond warehouse, including such items as letters written by Confederate generals, inkstands carved from bones of horses killed in battles, paintings, and buttons from Stonewall Jackson's coat. The bazaar was such a success that the HMA extended it for two weeks, collecting more than $18,000.[44] Despite the South's poverty, these women excelled at raising funds for their memorial work.

But even more importantly, these groups served two very practical purposes. First, as the center of the war's Eastern theater, Virginia not only witnessed more battles than any other state, but lost more of her native sons as well. Decomposing bodies and bleaching bones covered the state's battlefields and farmland. With no official state agency to conduct the interments, Virginia (and other Southern states) relied upon private individuals and organizations to raise funds for collecting and transporting remains as well as furnishing an appropriate place for burial. Second, Victorian culture assumed that women were more emotional, and therefore more fitting to exhibit the sorrow and reverence necessary for proper mourning. During the mid-nineteenth century, women were expected to participate in rigid and often elaborate mourning rituals upon the death of a parent, husband, or child. For example, during mourning women donned a black wardrobe, wrote on special stationery, and restricted their social activities to reflect their loss. Karen Mehaffey has noted that mourning fell primarily on the shoulders of women because they symbolized the nucleus of the family. Mourning became a natural part of women's lives, a role for which they were groomed from a small age. The war thus threw many women into a state of perpetual mourning and simultaneously prevented them from observing many of the rituals associated with mourning. Households and farms still had to be run even in their grief.[45] But in the aftermath of war, many women returned to the deep mourning war had forced them to put aside and took up the cause of caring for the dead, both kin and stranger.

While the men and women of Winchester were busy planning their Confederate cemetery, Northern troops had been preparing national cemeteries to honor their own dead near battlefields across the commonwealth. During the war, Winchester women had criticized the irreverent treatment of Northern bodies by the Federal armies. Kate Sperry noted in her diary that "the Yanks have been carrying off their dead since Sunday—all day today—and have buried a great many in trenches out on the field." They would "dig a trench, lay in a Yank, put a board on him—lay another Yank on top of board. By that time the hole is pretty well filled, so shoveling in some dirt, they put a board at the head with one name on it—so three men have one name—it's awful to think of." Despite Confederate criticism of Northern burial practices, it was the Union rather than the Confederacy that had the manpower to provide not only burials, but Federally sanctioned cemeteries. With the aid of the Sanitary Commission, the War Department utilized Union soldiers to gather bodies and inter them in national cemeteries throughout the South within a year of surrender. Supported by funds from Congress, these well-tended, neatly organized cemeteries stood in stark contrast to the shallow graves of Southern soldiers that were being uprooted by farmers and scavenging animals. By 1867, the federal government had organized nearly a dozen national cemeteries, including those in Fredericksburg, City Point (near Petersburg), Richmond, and Winchester.[46]

Every community in which a Virginia LMA formed in the years immediately after the war had been either the site of a battlefield (Winchester, Petersburg, and Fredericksburg) or had served as a large hospital complex where many soldiers had died of wounds or illness (Richmond and Lynchburg). Women in battle-torn sections of the commonwealth therefore set forth on their task to follow the path of Winchester's women and organize parties to gather and inter bodies, while those in hospital districts focused on tending the cemeteries that had been created during the war. In late May 1866, the Petersburg LMA noted that "a mysterious providence has devolved on us a duty, which would otherwise have been a nation's pride to perform." They requested "that the bones of our brave soldiers, now bleaching before Fort Stedman, be at once gathered" to be reinterred as part of memorial services at the Old Blandford Church. The association hired fourteen local men and boys to search for bodies (nearly five thousand in all) in the surrounding battlefields, lay off cemetery plots, inter the bodies, and mark and paint headboards for the identified graves.[47] The Ladies of the Fredericksburg LMA (FLMA) asked those living on or near battlefields to help them identify burial sites, and by June reports of grave locations began flooding the association.[48]

Identifying scattered graves and gathering bodies in a central location was the primary objective for women in Petersburg, Winchester, and Fredericksburg, but LMAs developed elsewhere to provide more aesthetic roles. Until the final days of the war, neither Lynchburg nor Richmond had experienced a battle in the immediate vicinity of their city. But both had housed numerous hospitals that cared for sick and wounded soldiers, and therefore, both became the final resting place for thousands of soldiers from across the South. The women of Church Hill and Union Hill in Richmond organized their LMA to care for graves already located in Oakwood Cemetery. The OMA women believed "that the dead rest better in beautiful places, and it is for the living too that such memorials are held, to inspire their lives with the memory of the lives and deeds of the great and noble dead."[49] In their constitution, adopted May 1, 1866, they explicitly noted that their objective was to have the soldiers' portion of Oakwood Cemetery "well enclosed and each grave turfed and marked by a neat headpiece, properly inscribed."[50] Similarly, the Ladies of Lynchburg believed that they should enclose the space around the graves in order to protect them for future generations.[51]

But the LMAs' activities did not end once comfortable graves had been secured for those Confederates scattered across the countryside. Having interred most of the bodies on the battlefield, the Petersburg Ladies' Memorial Association (PLMA) decided to expand the scope of their project. In February 1867, the Petersburg association resolved that the Old Blandford Cemetery should be the primary spot to bury the city's Confederate dead. They petitioned the city's Common Council, still dominated by conservative antebellum Democrats and Whigs, to appropriate free of charge to the association enough land for the interment of five hundred bodies. In May 1867, the Common Council agreed to support the Confederate cemetery by donating an acre of Blandford Cemetery to the association. With this newly acquired space, the PLMA appointed Reverend Thomas H. Campbell and "any sergeants he deemed necessary" to retrieve the bodies of soldiers from distant battlefields.[52]

While the LMAs might direct the interment and marking of graves, they could ill afford to finance these ever-increasing projects on their own. From Winchester to Lynchburg, each community appealed to the solidarity of the South to raise funds to continue their work. In order to reach those sympathetic to their cause, each of the LMAs prepared circulars they sent to newspapers across the South requesting cooperation and aid. The FLMA's circular noted that Fredericksburg and the surrounding counties had been "stripped of enclosures and forests, desolated and impoverished" such that "we cannot, without aid guard [the Confederate] graves from exposure and possible desecration; we can only cover them with our native soil. And, with pious care, garland them with the wild flowers of the fields." But, the circular continued, the Ladies wished to do much more. "With the generous aid and cordial cooperation of those who have suffered less," the FLMA hoped to "purchase and adorn a cemetery" and to erect "some enduring tribute to the memory of our gallant dead." The group appealed to every state of the former Confederacy, observing that scarcely a town or a county was unrepresented on the city's battlefields. Towns and organizations from across the South contributed to Fredericksburg's cemetery fund. An anonymous gift of $20 in gold arrived from Mobile, Alabama, while the Ladies' Memorial Association of Montgomery, Alabama, offered the FLMA not only their cooperation in caring for the Alabama dead, but pledged to donate the proceeds from a charity ball held in Montgomery.[53]

If providing Christian burials motivated Virginia's women to organize LMAs, their most visible and popular activity was the celebration of memorial or decoration days. Although white Southerners celebrated these days in the spring as a sign of renewal and rebirth, each community chose their own symbolic date on which to gather. Fredericksburg, Lynchburg, and Oakwood in Richmond all selected May 10, the anniversary of Stonewall Jackson's death, for their sentimental tributes. The women of Hollywood agreed on May 31, the anniversary of the day Richmonders first heard the cannons of war. Petersburg's LMA chose June 9, the day on which the "grey haired sires and beardless youths" of the home guard defended the city until Lee's troops could arrive. Finally, Winchester's Ladies settled on June 6, the day the Valley's hero, General Turner Ashby, was killed.

Regardless of date, each group's Memorial Day tended to follow a similar pattern. The women of the LMAs would gather on the days preceding the event to make evergreen and flora arrangements and would ask young men or boys to do any physically toiling work, such as remounding. On Memorial Day, hundreds and even thousands of citizens gathered at some central location in town, perhaps a church or town hall, and then marched in procession to the cemetery, where the Ladies and children would decorate the graves with flowers and evergreens. Subsequently, orators chosen by the LMA would deliver prayers and evocative speeches. Even though the featured guests and speakers were always men, everyone understood that the LMAs ran the show—they selected the date, chose the orators, invited groups to participate in the procession, and even chose the musical selections.

Despite the omnipresent rhetoric of mourning at these Memorial Days, white Virginians knew they were treading on dangerous ground when they invoked the "sacred" memory of the Confederacy so soon after defeat and while Union troops still occupied their soil. On Lynchburg's first Memorial Day, May 10, 1866, the city newspaper noted that the services would "doubtless excite harsh and malignant remarks in certain quarters of the North, and be taken as evidence of a mutinous, malcontent spirit pervading our people." But, the writer maintained, "we are sure" that "this sentiment will for the main part be confined to men who took no active battle-part in the war." Northern soldiers, and perhaps their devoted wives and daughters, would surely recognize the need to honor the remains of those who had died "valiantly in the opposite ranks."[54] Indeed, ex-Confederates had every reason to suspect that the Union army and Northern press were closely monitoring their actions. In May 1866, the

Chicago Tribune denounced the Ladies' Memorial Association of Richmond for strewing flowers on the graves of the Confederate dead, charging that these women sought "to keep alive the political feeling of hostility to the Union."[55] But couched safely in the shroud of "motherly and sisterly undertaking," Southerners defended their actions. "This poor privilege is all that is left us now," they claimed.[56] The *Richmond Whig* likewise responded that "political significance is not attached to these funeral ceremonies in the South," as it was not the habit of Southern white women to form political conspiracies. Rather, the paper proclaimed, "if the men of the South contemplated treason and 'civil war,'" they would not put "forward their wives and daughters to do the dangerous work."[57] But for all their reasoning and justifications, Southern white men did just that.

Just a little more than a year after Mrs. Williams of Winchester had suggested a collective effort to reinter the dead, the town was planning its first official Memorial Day for June 6. General Turner Ashby had been one of the central Confederate heroes in the Shenandoah Valley, leading cavalry troops under Stonewall Jackson. On June 6, 1862, Ashby died during a Federal assault on the rear of a Confederate column retreating to Port Republic. Born in Fauquier County, Ashby's connection to Winchester was due solely to his cavalry's defense of the town through the first two years of war. Following his death, the Confederate military buried him in an elaborate funeral at Charlottesville's University Cemetery.[58]

On June 6, 1866, Winchester businesses closed while thousands of locals and visitors filled the town's streets for its inaugural Memorial Day. Three hundred former Confederates, primarily survivors of Stonewall Jackson's and Major General Arnold Elsey's brigades, were followed by fourteen young girls wearing white dresses and black sashes, accompanied by other citizens in a procession from the Episcopal Church to the new cemetery. Upon reaching the cemetery, the women and young girls decorated every grave, no matter how humble, with wreaths and garlands of fresh flowers and greenery. Finally, the crowd gathered to hear three speakers, all former Confederate majors, pay tribute to the fallen soldiers.[59] Surely Northern troops stationed in Winchester must have—or at least should have—frowned upon the large gathering of Southern sympathizers, not to mention the hundreds of ex-Confederate soldiers who paraded through town only a year after the war's end. But Winchester's men consciously framed the day's blatant displays of Confederate nationalism in the sphere of mourning women in order to avoid cries of treason from Northerners.

"The mothers and daughters of Virginia are the chief mourners and actors in these touching obsequies," one of the day's speakers, Colonel Uriel
Wright, proclaimed. For Wright and other former Confederates, the language of mourning and feminine virtue were virtually inseparable when
justifying tributes to their "lost cause." It was this rhetoric, if not full-
fledged belief, that allowed them to subtly protest not only the outcome of
the war, but the uncertainty of what a reconstructed South might look like
in those first years after Appomattox. Who knew what changes might lie
ahead? Already the region's labor and racial systems had been overturned.
By placing the responsibility for protecting the past in the firm but gentle
hands of women, white Southern men could claim that memorializing the
Confederacy was by no means a political gesture.[60]

Wright made sure that white Southerners, as well as any Northerners
that might be watching, understood that despite Confederate veterans'
support, these ceremonies were solely the work of the South's women.
"Mothers and daughters of Virginia," he exclaimed, "this noble enterprise
is your work. Scenes like this, rising up wherever our dead lie, gild with
melancholy light the desolation of the land. They took their origin in the
brains of no politician, no schemer, seeking individual distinction or plot-
ting the renewal of strife." Because this tribute had been born in the heart
of women, he argued, it could only be interpreted as true and pure. These
women certainly could not be viewed as traitorous—they were simply exhibiting the qualities nineteenth-century Victorian ideology attributed
to women: sentiment, emotion, and devotion to one's menfolk. In fact,
Wright declared that Southern white women "were not political casu-
ists." They had not paused "to enquire whether the teachings of Jefferson,
Madison, or Macon furnished the true interpretation of the Constitution, and correctly marked the boundaries of State and Federal powers."[61]
Just as members of the Southern Whig party had done since the 1830s,
postbellum Virginians agreed that women were naturally "disinterested"
in politics and therefore their motives must be "pure."[62] If women were
not political, then by extension their actions could not be construed as
such. Therefore, memorial activities, clearly within the province of female
mourning, were no threat to sectional reunion.

In continually denying women's political nature, Wright simultaneously acknowledged the very political nature of their work. During the
war, he said, women had supported the efforts of their fathers, husbands,
sons, and lovers—implying that women merely followed their men's lead.
Yet he noted that these same women were "bound by every heart tie to

one cause," thereby acknowledging white women's sense of nationalism. The ideal of "Confederate womanhood" had helped to ensure the rise of Southern nationalism. As historian Elizabeth Varon has pointed out, Confederate propagandists held that women were purer patriots than men. Because of women's superior moral virtue, the ideal held, women must possess a greater love and devotion to country than their men. As such, it was women's special role to accept the loss of their husbands and sons in defense of Southern independence.[63] As they had done during the war years, these Southern white women proudly displayed their Confederate nationalism through their memorial activities.

If Winchester's first Memorial Day in June 1866 should have been enough to raise Northern eyebrows, then the elaborate reburial of General Turner Ashby and three other Confederate officers the following autumn should have been seen as outright treason. Believing that Winchester rather than Charlottesville would be a more appropriate burial location for Winchester's dashing hero, the WLMA proposed that Ashby and his brother, killed fighting on Kelly Island, Maryland, in 1861, be reinterred in Stonewall Cemetery.[64] In early October the bodies of both Ashbys were disinterred. Turner Ashby's body was placed in an elaborate coffin paid for by the "patriotic women" of Jefferson County, West Virginia. Made of black walnut and covered with black cloth of the finest fabric, it was, the newspaper noted, "nearly enveloped in silver fringe and platings." The brothers' bodies were transported first to Charlestown, West Virginia, and then on to Winchester, where they joined the remains of two other comrades on the night of October 24. The final procession included former military officers and local officials. What followed must have been a spectacle reminiscent of Confederate military parades through towns during the war.[65]

On Thursday morning, October 25, nearly ten thousand Valley residents and guests gathered in the small town awaiting the solemn burial of the Confederate officers and the dedication of Stonewall Cemetery.[66] Morning trains on the Winchester and Potomac line brought eleven passenger cars crowded with anxious spectators from Virginia and Maryland. Even West Virginia was well represented by the "fair women and brave men" of Jefferson and Berkeley counties. According to the local paper they ignored "their unnatural separation which has, temporarily we trust, deprived them of their birth rights as Virginians," and "gathered around the tombs of the Confederate dead."[67] But if men and women alike thronged the bustling streets of this quaint Valley town, all recognized the vital role the fairer sex played in the day's events. "An early visit to the cemetery revealed to us the fact that, while man had shown energy and industry in preparing and mounding the graves of the dead, the hand and heart of woman had been enlisted in the decoration of the sacred ground," noted one observer. Women from West Virginia to North Carolina had contributed to the affair. A collection of flowers sent by the LMA of Sherpherdstown and an elegant floral cross, a gift of Ladies present from North Carolina, decorated Ashby's grave. The monuments marking the location of the lots appropriated to each state for the burial of the dead had been "wreathed and twined with evergreens, myrtle, and cedar, whilst the numberless bouquets resting on the hills marking the repository of the heroic dead, told plainly the sympathizing daughters of Virginia had been thus early at the tomb."[68] Like Mary Magdalene at Christ's tomb, the women gathered to witness the Confederacy arise from the ashes of defeat crowned in glory.

The Winchester LMA and their sisters from surrounding areas, however, served a more valuable purpose than mere decorators. As had been the case only months before at Winchester's Memorial Day, women once again proved to be an important political symbol for the ex-Confederacy's message of triumph through defeat. As the keynote speaker at the dedication, former governor Henry A. Wise spoke neither of mourning nor reunion. Instead he encouraged the crowd to look to the dead for the power and strength to deal with surrender and submission. He told them to ask themselves what the mighty Stonewall would do in their situation. "Would he have praised proclamations of peace! Peace! When there is no peace?" he asked. "Would he not have demanded as lawful rights the withdrawal of military force and of Freedman's Bureau, and the restoration of Civil Rule and the writ of Habeas Corpus?" Wise proclaimed that Jackson would have never disavowed the cause for which his comrades died. Finally, with the Federal troops watching from across the field, he shouted "A lost cause! If lost it was false; if true, it is not lost!" As William Blair has pointed out, Turner Ashby was reinterred in a town in which he had never resided, in a cemetery named after Jackson (who also had never lived in Winchester, nor was he buried there), at a dedication that featured a recalcitrant rebel such as Wise. How could Northerners not look upon the spectacle in the Valley as anything other than pro-Confederate political behavior?[69] Surely the U.S. Burial Corps encamped in the adjacent national cemetery must have felt dismayed.[70]

Apparently Northerners and the Republican government could tolerate only so much praise for the defeated Confederacy, even in the tender hands of Southern women. Following the elaborate ceremonies throughout Virginia in 1866, the federal government cracked down on open expressions of Confederate celebrations the next year. In 1867, the commanding federal officer in Lynchburg prohibited H. Rives Pollard, Esq., from delivering a lecture regarding the chivalry of the South during war. That spring the local LMA chose only to gather at the cemetery to deposit flowers on the graves. The Oakwood Memorial Association refrained altogether from organizing a decoration day.[71] And although nearly sixty thousand Richmonders turned out to place flowers on the graves at Hollywood, the HMA likewise held no formal procession and prohibited orations in eulogy of the dead.[72] But even without the parades and speeches, one Richmond resident noted that if the affair "had not been under the control of the Ladies," then a "thousand bayonets would have bristled to prevent the celebration."[73] Despite the strictures implemented by the federal troops stationed throughout the commonwealth during the spring of 1867, a Lynchburg paper concluded that "we yet have left us the right to love and to mourn"[74]

Although Appomattox signified the death of the Confederate nation, it did not extinguish feelings of Confederate womanhood or Confederate sentiment. Even in the aftermath of defeat, Southern white men realized that their women played a pivotal role in maintaining and recreating Confederate identity through elaborate reburial efforts and memorial celebrations. White Southerners recognized the potency of these women's organizations that managed to attract hundreds of members as early as 1865 and 1866 and collect thousands of dollars from a war-torn region. And while these middle- and upper-class white women may not have engaged in the public debate concerning the political role they played in the occupied South, they certainly believed that their efforts were vital to preserving the memory of the Confederate dead. Behind their Southern drawl and sweet demeanor, Virginia's upper- and middle-class white women provided a space—cemeteries—within which defeated Southerners might reclaim some bit of honor and respect. It had been the women who sponsored elaborate Confederate tributes, such as Ashby's reinterment, and women who had staged symbolic rituals such as decoration days. It was the women, in their cloak of feminine mourning and weakness, who triumphed in their efforts to fashion a positive memory of the defeated Confederacy and maintain their own image as true and faithful "ladies." As the *Winchester Times* gushed in the fall of 1866, "their labors have been crowned with success, and in preparing sepulchers for the dead, they have erected monuments to themselves."[75]

Notes

1. Throughout the late nineteenth and early twentieth centuries, representatives from Ladies' Memorial Associations (LMAs) across the South debated which group had been the first to organize. My research suggests that Winchester was at least the first LMA in Virginia, if not in the South. In addition, these same groups disputed who first celebrated Memorial Days. For more on this debate, see David W. Blight, *Race and Reunion: The Civil War in American Memory* (Cambridge, Mass.: Belknap Press of Harvard University Press, 2001), and the Mildred Rutherford Scrapbook Collection, Museum of the Confederacy, Richmond, Va. (hereafter cited as MOC).

2. *History of the Confederated Memorial Associations of the South* (New Orleans: Graham Press, 1904), 314–15; Frederick Morton, *The Story of Winchester Virginia: The Oldest Town in the Shenandoah Valley* (Strasburg, Va.: Shenandoah Publishing House, 1925), 247.

3. See Ann Douglas, *The Feminization of American Culture* (London: Papermac, 1996), 200–226. Douglas argues that mourning rituals were a source of authority for women and ministers, thereby widening their sphere of influence.

4. Virginia was selected for this study because of its prominence during the years of the Confederacy and its significance as a bastion of early Lost Cause rhetoric and leaders. The cities of Winchester, Fredericksburg, Petersburg, Lynchburg, and Richmond were chosen because of the diversity of their wartime and postwar experiences. Several other communities in Virginia, including Portsmouth (1866), Manassas (1867), Front Royal (1868), and Danville (1872), established Ladies' Memorial Associations in the years after the war. Likewise, women in states throughout the former Confederacy, notably North Carolina, Georgia, and Alabama, formed Ladies' Memorial Associations. *History of the Confederated Memorial Associations.*

5. The standard definition of the Lost Cause claims that in the postwar climate of economic, racial, and gender uncertainty, many white Southerners began to reshape, reimagine, and herald the "true" story of the antebellum South. Rather than forsaking the defeated Confederacy, they created and romanticized the "Old South," thus factually and chronologically distorting the way in which the past would be remembered. This nostalgia for the past accompanied a collective forgetting of slavery while defining Reconstruction as a period of "Yankee aggression" and black "betrayal." The Lost Cause provided a sense of relief to white Southerners who feared being dishonored by defeat, while its rituals and rhetoric celebrated the memory of personal sacrifice in a region rapidly experiencing change and disorder. Fictional stories of the plantation past blurred the concept of time, as the past mingled with the present and yet remained isolated in "history" by the war. (C. Vann Woodward, *Origins of the New South 1877–1913* [Baton Rouge: Louisiana State University Press, 1951], 154–55; Grace Elizabeth

Hale, *Making Whiteness: The Culture of Segregation in the South, 1890–1940* [New York: Pantheon Books, 1998], 47–49; Gaines M. Foster, *Ghosts of the Confederacy: Defeat, the Lost Cause, and the Emergence of the New South* [New York: Oxford University Press, 1987], 3–10; Pete Daniel, *Lost Revolutions: The South in the 1950s* [Chapel Hill: University of North Carolina Press, 2000], 26.)

6. On Confederate memory and the Lost Cause, see William Blair, *Cities of the Dead: Contesting the Memory of the Civil War in the South, 1865–1914* (Chapel Hill: University of North Carolina Press, 2004); Karen L. Cox, *Dixie's Daughters: The United Daughters of the Confederacy and the Preservation of Confederate Culture* (Gainesville: University Press of Florida, 2003); Catherine W. Bishir, "'A Strong Force of Ladies': Women, Politics, and Confederate Memorial Associations in Nineteenth-Century Raleigh," in *Southern Built: American Architecture, Regional Practice* (Charlottesville: University of Virginia Press, 2006), 215–53; David W. Blight, *Race and Reunion: The Civil War in American History* (Cambridge, Mass.: Harvard University Press, 2001); Gary W. Gallagher and Alan T. Nolan, ed. *The Myth of the Lost Cause and Civil War History* (Bloomington: Indiana University Press, 2000); Cecelia Elizabeth O'Leary, *To Die For: The Paradox of American Patriotism* (Princeton, N.J.: Princeton University Press, 1999), 122–23; Kirk Savage, *Standing Soldiers, Kneeling Slaves: Race, War, and Monument in Nineteenth-Century America* (Princeton, N.J.: Princeton University Press, 1997); W. Fitzhugh Brundage, "White Women and the Politics of Historical Memory in the New South," in *Jumpin' Jim Crow: Southern Politics from Civil War to Civil Rights*, ed. Glenda Gilmore, Bryant Simon, and Jane Daily (Princeton, N.J.: Princeton University Press, 2000), 115–39; Hale, *Making Whiteness*, 79–80; Parrott, "Love Makes Memory Eternal," 219–38; Foster, *Ghosts*; Charles Reagan Wilson, *Baptized in Blood: The Religion of the Lost Cause* (Athens: University of Georgia Press, 1980); C. Vann Woodward, *The Strange Career of Jim Crow* (New York: Oxford University Press, 1974); Rollin G. Osterweis, *The Myth of the Lost Cause, 1865–1900* (Hamden, Conn.: Archon Books, 1973).

7. Foster, *Ghosts*, 36–62; Brundage, "White Women and the Politics of Historical Memory in the New South," 115.

8. See Foster, *Ghosts of the Confederacy*, for the argument that in the 1870s the Lost Cause movement was led by veterans and members of the officer corps, primarily from Virginia. He contends that their anti-Northern tone and elitist attitude discouraged most white Southerners from joining. For argument similar to the author's, see Bishir, "A Strong Force of Ladies." Cox argues in *Dixie's Daughters* that the United Daughters of the Confederacy aspired to "transform military defeat into a political and cultural victory, where states' rights and white supremacy remained intact" (1). I am arguing, however, that their predecessors, the LMAs, had already established this transformation by the time of the UDC's organization in 1894.

9. Memoir of Sallie Brock Putnam, 1867, in *Richmond during the War: Four Years of Personal Observation* (New York, N.Y.: G. W. Carleton & Co., 1867), 389.

10. Lucy Muse Walton Fletcher diary, April 12, 1865, Perkins Library, Duke University, Durham, N.C. (hereafter cited as DU).

11. Garland R. Quarles, *Occupied Winchester, 1861–1865: Prepared for Farmers and Merchants National Bank, Winchester, Virginia* (Stephens City, Va.: Commercial Press, 1976; reprint, Winchester, Va.: Winchester-Frederick County Historical Society, 1991), 123; Morton, *The Story of Winchester*, 193.

12. William Blair, "Barbarians at Fredericksburg's Gates, The Impact of the Union Army on Civilians," in *The Fredericksburg Campaign*, ed. Gary Gallagher (Chapel Hill: University of North Carolina Press, 1995), 161.

13. W. Asbury Christian, *Lynchburg and Its People* (Lynchburg: J. P. Bell Company, Printers, 1900), 241.

14. William Blair, *Virginia's Private War: Feeding Body and Soul in the Confederacy, 1861–1865* (New York: Oxford University Press, 1998), 136.

15. George W. Munford to Elizabeth T. Munford, April 28, 1865, Munford-Ellis Papers, DU.

16. *Lynchburg Daily Virginian*, April 1865 (hereafter cited as *LDV*); Michael Chesson, *Richmond after the War, 1865–1890* (Richmond, Va.: Virginia State Library, 1981), 57.

17. *LDV*, June 6, 1865; Henderson, *War at the Door*, 143–48; Foster, *Ghosts*, 20–21; Dan T. Carter, *When the War Was Over: The Failure of Self-Reconstruction in the South* (Baton Rouge: Louisiana State University Press, 1985).

18. Emmy Wellford to brother, Phil, April 20, 1865, John Rutherfoord Papers, DU.

19. Elizabeth Munford to George Munford, May 2, 1865, May 18, 1865, Munford-Ellis Papers, DU.

20. George Rable, *Civil Wars: Women and the Crisis of Southern Nationalism* (Urbana: University of Illinois Press, 1989), 221–37; Drew Faust, *Mothers of Invention: Women of the Slaveholding South in the American Civil War* (Chapel Hill: University of North Carolina Press, 1996), 248–57.

21. For explanation of the Southern Lady see Anne Scott Firor, *The Southern Lady: From Pedestal to Politics, 1830–1930* (Charlottesville: University Press of Virginia, 1970).

22. Suzanne Lebsock, preface to *A Woman's War: Southern Women, Civil War, and the Confederate Legacy*, ed. Edward D. Campbell and Kym S. Rice (Museum of the Confederacy, Richmond, Va., and the University Press of Virginia, Charlottesville, Va., 1996).

23. *LDV*, April 20, 1866; Christian, *Lynchburg and Its People*, 241; Rable, *Civil Wars*, 236.

24. Mary Cabell diary, April 9, 1865, Early Family Papers, Virginia Historical Society, Richmond, Va.

25. Judith Brokenbrough McGuire, quoted in Katharine M. Jones, *Heroines of Dixie: Confederate Women Tell Their Story of the War* (Indianapolis and New York: Bobbs-Merrill Company, 1955).

26. Lucy Muse Walton Fletcher diary, DU.

27. Quoted in Blair, *Virginia's Private War,* 135.

28. Lucy Muse Walton Fletcher diary, DU.

29. Emmy Wellford to brother, Phil, April 20, 1865, DU; Mrs. Charles Ellis Sr. to unknown, April 1865, Munford-Ellis Papers, DU.

30. Nina Silber, *Romance of Reunion: Northerners and the South, 1865–1900* (Chapel Hill: University of North Carolina Press, 1993), 26–29.

31. Morton, *The Story of Winchester,* 247–48; *History of the Confederated Memorial Associations,* 316.

32. Rable, *Civil Wars,* 240–64.

33. Stonewall Cemetery Records, Winchester Frederick County Historical Society, Winchester, Va. (hereafter cited as WFCHS).

34. Morton, *The Story of Winchester,* 248; *History of the Confederate Memorial Associations,* 316.

35. During the first week of May, Northern school teachers in Richmond had tended the graves of Federal soldiers on Belle Isle and in Hollywood (*New York Daily News,* June 5, 1866).

36. Davidson's father, Thomas D. Davidson, head of the Davidson School, along with other prominent businessmen, had been taken captive following the June 9, 1864, standoff between the old men and young boys left to defend the city and Federal cavalrymen. Henderson, *War at the Door,* 110; Davidson, *Cullings from the Confederacy* (Washington, D.C.: Rufus H. Darby Printing Co., 1903), 19. It was the graves decorated by Miss Nora and her students on June 9, 1867, that Mrs. John A. Logan saw on her visit to Petersburg in 1868. "It was from this celebration that Mrs. Logan, wife of the gallant Federal general, who was in Petersburg at that time, gained her inspiration which caused the National Decoration Day which is now in existence" (*Petersburg Progress-Index,* February 11, 1929).

37. *LDV,* April 24–25, 1866.

38. The April 25 edition of the *LDV* issued a call by "several Ladies" to meet and take into consideration "and adopt the most speedy and effective measures for inclosing the graves of the Confederate soldiers" buried in the city. The newspaper followed the announcement with an endorsement of the proposal, noting that the thousands of graves were exposed to the elements and that this was "a shame, and a reflection on the people of Lynchburg"—"a fitting work lies before the Ladies. We doubt not they will do it well and promptly." The next day the paper noted that "every lady ought to be glad to do something towards an object which appeals so warmly in their sympathies and to humanity." Mary H. Mitchell, *Hollywood Cemetery: The History of a Southern Shrine* (Richmond, Va.: Virginia State Library, 1985), 26, 64; number of Lynchburg women determined by list of names in *LDV,* April 28, 1866.

39. Petersburg Ladies' Memorial Association (hereafter cited as PLMA) Minutes, May 6, 1866, Library of Virginia, Richmond, Va. (hereafter cited as LOV).

40. Hollywood Memorial Association (hereafter cited as HMA) Minutes, MOC; Mitchell, *Hollywood Cemetery,* 64; *Lynchburg News,* April 20, 1866.

41. "A leaf from the Past: from the records of the Ladies' Memorial Association of Fredericksburg, VA," pamphlet, Central Rappahannock Regional Library.

42. Robert Hodge, ed., *Confederate Memorial Days* (Fredericksburg, Va.: R. A. Hodge, 1987), 1.

43. *LDV,* April 24, 1866.

44. Mitchell, *Hollywood Cemetery,* 72–73.

45. Karen Rae Mehaffey, *The After-Life: Mourning Rituals and the Mid-Victorians* (Pipestone, Minn.: Laser Writing Publishing, 1993).

46. National cemeteries in Virginia include: Alexandria, Balls Bluff, City Point, Cold Harbor, Culpeper, Danville, Fort Harrison, Glendale, Hampton, Richmond, Seven Pines, Staunton, and Winchester. While the national cemetery at Winchester was dedicated April 8, 1866, the deed for the property was not drawn until December 1, 1870, when Jacob Baker formally conveyed the property to the U.S. government. The cemetery contains the bodies of Union soldiers from the battlefields of Winchester, New Market, Front Royal, Snickers Gap, Harpers Ferry, Martinsburg, and Romney. There are 4,491 Union soldiers buried in the cemetery, 2,396 of whom are unknown. Quarles, *Occupied Winchester,* 130; Morton, *The Story of Winchester,* 249–50.

47. PLMA Minutes, July 11, 1866, July 18, 1866, October 12, 1866, October 16, 1866, LOV; *History of the Confederated Memorial Associations,* 288–90.

48. Minutes of the Fredericksburg Ladies' Memorial Association (hereafter cited as FLMA minutes), June 28, 1866, July 26, 1866, September 6, 1866, October 1866, LOV.

49. Oakwood Memorial Association Minutes (hereafter cited as OMA Minutes), MOC, 1897.

50. OMA Minutes, MOC.

51. *LDV,* April 27, 1866.

52. The men named included Colonel William Brown, Colonel D. G. Potts, and Captain L. L. Marks. Both Potts's and Marks's wives were members of the PLMA. PLMA Minutes, May 30, 1867, LOV.

53. FLMA minutes, May 24, 1866, LOV; Silvanus Jackson Quinn, *The History of the City of Fredericksburg,* (Richmond, Va.: Hermitage Press, 1908), 186–87; Other anonymous donations poured in during the summer and fall of 1866 ranging from $5 to $100. FLMA minutes, June 28, 1866, July 26, 1866, September 6, 1866, October 1866, LOV. In Petersburg, as soon as a central site for a cemetery had been secured, the PLMA prepared a circular appealing to the legislatures of all the Southern states requesting aid from the people of the South for the cemetery, which now held nearly four thousand soldiers.

54. As early as a mere twelve months after Lee's surrender, white Southerners were already employing the rhetoric of what would come to be the primary tenants of the "Lost Cause" by the 1890s. The Lynchburg paper argued that Confederate armies had fought well—as had the Union—and therefore, both sides should honor the other's dead. In fact, he noted that "the southern people would indeed

deserve eternal dishonor were they to fail in paying all becoming consideration to their illustrious dead" (*LDV,* May 10, 1866).

55. *New York Times,* May 21, 1866.

56. *LDV,* April 28, 1866, May 14, 1866.

57. *New York Times,* May 21, 1866.

58. Blair, *Cities of the Dead.*

59. *Winchester Times,* June 13, 1866.

60. Ibid.

61. Ibid.

62. For explanation of antebellum Southern white women and politics, see Elizabeth Varon, *We Mean to Be Counted: White Women and Politics in Antebellum Virginia* (Chapel Hill: University of North Carolina Press, 1998).

63. For discussion of Southern white women and Southern nationalism, see: Faust, *Mothers of Invention;* Rable, *Civil Wars;* and Varon, *We Mean to Be Counted,* 4, 137–68. Varon argues that Confederate womanhood represented "not only the beginning point but an end point in Southern women's political history, the end of a long and complicated transition from partisanship to sectionalism to Southern nationalism as the dominant theme of political life" (138).

64. The WLMA asked the Ashbys' surviving sisters for permission to disinter the bodies and rebury them in Winchester, and the sisters consented. Blair, *Cities of the Dead.*

65. Reverend James B. Averitt, *The Memoirs of General Turner Ashby and His Compeers* (Baltimore: Selby & Dulany, 1867), 243–55; Stonewall Cemetery Records, WFCHS; *Winchester Times,* October 31, 1866.

66. The October 31, 1866, *Winchester Times* estimated that ten thousand people attended the ceremony; however, the *New York Times*'s correspondent (October 29, 1866) estimated only four to five thousand people participated.

67. *Winchester Times,* October 31, 1866.

68. Ibid.

69. Blair, *Cities of the Dead.*

70. Morton, *The Story of Winchester,* 249; *New York Times,* October 29, 1866.

71. OMA Minutes, April 30, 1867, MOC.

72. *New York Times,* June 3, 1867.

73. Quote copied from Blair, *Cities of the Dead.*

74. *LDV,* May 1, 1867, May 11, 1867.

75. *Winchester Times,* October 31, 1866.

Reconciliation in Reconstruction Virginia

Susanna Michele Lee

Once the fighting on the battlefield ended, black and white Virginians turned their attention to adjusting to the changes wrought by the Civil War. In the aftermath of the conflict, Virginians confronted the monumental tasks of reconfiguring race relations without slavery, restoring farms and businesses to their former productivity, and renewing relations with the federal government. While undertaking these tasks, Virginians reflected upon the war in light of their postwar circumstances. Confederate defeat, the preservation of the Union, and the abolition of slavery prompted Virginians to assess their opinions on the war and decipher its ultimate meaning.

How did Virginians make sense of the Civil War during Reconstruction? Most white Virginians recognized the need to reconcile with the federal government for the sake of resuming peaceful relations and rebuilding the war-torn South. In seeking the benefits of postwar citizenship, white Southerners were forced to conciliate Northerners. Despite these compromises, they articulated an interpretation of the war that attempted to take into account their particular experiences as Southerners. Black Virginians, in contrast, resorted to fewer compromises in their representations of the Civil War.

The fighting had ended on the battlefield, but the struggle over the interpretation of the war had just begun. Though many public figures asserted that states' rights principles rather than the preservation of slavery had spurred the South to war, private citizens in the South focused on the institution as the issue in contention between the sections. But quite often, for the sake of reconciliation, Northerners and Southerners avoided a debate over the causes of the war altogether. Whether they discussed the institution of slavery or not, both Northerners and Southerners contested the memory and the meaning of the war in order to shape the contours of postwar politics and the direction of the reunited nation.

In the postwar South, the federal government held the preponderance of power. In particular, federal officials in the South required Southerners to demonstrate their willingness to accept the dominion of the federal government in exchange for the rights of citizenship, such as voting and office holding. But the government also demanded loyalty in exchange for benefits of citizenship, directly impinging upon Southerners' day-to-day existence, including the ability to secure rations to survive, apply for licenses for certain occupations, receive compensation for lost property, and halt confiscation proceedings. Virginians who wished to resume their everyday lives in the aftermath of the war found that they had to reconcile, or at least pretend to reconcile, with the federal government to do so. Amnesty applications submitted by admitted Confederates and Southern Claims Commission petitions submitted by self-identified Unionists chronicle the process of reconciliation. These documents reveal the debate and dialogue between and among Northerners and Southerners over the meaning of the Civil War.

White Southerners who had supported the Confederacy sought pardon and amnesty to restore their relations with the federal government. In May 1865, President Andrew Johnson offered general amnesty to Southerners, except fourteen classes of prominent Confederates. Johnson required Southerners who were denied amnesty under his fourteen exceptions to submit individual petitions. Approximately fifteen thousand former Confederates followed this course of action. Johnson imposed only two conditions on Southerners who desired to reestablish their rights of citizenship in the Union. First, he required that Confederates pledge an oath to support, protect, and defend the Constitution of the United States, and, second, that they pledge to support all laws and proclamations concerning the emancipation of slaves. In this manner, Johnson required Confederates to accept the defeat of secession and the abolition of slavery as permanent realities stemming from the war. In their petitions for pardons, former secessionists in Virginia just barely met Johnson's requirements. For the sake of regaining their rights of citizenship, former secessionists conceded certain points to appease their Northern victors, but they maintained clear limits in their concessions.[1]

Virginians who requested pardons were willing to compromise on President Johnson's first requirement. Johnson's oath required no repudiation of the doctrine of secession. Nevertheless, many Virginians who requested pardons asserted that they had initially opposed secession. Thomas C. M. Anderson "honestly and bitterly" opposed the "dogma of secession," which he condemned as a "political heresy." More commonly, pardon petitioners refrained from commenting upon constitutional questions and instead identified secession as unwise and disastrous. William C. Allen denounced secession as "the greatest calamity that could have befallen the southern people." In fact, many white Virginians referred to the war not as "the war between the states" or "the war of Northern aggression," as they would in later years, but as "the unfortunate war." In the aftermath of Confederate defeat, with the emancipation of Virginia's nearly half million slaves and the devastation of the state's landscape and economy, former Confederates could readily make the argument that secession did indeed seem an imprudent and destructive course.[2]

Though white Virginians repudiated secession in their petitions, they also emphasized their sympathy with the Southern people and the Southern cause. Joseph R. Anderson presented himself as a reluctant secessionist. He originally opposed secession because he thought that "all differences between north and south ought to have been settled amicably within the Union," but "I would consider it dishonorable to ignore the fact that I went with my state, sympathized in the cause of the south and aided it to the extent of my ability." Beyond questions of honor, former Confederates who did not honestly admit that they "went with their state" ran the risk of being challenged by Unionist neighbors or federal officials. Most pardon petitioners asserted that they had initially opposed secession, but admitted that they had subsequently supported the Confederacy.[3]

Even in their petitions for pardon, a few Virginian secessionists avoided all concessions to the federal government. These stalwarts rejected any renunciation of the doctrine of secession and represented their actions as justifiable. Robert A. Banks, for example, refused to identify secession as unconstitutional, or even unwise. During the war, Banks concluded that his "beloved State" of Virginia had been justified in exercising "her" sovereign powers by waging war in response to the "imminent peril" of Northern invasion. By positioning Virginia as the innocent party, Banks shifted responsibility for the war to the federal government. Consequently, Banks denied that he had been a "traitor or a rebel," thereby challenging the legitimacy of the president's requirement that Confederates request pardon. Samuel Andrews, like Banks, also followed the dictates of his state. After the approval of secession by the Virginia convention and the ratification of the ordinance by Virginia's voters, Andrews considered it "my duty to sustain the constituted authorities of the people." Other white Virginians who shared the beliefs of Banks and Andrews simply refused to ask the federal government for pardon for actions they believed had been just.[4]

Still, uncompromising secessionists recognized that their attempt to establish sovereignty had collapsed. Banks acknowledged that "his State failed to consummate her attempt at secession and separate independence" and even resigned himself to the fact that "now her citizens are subjected to certain pains and penalties." Other former Confederates, like Thomas G. Turner, declared themselves "determined to do all in my power to promote harmony and peace in the Union." Whether or not Confederate defeat settled the constitutionality of secession, pardon petitioners recognized that the Civil War had rendered secession a dead issue in practical terms.[5]

On President Johnson's second requirement, most former slaveholders merely repeated his required oath and acknowledged abolition, but some emphasized their willingness to abide by emancipation. In going beyond President Johnson's requirements, these white Virginians asserted their readiness to compromise with the federal government. A few slaveholding Virginians even claimed to welcome the emancipation of slaves. P. H. Aylett "cheerfully" pledged to "renounce and disclose all right title interest and claim, whatsoever to any one all slaves now and heretofore possessed by me." Few slaveholders, however, greeted emancipation as "cheerfully" as Aylett. In exchange for his pardon, Elijah Baker simply "consent[ed]" to the emancipation of his fifteen slaves and disavowed the restoration of slavery in Virginia. Though important symbolically, in practical terms these actions did not mark much of a concession. In accepting the emancipation of slaves, white Virginians merely acknowledged wartime and postwar realities. Philip St. George Ambler noted that he had been the owner of a large number of slaves, whom "with my assent are free and will continue so." Ambler, however, had little choice but to assent in his slaves' freedom, as many of them had escaped to the federal lines during the war or, as Ambler termed it, were "carried off by the Fed. Forces." These former slaveholders asserted their willingness to accept emancipation in exchange for peace.[6]

A minority of pardon petitioners took their acceptance of emancipation one step further. They attempted to distance themselves from the issue of slavery, which they recognized as the cause of the war. In explaining his opposition to secession, William B. Allegre emphasized that "I have never owned any interest in slaves." Moreover, Allegre asserted that he had "always believed the institution of slavery detrimental to the true happiness and prosperity of the people of the Union." He assured President Johnson that "of course am now pleased to know that the institution has been forever abolished in this country."[7]

These Virginians drew upon the antebellum Southern argument that slavery had been a necessary evil which had been imposed upon the South, but which could not be safely eliminated. Some white Virginians before the war may have regretted the institution of slavery, but they saw no method for relieving the state. Once the federal government had enacted emancipation, former slaveholders could console themselves that their slave dependents had been more of a burden than a benefit. Nonslaveholding Virginians, with the prospect of future slaveholdings dashed, could also pronounce slavery as antithetical to their interests. In any case, though some pardon petitioners identified slavery as adverse to the interests of Virginia, they did not push the boundaries of Southern sentiment by questioning Southerners' constitutional rights to their slave property.

While there were a few exceptions, most former Confederates who petitioned for pardons were willing to concede the impracticality of secession and the reality of emancipation. On the other hand, few pardon petitioners openly called into question the constitutionality of secession or slavery. In these actions—or more precisely, inactions—white Virginians mirrored the sentiments underlying discussions within state constitutional conventions across the South. Convention delegates fought over the precise wording of their repudiation of secession and their acceptance of emancipation. On the secession issue, most conventions declared the ordinances "null and void," rather than repealing them, which some delegates feared could be interpreted as a criticism of antebellum Southern leaders. On the slavery issue, delegates opposed any language that would later prevent Southerners from obtaining compensation for their lost slave property or would suggest that slavery had been unconstitutional. Most former Confederate states adopted clauses that simply recognized emancipation as an established fact.[8]

In the end, former secessionists' concession of defeat proved enough to regain citizenship in the Union. President Johnson liberally granted pardons to Confederates initially excluded from his general amnesty.

Johnson sometimes granted hundreds of pardons in a single day, indicating that the very act of requesting pardon was sufficient for its bestowal. With his pardon policy and other actions, Johnson incurred the wrath of Republicans. Nevertheless, by the end of 1868 he had pardoned all former Confederates.[9]

While Virginians who requested presidential pardons acknowledged that they had supported the Confederacy, petitioners before the Southern Claims Commission swore that they had been loyal to the federal government during the Civil War. Johnson proved relatively lenient in accepting white Southerners into the reunited nation, but the claims commissioners, under the oversight of the House of Representatives, proved less forgiving. The commission provided an even more contentious forum to debate the meaning of the war and the requirements for loyal citizenship.

Congress created the commission in 1871 to award compensation to "loyal" Southerners for their wartime losses. With this action, congressmen shifted from an assumption that all Southerners had been Confederates toward a recognition that some Southerners had supported the Union. The year 1871 also marked the first congressional session with all the former Confederate states represented. In addition, the Liberal Republican movement indicated that growing numbers of Northerners favored the end of Reconstruction. The establishment of the commission, then, represented another step by the federal government in the growing movement toward reconciliation with the South.[10]

The commissioners placed secession at the center of their interpretation of the Civil War. They primarily viewed the war as a constitutional crisis. The commissioners undoubtedly recognized that disagreements over slavery prompted secession, but from a legal standpoint they identified secession as the ultimate cause of the Civil War. As a result, the commissioners only rarely asked claimants about slavery or slaveholding. They did not ask petitioners if they had owned slaves, if they had supported or opposed the institution of slavery, or if they had approved or disapproved of the Emancipation Proclamation. Instead, the commissioners asked claimants where they had stood on the secession issue.

As Northerners, the commissioners assumed their duties with certain presuppositions about Southern Unionists. They initially employed strict standards for the proof of Southern loyalty. First, they identified voluntary residence in a seceded state as evidence of disloyalty to the Union and required claimants to disprove this presumption. Second, they demanded so-called iron-clad loyalty, which mandated adherence to the Union from secession to surrender. The commissioners, who were based in Washington, D.C., formulated a series of questions for the use of special commissioners in Southern communities to test claimants on their loyalties during the war. These questions concentrated on claimants' voting record and military service, revealing that the commissioners envisioned the Southern Unionist as a white man who had voted against secession at the ballot box and had fought secession on the battlefield. The commissioners also queried claimants on a plethora of disloyal acts and only excused these acts if they had been performed under the threat of physical coercion.[11]

Virginians prompted the commissioners to reevaluate these standards for loyalty in the South. Because Virginians submitted the second largest number of claims following Tennessee, the experiences and perspectives of Virginians were well represented among the claims. More important, the commissioners formulated their policies in the first four years of their tenure, from 1871 to 1874, during which claims from Virginia dominated the docket in three out of four of these years. Not only did the commissioners decide more claims from Virginia in their early years, but they probably personally examined more claimants from Virginia than any other state. They required that Southerners with large claims testify in Washington, rather than record their depositions with their local special commissioner. Because of their proximity to Washington, Virginians numbered among the earliest Southerners to appear before the commissioners. Rigorous examination of claimants and their witnesses and the dialogue made possible by their physical presence provided the commissioners a better opportunity to appreciate the position of the Southern Unionist than the reading of a deposition allowed.[12]

Testimony by Virginians convinced the commissioners to alter their assumptions about the experience of war in the South. Once they began reviewing evidence from claimants and their witnesses, the commissioners realized that they had set too strict a test for Southern loyalty. After exposure to stories of Virginians' war experiences, the commissioners drastically altered their attitude toward the issue of duress. Claimant after claimant told harrowing tales of terror and violence meted out by Confederates intent upon enforcing unanimity on the question of secession. The commissioners learned that the harassment suffered by Southerners "is rarely of actual force." Instead, the commissioners discovered that "the real imminent danger of injury" originated with the "terrorism and intimidation" of "constant and oppressive apprehension of lawless violence."

They recognized that "to escape these perils, men who were at heart true friends of the Union felt compelled to appear friendly to the confederate cause and to do disloyal acts." Under this new policy, the commissioners excused a disloyal act made under such conditions if the claimant otherwise had proven himself or herself loyal to the Union. Though the commissioners were not willing to adopt a Southern perspective on the Civil War, they were willing to grant some concessions to Southern experiences.[13]

Self-identified Unionists found common ground with the commissioners in their condemnation of secession. In response to the commissioners' questions, claimants generally repudiated secession. Richard Ennis identified secession as an attempt to subvert proper governance. He argued that, despite Lincoln's positions on the issues of the day, "the president has a right to his office, the same as any other president." Martin Ellis opposed secession for more practical reasons. He believed that "we had better stay together" because "if divided, I thought other nations might break in on us and destroy us."[14]

While many white Virginians criticized secession, they often refrained from condemning secessionists. To claim indifference to the fate of a Confederate neighbor would have earned a claimant the antipathy of his or her community. A claim of opposition to secession would not have necessarily roused anger or warranted retaliation from one's Confederate neighbors since many white Virginians, even those who eventually supported the Confederacy, had initially opposed secession. But a steadfast defense of the Union generated hostility and occasionally provoked vengeance in a claimant's community. Virginians who did not disclose their Southern sentiments, or seemed to express positions that former Confederates deemed too "Northern," incited the enmity of their neighbors. Caroline Heater petitioned the Southern Claims Commission, asserting that "my feelings were always in favor of the Union cause." On the basis of these assertions, members of Heater's church tried her for committing perjury, but they eventually acquitted her for lack of evidence. Thaddeus Higgins incurred the wrath of the "Ku Klux" in submitting his claim to the commission. Higgins reported that one enemy swore that "I ain't going to stand that. Before I will stand that I will bring on another war." The rebel then threatened that "we will hang him sure, to the first tree, if we get him." White Virginians did not hesitate to attack neighbors who claimed to have favored the Union side during the Civil War.[15]

While most claimants had little difficulty expressing hostility to the Confederate cause and thereby gaining the sympathy of the commissioners, many refused to condemn their Confederate families and friends. Quick-witted Virginians reconciled their conflicting loyalties by distinguishing between their personal sentiments and their political principles. These Virginians claimed that they had opposed the war but had remained concerned for the welfare of their Confederate acquaintances, especially those in the Confederate army. Winfield Scott Berry sympathized "on the score of humanity with his neighbors and friends," but he continued to oppose the war, arguing that Virginia had not had sufficient cause to secede. Mary L. White admitted that "I was born and raised in the South and it was natural that my sympathies were with the South," but she also suggested that it was only natural for her to share the same sentiments as her husband, who had opposed the war. To profess disinterest in the fate of a loved one in the Confederate army would have seemed disingenuous to the commissioners. But to express too much compassion for the Confederate people could possibly provoke a ruling of disloyalty to the Union. Claimants found striking a balance nearly impossible. The commissioners routinely judged white Virginians disloyal if they sympathized with Confederates, even if they opposed the political doctrine of secession.[16]

White Virginians readily challenged claimants who submitted too easily or too completely to the Northern invaders, but former Confederates faltered in challenging neighbors who did not veer too far in the direction of a Northern perspective. Samuel W. George Sr. identified himself as an opponent of the war, but the tenor of his testimony indicated neutrality more than anything else. George claimed that during the war "I attended to my own business and just went on the same, farming as I always had done." The commission's investigator reported that George's neighbors considered him a "rebel" but hesitated in speaking against him because as "old differences are dying out his neighbors would prefer to not do anything to create unkind feeling," especially against a "good neighbor" who voted and acted with the "rebel party." A Virginian could count upon the silence of his neighbors if he or she did not offend Southern sensibilities with boisterous Unionist sentiments and otherwise returned to the Confederate side in the new battles over postwar politics.[17]

White Virginians who submitted claims to the commission could not escape the secession question, but the slavery issue could more easily be ignored. Many white claimants probably avoided dealing with the issue altogether by refraining from introducing the subject. Because the commissioners also neglected the issue of slavery, many claimants never mentioned their status as slaveholders. In some cases, the only indication in their claims that they had owned slaves emerged through the testimony of their former slaves who had been called upon to certify the quantity of property appropriated by the Union army. Though the commissioners only rarely questioned white Virginians on their status as slaveholders and even less frequently on their opinions on the institution of slavery, some white Virginians inserted discussions of slavery into their commentary on the war.

Despite the necessity to win the favor of the federal government in order to gain compensation for their lost property, some white Virginians could not resist the opportunity to condemn President Lincoln's policy of emancipation. A few slaveholding Unionists expressed opposition to abolition, but claimed to have otherwise supported the Union. William C. Lipscomb testified that "so far as the management of matters was concerned, subsequently to the proclamation, in regard to the question of slavery and things of that kind, . . . I certainly did not approbate it." Some claimants did not disguise their hostility toward the federal government. These Virginians blamed the federal government for instigating the war through its aggressive actions against the institution of slavery. Thomas M. Mills and his wife owned twenty-two slaves when the war commenced. Mills explained that "I and my wife both understood that if the South succeeded her Slave property was safe to her and if the Federal Government succeeded it would be taken from her or set free." He dedicated himself to the Confederate cause as the best protection for his family's economic interests.[18]

Complaints over abolition demonstrated white Virginians' refusal to concede the slavery question to Northerners, their belief in the legitimacy of slaveholding and the illegitimacy of emancipation, and their identification of the institution as a crucial issue in the Civil War. It was a claimant's introduction of the subject of slavery, their unwillingness to overlook the issue, and their continued bitterness over the loss of their slaves that prompted the commissioners to rule against them and deem them disloyal to the Union during the war. Former slaveholders in Virginia would have been better off in the claims process—and, ultimately, in the reconciliation process—if they had forgotten the issue of slavery, as many white Southerners by the turn of the century would do.[19]

In contrast, some white Virginians, usually nonslaveholders, found common ground with Northerners, particularly Republicans, by embracing the abolition of slavery or distancing themselves from the institution. A few expressed their outright opposition to holding slaves in bondage. Rebecca Sexsmith claimed that "our family never had any sympathy with slavery." In fact, her family had demonstrated their aversion to the institution by manumitting their "servants" long before the war. Most nonslave-holders who introduced the issue of slavery emphasized their disinterest in the institution. Peter P. Perkins, a former overseer, asserted that he "took no part" in the war because "I never owned a slave and never wanted to." Some white Virginians cited their religious principles in explaining their opposition to slavery and the war. As a Mennonite, Jacob Brunk opposed the institution of slavery. He felt in "perfect accord" with his faith, noting that "we were conscientiously opposed to slavery and no slaveholder could become a member of our society until he manumitted his slaves."[20]

Some nonslaveholding white Virginians explicitly identified slavery as the central issue of the Civil War. They argued that slaveholders had in-stigated the war to preserve their slave property. James W. Spicer asserted that he "had no sympathy with the slaveholders war on the union, or their attempt to break it up." John Peterson likewise "had no use for slavery" and opposed what he considered a "war to sustain slavery." These non-slaveholders asserted that they had refused to fight in a war fought in the interest of slavery. Richard Ennis owned "no negroes to fight for" and so he argued that "those that wanted to hold them might do the fighting." Nonslaveholders explained their hostility toward slaveholders and the "slaveholders war" as the result of class antipathy rather than abolitionist sentiment. They distinguished themselves as "poor" and "hardworking" in contrast to wealthy slaveholders who exploited the labor of their slaves. Moreover, nonslaveholders feared that the Confederacy would favor the slaveholding elite. Simeon Shaw charged that "if the South had gained their independence, a poor man like [me] would stand no chance at all here." Nonslaveholders doubted that a government formed for the preser-vation of slavery would serve their interests.[21]

Nonslaveholders mentioned slavery despite the commissioners' neglect because they believed the issue to be a relevant topic in their discussion of the Civil War and because they recognized that their distance from the in-stitution would help gain the sympathy of federal officials. With such anti-slavery expressions, this small minority of white Virginians allied their sentiments, however obliquely, with the Northern course of abolition.

White petitioners before the Southern Claims Commission more closely approximated a Northern perspective on the Civil War than petitioners for pardon. Still, their positions did not thoroughly repudiate Southern principles and did not completely recapitulate Northern perspectives. While they routinely condemned secession, white claimants generally re-mained silent on the question of slavery. Whites in Virginia believed that opposition to secession constituted sufficient qualifications for favorable consideration by the federal government. For many white Virginians, especially former slaveholders, the issue of slavery was better off left alone.

Some white Virginians evaded all discussion of the causes and issues of the Civil War. They did not comment upon the doctrine of states' rights or the institution of slavery as either practical or constitutional questions. Instead, they avoided choosing sides between the North and the South in their remembrances of the war. Rather than claim Confederate or Unionist identities, these Virginians, in effect, disowned the war. Some white claimants specifically identified themselves as neutral. John H. Bowles testified that "I acted as a neutral, desired to be considered such and was not willing to contribute to either side." White women, especially, stressed their marginal role, dismissing the war and other public affairs as beyond the bounds of their feminine expertise. Eliza A. Clarke testified that "as a woman I took no part whatever in the war." Susan W. Peterson similarly explained that "it was not a woman's business to be meddling with men's affairs." These Virginians had primarily been civilians, whose limited participation in the war meant that they could make a plausible case to have favored either side.[22]

Though many women denied involvement in politics and public affairs, they did recognize the care, comfort, and safety of their loved ones as their domain. Eliza A. Lively claimed that she had no opinions on the war. Her dominant allegiance was not to a cause, an institution, or a political question, but to her family. Her son had been at school in Williamsburg when the war began, but he enlisted in the Confederate army. She reported that "I thought if I could get my son I did not care any thing about it." Many white women asserted that they had supported the Union, but had also supplied food, clothing, and even guns to their husbands and sons in the Confederate army. These women refused to connect their actions as wives and mothers in supporting their Confederate men to national questions of loyalty or disloyalty.[23]

With these strategies, white Virginian women exploited gender conventions to assume a conciliatory posture without compromising their loyalties to their state and their region. In this manner, women meddled in "men's affairs," all the while disclaiming any involvement. By defining realms of men's affairs and women's affairs, women attempted to maintain their loyalty to their friends and neighbors without calling into question their loyalty to their nation, rendering it, in effect, an irrelevant question as applied to women.

The commissioners believed that Confederate men frequently attempted to capitalize upon women's presumed apolitical nature by submitting claims in their wives' names in the hope that they would be held to less rigorous standards of loyalty. The commissioners negated this strategy by recognizing women as political actors and insisting that they prove their loyalty. In addition, the commissioners subjected female petitioners to thorough questioning on the ownership of their appropriated property and required them to submit deeds or wills as additional proof.[24]

Men also disclaimed involvement in politics, arguing that their personal affairs and economic endeavors absorbed all of their time and energy. John T. Mitchell concentrated on his private business and "took little or no part in politics or political discussions." Some men explained their inaction by emphasizing their ignorance. William Drake rooted his lack of interest in the war on the fact that "I had no learning." John W. Edwards testified that "I was confused and didn't know which was right." As a consequence, he "didn't vote either side." Because Virginian men could not call upon apolitical gender stereotypes, their neutrality worked against them. As fully enfranchised citizens, the commissioners expected white men in Virginia to have fulfilled their duty to their country and voted against secession.[25]

Discussion of the underpinnings of the Civil War would not serve the goal of reconciliation. By disclaiming knowledge of the causes and issues of the Civil War, Virginians evaded the question of loyalty to the North and disloyalty to the South. By claiming ignorance or indifference, these Virginians could possibly gain the sympathy of the federal government without alienating their friends and neighbors.

While many white Virginians had difficulties balancing their loyalties to their country and their friends, black Virginians who petitioned the Southern Claims Commission revealed little ambivalence. Almost unanimously, black Virginians represented the Civil War as a war for the abolition of slavery. They invariably identified the essential meaning of the war as freedom. The word "secession" rarely entered their lexicon. Even the most committed white Unionists regretted the costs of war, but black Virginians remembered the Civil War with virtually unmitigated joy.

Former slaves testified that they had immediately realized the centrality of slavery. Their proximity to Union troops had literally brought freedom to their doorsteps. While slaves deeper in the Confederate interior had received conflicting reports on the war, slaves in Virginia had quickly surmised that the war would bring emancipation. Richard Freeman re-membered that "I went for freedom for me and every body else." On the Union cause, Freeman noted that "I prayed for it and worked for it and the war ended as I wanted it to end: It made me a free man." Freeman perhaps adopted his name in line with his new circumstances.[26]

Black Virginians who had been free before the war also identified the Civil War as a war between slavery and freedom. John M. Dogans posi-tioned slavery as a primary issue in the Civil War. He opposed slavery and "was willing if nothing else could bring freedom to the black man to see the war go on." Isaac Pleasant also believed that "slavery was a good deal at stake in the conflict between the states." He understood that "the success of the North would improve the condition of the slaves, at least."[27]

Free blacks, one after another, condemned their disfranchisement under antebellum Virginia society. Some free blacks explained that though they had been legally free before the war, they had possessed few rights. Joseph Brown, a farmer, revealed that "I was born free and so was my wife, but we had no liberty. We had no chance for education and hardly any rights at all." Even slaveholders of color who had benefited from the South's pe-culiar institution made this argument. Alfred Anderson had been born free, but complained that "I had not the rights of a free man." Other free blacks emphasized that they had been "called" free by name, but had not been free in actual fact. Beverly Dixon recalled that "free born men" were "called free but we were denied the rights of a citizen." Free blacks pointed out the inconsistency between their status as free and their limited rights. They identified the misnomer in their categorization as "free" in a society that did not recognize freedom for blacks.[28]

Minimizing distinctions within the black community, free blacks lik-ened their status to slavery. William Wilkerson explained that "we had no liberty, any more than the slaves." Beverly Matteur, who described himself as "a free born man with fair skin but never clothed with citizenship until after the war," testified that "a free person whose blood was tinctured at all, had no more rights than a slave." In antebellum Virginian society, to be free meant to be white and to be black meant to be a slave. Free blacks resolved this contradiction by concluding that to be black in Virginia meant to be a slave, regardless of actual legal status. Free blacks criticized Virginia's antebellum version of freedom as fraudulent because it was not accompanied by rights of citizenship.[29]

The Union, according to free blacks, would offer genuine freedom. Al-exander Anderson, a farmer, explained that "I was told and believed that if the Union succeeded we should all be free and we would have the right to vote and carry arms and serve on the jury." Alfred Wilson, a fellow farmer, spoke for all black Southerners: "We all wanted freedom and our rights." For black Virginians, freedom and rights existed side by side. To truly offer freedom, the Civil War needed to offer black Virginians rights.[30]

Free blacks contrasted the Union war effort of freedom and citizenship with a Confederate war effort of enslavement. Over and over again, they charged that Confederates intended to chain all blacks in bondage, even those legally free before the war. Gabriel Jones explained that "I was just what you may call free, and they wanted to make me rest down in bondage, but I like freedom above all things." Some free blacks had feared that enslavement would be used to fund the Confederate war effort. Beverly Dixon remembered that "the rebels said they were going to sell the free colored people and give money to their soldiers wives and I believe they would have done it." Other free blacks accused Confederates of enticing whites to their cause through promises of future slave ownership. Henry Escridge, who narrowly escaped being sold as a slave in 1863, believed that "the strength of secession is to take those who are free and sell them, and I have been sold often enough." Even without the enslavement campaign, black Virginians recognized that the Confederacy did not serve their interests. William Peters, a Harrisonburg mechanic, condemned the South, which "never did anything for me or my race to help us."[31]

Black Virginians embraced the federal government as the salvation for their future. Reuben Gilliam had traveled in the North and had noticed "the difference in the condition of free people of color in the two sections." In the South he labored under "heavy burdens," but he believed that "I should be better off in every particular under the Union than under the Confederacy." Indeed, Gilliam's service as an election judge after the war indicated his increased political stature. Black Virginians repeatedly reminded the federal government of their bonds to one another. One black Virginian "set a great deal of store" in the Union soldiers and "treated them as if they were his friends." During the postbellum years, black Virginians continued to look toward their friend, the federal government, to help, in the words of one former slave, secure "a better chance in the world."[32]

Assessments of the meaning of the war did not simply tally the deaths and injuries of soldiers and civilians or calculate dollars lost in property and possessions. For most Virginians, these assessments were first and foremost personal and individualized evaluations. White Virginians measured the war in terms of the deaths of their friends and family, the loss of their property, including slaves, and the destruction of their livelihood. Black Virginians, in contrast, measured the war in terms of their freedom from bondage, or the freedom of their friends and family, and the security and reality of their rights as free citizens. Depending on their perspective, Virginians infused their interpretations of the war with feelings of grief, anger, uncertainty, or jubilation.

When Virginians attempted to identify a cause of secession and war, they almost always focused upon slavery. Former slaves and free blacks, more than any other group of Virginians, consistently focused upon slavery in their discussions of the war. Black Virginians celebrated the Civil War exclusively as a war for their freedom. Though black Virginians most frequently imbued the war with ideological meaning, white Virginians also occasionally revealed their beliefs. Nonslaveholders blamed slaveholders who preferred to drive their state into war rather than sacrifice their slave property for the preservation of the Union. Former slaveholders, in turn, denounced the war as an abolitionist attempt to deprive them of their slave property.

Despite their divergent perspectives, blacks and whites as well as Confederates and Unionists could find agreement on specific war experiences. All could recognize that the Civil War had inflicted much suffering. This focus on the experience of the war, particularly upon its hardships, however, ignored the ideological underpinnings of the war and therefore ignored the role of slavery. Nevertheless, this consensus came to dominate remembrances and celebrations of the Civil War by the turn of the century.

After the war, both black and white Virginians looked to the federal government to bestow their rights of citizenship. The federal government, under the Grant administration, accepted a compromise to readmit Virginia to the Union in 1870. Moderate and conservative Virginians succeeded in securing Confederate enfranchisement in exchange for black male suffrage in their new state constitution. These events cleansed most former Confederates of the taint of treason, but left the elimination of racial discriminations, primarily within the arena of civil rights, an unsettled question. Congressmen imposed disabilities upon influential Confederates through the Fourteenth Amendment, but Northerners and the federal government increasingly lost interest in the project of Reconstruction and the fate of the former slaves. Congress, in 1898, removed the last remaining distinctions between loyal and disloyal citizens. A few years later, in 1902, Virginia adopted a new constitution that effectively disfranchised much of its black population. This reconciliation between white Northerners and white Southerners excluded blacks, both North and South, from the rewards of postwar reunification and fostered a celebration of the Civil War that ignored the centrality of slavery.

Notes

I would like to thank Edward L. Ayers, Gary Gallagher, Watson Jennison, Dayo Mitchell, and Aaron Sheehan-Dean for their comments and suggestions.

1. In his December 8, 1863, amnesty proclamation, Abraham Lincoln excluded six classes, primarily leaders of the Confederacy, from the benefits of his general amnesty. To Lincoln's exceptions, Johnson in his May 29, 1865, proclamation, added, among others, Confederates with taxable property valued at over $20,000. Johnson also issued subsequent amnesty proclamations in which he increasingly narrowed the categories of Confederates excluded from general amnesty. Johnson finally granted an unconditional and full pardon to all Confederates on December 25, 1868. See Jonathan T. Dorris, *Pardon and Amnesty under Lincoln and Johnson: The Restoration of the Confederates to their Rights and Privileges, 1861–1898* (Chapel Hill: University of North Carolina Press, 1953), 33–35, 111–12, 339–61.

2. Thomas C. M. Anderson Pardon Application, William C. Allen Pardon Petition, and William B. Allegre Pardon Petition, all in Virginia Amnesty Papers, 1865–1867, Records of the Adjutant General's Office, RG 94, National Archives, Washington, D.C. (hereafter cited as Virginia Amnesty Papers).

3. Joseph R. Anderson Pardon Petition, Virginia Amnesty Papers. Some pardon petitioners argued that they had been coerced into supporting the Confederacy. In this manner, their stories of the war seemed little different than petitioners before the Southern Claims Commission.

4. Robert A. Banks Pardon Petition, and Samuel Andrews Pardon Petition, all in Virginia Amnesty Papers.

5. Robert A. Banks Pardon Petition and Thomas G. Turner Pardon Petition, both in Virginia Amnesty Papers.

6. P. H. Aylett Pardon Petition, Elijah Baker Pardon Petition, and Philip St. George Ambler Pardon Petition, all in Virginia Amnesty Papers.

7. William B. Allegre Pardon Petition, Virginia Amnesty Papers.

8. On new state governments under Johnson, see Eric Foner, *Reconstruction: America's Unfinished Revolution, 1863–1877* (New York: Harper and Row, 1988), 193–94; and Dan T. Carter, *When the War Was Over: The Failure of Self-Reconstruction in the South, 1865–1867* (Baton Rouge: Louisiana State University Press, 1985), 83–85.

206 SUSANNA MICHELE LEE

9. Foner, *Reconstruction*, 190–91; Dorris, *Pardon and Amnesty under Lincoln and Johnson*, 135–46.

10. Congress limited compensation to quartermaster and commissary stores that had been officially appropriated by the Union army. Southerners who desired compensation for rents, damages, or other property, such as cotton, could petition the Court of Claims for compensation. See Frank W. Klingberg, *The Southern Claims Commission* (New York: Octagon Books, 1978), 117.

11. Commissioners of Southern Claims, "First General Report of the Commissioners of Claims," 42nd Cong., 2nd sess., 1871, H. Doc. 18, 2–3, 27–29.

12. Virginians submitted 3,731 claims, which constituted approximately 17 percent of the total, and Tennessee submitted 4,027 claims, which constituted approximately 18 percent of the total. See Klingberg, *The Southern Claims Commission*, 157. The commissioners decided 262 claims (or 45 percent from Virginia) in 1871, 545 claims (or 25 percent) in 1872, 427 claims (or 17 percent) in 1873, and 475 claims (or 20 percent) in 1874. Only in 1874 did the commissioners decide more cases from a state other than Virginia. Specifically, they ruled on 554 claims from Tennessee, or 23 percent of the total for that year. For the number of claims submitted by state and by year, see Klingberg, *The Southern Claims Commission*, 174. The commissioners set the threshold for a claimant's appearance in Washington at a claim of $10,000 (see Klingberg, *The Southern Claims Commission*, 73).

13. Commissioners of Southern Claims, "Second General Report of the Commissioners of Claims," 42nd Cong., 3rd sess., 1872, H. Doc. 12, 5.

14. Richard Ennis Deposition, May 10, 1782, Richard Ennis Allowed Claim, Prince William County, Virginia, Southern Claims Commission, Records of the U.S. General Accounting Office, RG 217, National Archives II, College Park, Md. (hereafter cited as Allowed Claim); Martin Ellis Deposition, May 19 to 20, 1873, Martin Ellis Allowed Claim, Page County, Virginia.

15. Summary Report, 1879, Caroline Heater Disallowed Claim, Frederick County, Virginia, in Court of Claims, Docket No. 3,580, Records of the U.S. House of Representatives, RG 123, National Archives, Washington, D.C. (hereafter cited as Court of Claims); Thaddeus Higgins Deposition, June 22, 1871, Thaddeus Higgins Disallowed Claim, Hanover County, Virginia, Barred and Disallowed Claims, 1871–1880, Southern Claims Commission, RG 233, National Archives, Washington, D.C. (hereafter cited as Disallowed Claim). Virginia did not witness the same Ku Klux Klan outrages as other states of the former Confederacy. Much of the Ku Klux Klan activity in Virginia occurred in the spring and summer of 1868. The "Ku Klux" mentioned by Higgins in 1871 probably refers to a local group not directly affiliated with other Ku Klux Klan groups across the South. (See Allen W. Trelease, *White Terror: The Ku Klux Klan Conspiracy and Southern Reconstruction* [Baton Rouge: Louisiana State University Press, 1995], chapter 3.)

16. Winfield Scott Berry Deposition, February 5, 1878, February 15, 1878, Winfield Scott Berry Disallowed Claim, Prince Edward County, Virginia; Mary L.

White Deposition, July 1, 1872, Mary L. White Disallowed Claim, Albemarle County, Virginia.

17. Samuel W. George Sr., Deposition, March 19, 1873, Samuel W. George Sr. and Samuel L. Steer to George Tucker, November 4, 1873, both in Samuel W. George Sr. Disallowed Claim, Loudon County, Virginia, in Court of Claims, Docket No. 1,052.

18. William C. Lipscomb Deposition, February 18, 1879, William C. Lipscomb Disallowed Claim, Fairfax County, Virginia; Thomas M. Mills Deposition, March 13, 1878, Thomas M. Mills Disallowed Claim, Orange County, Virginia.

19. On slavery and the memory of the Civil War, see David W. Blight, *Race and Reunion: The Civil War in American Memory* (Cambridge, Mass.: Harvard University Press, 2001), especially chapters 5 to 8.

20. Rebecca Sexsmith Deposition, October 3, 1873, Rebecca Sexsmith Allowed Claim, Prince William County, Virginia; Peter P. Perkins Deposition, April 25, 1872, Peter P. Perkins Disallowed Claim, Halifax County, Virginia; Jacob Brunk Deposition, December 19, 1873, Jacob Brunk Allowed Claim, Rockingham County, Virginia.

21. James W. Spicer Deposition, April 4, 1877, Simeon Shaw Allowed Claim, Culpepper County, Virginia; John Peterson Deposition, September 5, 1873, Susan W. Peterson Disallowed Claim, Warren County, Virginia, in Court of Claims, Docket No. 8,707; Richard Ennis Deposition, May 10, 1782, Richard Ennis Allowed Claim, Prince William County, Virginia; James W. Spicer Deposition, April 4, 1877, Simeon Shaw Allowed Claim, Culpepper County, Virginia; Simeon Shaw Deposition, April 4, 1877, Simeon Shaw Allowed Claim, Culpepper County, Virginia.

22. John H. Bowles Deposition, August 25, 1871, John H. Bowles Disallowed Claim, Goochland County, Virginia; Eliza A. Clarke Deposition, April 25, 1872, Eliza A. Clarke Disallowed Claim, Halifax County, Virginia; Susan W. Peterson Deposition, September 5, 1873, Susan W. Peterson Disallowed Claim, Warren County, Virginia, in Court of Claims, Docket No. 8,707. In Klingberg's study of large claims (worth over $10,000), the commissioners rejected six Virginia claimants for neutrality (approximately 6 percent of the total disallowed for the state). This approximated the 7 percent for all twelve states (Alabama, Arkansas, Florida, Georgia, Louisiana, Mississippi, North Carolina, South Carolina, Tennessee, Texas, Virginia, and West Virginia). Overall, in terms of the loyalty question, neutrality was the fourth likeliest category for rejection, following overt disloyalty, circumstantial or interrupted Unionism, and borderline loyalty. See Table 4 and Table 5 in Klingberg, *The Southern Claims Commission*, 160, 162.

23. Eliza A. Lively Deposition, November 12, 1872, Eliza A. Lively Disallowed Claim, Elizabeth City, Virginia.

24. The commissioners also suspected that former Confederates submitted claims in the names of their former slaves and therefore required proof of property ownership from blacks as well as women.

25. Joseph T. Mitchell Deposition, February 22, 1875, Joseph T. Mitchell Disallowed Claim, Augusta County, Virginia, in Court of Claims, Docket No. 478; William Drake Deposition, December 23, 1873, William Drake Disallowed Claim, Southampton County, Virginia; John W. Edwards Deposition, November 11, 1875, John W. Edwards Disallowed Claim, Prince George County, Virginia.

26. Richard Freeman Deposition, September 5, 1871, Richard Freeman Allowed Claim, Norfolk County, Virginia.

27. John M. Dogans Deposition, June 16, 1873, John M. Dogans Allowed Claim, Page County, Virginia; Isaac Pleasants Deposition, February 24, 1873, Isaac Pleasants Allowed Claim, Henrico County, Virginia.

28. Joseph Brown Deposition, March 13, 1874, Joseph Brown Allowed Claim, New Kent County, Virginia; Alfred Anderson Deposition, September 9, 1872, Alfred Anderson Disallowed Claim, Amelia County, Virginia, in Court of Claims, Docket No. 1,913; Beverly Dixon Deposition, March 1, 1877, Joseph Brown Allowed Claim, New Kent County, Virginia.

29. William Wilkerson Deposition, March 1, 1877, Joseph Brown Allowed Claim, New Kent County, Virginia; Beverly Matteur Deposition, September 19, 1874, Beverly Matteur Allowed Claim, Appomattox County, Virginia.

30. Alexander Anderson Deposition, September 9, 1872, Alexander Anderson Disallowed Claim, Amelia County, Virginia; Alfred Wilson Deposition, September 9, 1872, Alexander Anderson Disallowed Claim, Amelia County, Virginia.

31. Beverly Dixon Deposition, February 1, 1873, Beverly Dixon Allowed Claim, New Kent County, Virginia; Henry Escridge Depositions, October 2, 1873, June 18, 1877, Henry Escridge Allowed Claim, Fairfax County, Virginia; William Peters Deposition, June 16, 1875, William Peters Allowed Claim, Rockingham County, Virginia.

32. Reuben Gilliam Deposition, March 19, 1872, Reuben Gilliam Allowed Claim, Prince George County, Virginia; Jerry Hughes Deposition, n.d., Richard Pinn Allowed Claim, Fauquier County, Virginia; Elias Peyton Deposition, April 25, 1873, Elias Peyton Allowed Claim, Fauquier County, Virginia.

Conclusion

Edward L. Ayers

Like flanking maneuvers on Civil War battlefields, these essays attack questions from surprising directions, exposing sides to problems and opening up opportunities we had not expected. The questions are the same ones that always concern historians of the Civil War, especially those of Virginia. How did this state, so central to the building of the United States, come to secession? What motivated men such as Robert E. Lee, who had dedicated their lives to the United States and its defense, to renounce their loyalty? What held the Confederacy together across its divides of class, locality, gender, ethnicity, and political division? How did the institution of slavery fare during the war? How did people's most profound religious beliefs confront the challenges of civil war? How did proud Confederates reconcile themselves to defeat and the loss of so much that had defined their lives before 1861? How did people of all sorts make sense of the changes they had undergone during the tumult of secession, war, emancipation, and aftermath?

Historians and others have attacked these classic questions head-on and have often offered straightforward answers. Some say Virginians seceded because of slavery; others say that secession came from deeply held political beliefs that had nothing to do with slavery. Robert E. Lee fought for the Confederacy because his ideals of honor and duty left him no choice— or because he was, beneath it all, a slaveholder. Men from places where slaves were relatively scarce fought only reluctantly—or with eagerness and dedication. Slaves remained loyal and slavery remained strong to the very end of the war—or slavery began disintegrating almost immediately. White Christianity sustained the Confederacy through great trials—or slaveholder guilt undermined the Confederacy and destroyed its will to win. Former Confederates wrapped themselves in nostalgia and evasion— or honorably treasured the memories of their lost relatives. Southerners buried their political differences after the war—or deep conflicts churned under the surface, emerging as political backlash at the first opportunity.

Why don't these essays come to the same kind of straightforward conclusions? It is not because the authors lack opinions and it is not because the authors' arguments are limited by their focus on particular places and groups. Rather, these historians deliver supple interpretations because they assume that people act from complex motivations in complicated contexts. Each author in each essay sets a scene that by its very nature requires that the historical actors make decisions: how to vote, how to decide loyalty, how to act during wartime, how to behave in a time of uncertainty, how to judge God's will when things are falling apart, how to remember disaster. These historians weave conflict and choice into the very fabric of the stories they tell.

Once they have established the drama of the situations black and white Virginians faced, the authors of this volume look for evidence to reveal the rationales behind the choices people made. Sometimes the historians turn to direct indications of these decisions, using evidence such as votes, prices, and enlistment dates. Other times the authors look to the words in newspapers, letters, speeches, and court testimony, finding that the words often turn out to be changeable, ambiguous, and self-deceptive.

The essays of this book pursue case studies because merely gathering quotes to support any particular argument on the Civil War is all too easy. Without the discipline of looking intently at particular people in particular places and circumstances, generalizations tend toward the banal. Close analysis is the only way to see how people triangulated among competing motives, desires, and forced decisions. The authors here are more interested in understanding why people did the things they did than in passing judgment on people long dead. All these historians are sympathetic to the dispossessed, black and white, but recognize that the poor and the oppressed lived lives at least as complicated as those of the wealthy and powerful.

By looking at new kinds of evidence, by including people often ignored in more traditional studies, and by asking novel questions as well as older ones, these young historians point us toward a more vital kind of Civil War history, a Civil War history sure to emerge over the next decades. That history will focus on the connections among various facets of life, on the interactions among different kinds of people.

Let us imagine, for example, the course of a young white man's life as he traversed the terrain of this book's essays. As he considered the choices before him in the election of 1860, in most parts of Virginia our young man would confront a complicated decision. As Andrew Torget shows us, for example, three contiguous Valley counties displayed directly contrary political patterns before 1860: strongly Democrat, strongly Whig, and strongly mixed. The reasons for those differences are hard for us to see at this distance, but surely they had much to do with the political leanings of powerful men in the past, with the messages conveyed in church, and with family tradition. Whatever his loyalties before 1860, however, after Abraham Lincoln called for Virginia militia this young man found himself swept up in the new Confederacy. Aaron Sheehan-Dean tells us of the overwhelming power of mobilization. Our young man, like his neighbors and kin, directed his loyalty toward the nation to which he suddenly belonged. Slaveholder or not, he would fight for a slaveholding nation. If he was a product of West Point or the prewar army, our young man had especially hard decisions to make, on a different calculus of loyalty and loss, as Wayne Hsieh details.

Or let us assume that our central character is an African American woman. She had no voice in the coming of the war, of course, but found herself in the middle of war nevertheless. Perhaps her master quickly put together a sale of slaves to lessen his risk or to make a profit while the chance presented itself. As Jaime Martinez reveals, the slave market did not fall silent during the Civil War, but worked on relentlessly if spasmodically. That woman might find, until the minute the guns fell silent at Appomattox, her children sold away from her. Just as the slave market operated without ceasing during the conflict, so did the church. Andrew Witmer visits churches in central Virginia throughout the war and finds that antebellum patterns of religious fellowship gradually gave way to new patterns. Black Christians pressed slowly yet steadily for self-determination, for churches and worship services of their own. White Christians sometimes helped their formerly enslaved coreligionists and sometimes blocked their movement away from the white-dominated church.

Perhaps we are interested in a white woman's path through the war. She would likely be swept up in the same enthusiasm her husband or sons or father experienced, the same determination to fight for independence from the United States. But she could only do so much. She could sew uniforms or tents, she could write letters, and she could attend meetings. She could also maintain the family's respectability, as Amy Minton shows us, by behaving according to scripts appropriate to wartime's demands. Perhaps she would contribute to the common good by her labor or aid a needy friend; perhaps she would set aside her favorite dress or attend church with greater fidelity; perhaps she would mourn the loss of a cherished son or husband with grace and strength. At war's end, Carrie Janney shows us, such women took the lead in honoring the dead, making certain that even strangers found a burying place worthy of a Confederate soldier, ensuring that those too young to have known the war firsthand would remember the Confederate version of its history and of the sacrifices it demanded.

Everyone recalled things a bit differently after a few years passed. Susanna Lee tells us about the ways that Southerners, whatever their race or gender or political loyalties, shaped their memories to fit new needs. Some white people imagined a past in which they had been strong Unionists, others imagined themselves as steadfast Confederates. Black people's memories seem to have strayed less often, for they knew, start to finish, that they desperately wanted to be free of slavery and its relentless costs for African Americans.

The Civil War proved a crucible for all who lived in Virginia. The state's rivers and mountains shaped plans of attack and routes of retreat; the names of its rivers and towns became synonymous with the names of the war's victories and losses. Its men and women were tried in the war's heat and found battlefield and home front all too often one and the same. Whatever their race or gender, whether they lived in the Tidewater, Piedmont, Valley, or mountains, whether they entered the war as Unionists or secessionists, slave or free, the war changed them all. We have only begun to understand their stories.

Contributors

Edward L. Ayers is the Hugh P. Kelly Professor of History and the Dean of the College and Graduate School of Arts and Sciences at the University of Virginia. He is the author of *In the Presence of Mine Enemies: War in the Heart of America, 1859–1863, What Caused the Civil War? Reflections on the South and Southern History,* and the founder of *The Valley of the Shadow: Two Communities in the American Civil War,* a large digital archive.

Gary W. Gallagher is the John L. Nau III Professor in the History of the American Civil War at the University of Virginia. His books include *The Confederate War, Lee and His Army in Confederate History,* and a forthcoming study of how the Civil War has been presented in recent film and art.

Wayne Wei-siang Hsieh is an Assistant Professor of History at the U.S. Naval Academy. His 2004 dissertation, "The Old Army in War and Peace: West Pointers and the Civil War Era, 1814–1865," was co-directed by Edward L. Ayers and Gary W. Gallagher at the University of Virginia, and is currently being revised for publication.

Caroline E. Janney received her Ph.D. in 2005 from the University of Virginia, where her dissertation, "If Not for the Ladies: Ladies' Memorial Associations and the Making of the Lost Cause," was directed by Gary W. Gallagher.

Susanna Michele Lee received her Ph.D. in 2005 from the University of Virginia, where she worked with Edward L. Ayers. Her dissertation, "Claiming the Union: Stories of Loyalty in the Post–Civil War South," examines Southern citizenship in the aftermath of the Civil War. She is currently at work on a history of the civilian experience in Virginia during the Civil War for the National Park Service.

Jaime Amanda Martinez is a Ph.D. candidate at the University of Virginia, where she holds a John L. Nau III graduate fellowship from the Jefferson Scholars Foundation. She is writing a dissertation on slave impressment in Confederate Virginia, under the direction of Gary W. Gallagher.

Amy R. Minton is a Ph.D. candidate at the University of Virginia, where she works with Edward L. Ayers. Her dissertation is titled "A Culture of Respectability: Southerners and Social Relations in Richmond, Virginia, 1800–1865." She has taught courses at the University of Virginia and is currently teaching at George Mason University in Fairfax, Virginia.

Aaron Sheehan-Dean received his Ph.D. from the University of Virginia in 2003 and is an Assistant Professor of History at the University of North Florida. He has published articles on the Civil War and on the use of digital technologies in history and is currently working on a manuscript titled *Creating Confederates: Family and Nation in Civil War Virginia.*

Andrew J. Torget is a Ph.D. candidate at the University of Virginia. He is the project manager for the *Valley of the Shadow* project at the Virginia Center for Digital History and co-editor of the forthcoming book *Two Communities in the Civil War: A Norton Casebook in History.* His dissertation, directed by Edward L. Ayers, examines the expansion of American-style slavery into northern Mexico in the years between 1820 and 1845.

Andrew Witmer is a Ph.D. candidate and a fellow of the Institute for Advanced Studies in Culture at the University of Virginia. His dissertation, directed by Joseph Kett, examines how foreign missionary work in Africa influenced American thought in the nineteenth and early twentieth centuries about race and race relations.

Index

Charles (slave), 124
Charleston, S. C., 39, 43, 107, 116
Charleston, W.Va., 69, 180
Charlotte (slave), 140
Charlottesville, Va., 68, 115, 116, 138,
    139, 141, 142, 145, 147, 148, 150, 153,
    154, 155, 156, 157, 178, 180
Chestnut Grove Baptist Church
    (Albemarle Co., Va.), 140, 141, 144,
    146, 147, 148, 149, 150, 151, 156
Chicago Tribune, 178
Chickamauga, battle of, 37
Christ Church Episcopal (Albemarle
    Co., Va.), 139, 140
Christianity. *See* religion
Church Hill (Richmond, Va.), 175
City Point, Va., 175
Clark, Cyrus, 124
Clark, Granvill, 119
Clarke, Eliza A., 200
Clover Hill rock pits, 110
Confederate army, 1, 4, 45, 46, 69,
    110, 114, 125, 127, 128, 130, 148, 197;
    Army of Northern Virginia, 1, 4, 5,
    147, 168, 177; Army of Tennessee, 37;
    Army of the Valley, 70; enlistment
    in, 37t, 68f, 86, 99, 148–49, 200;
    soldiers of, 2, 3, 4, 7n7, 29, 46–48,
    64–66, 68, 70, 71, 72, 73, 84–85,
    87–88, 89, 90, 93, 94, 100, 147,
    148, 150, 165, 171, 172, 175, 180, 212;
    veterans of, 5, 167, 168, 177, 178, 179;
    women in, 92
Confederate nationalism, 6, 59, 62,
    64, 65, 69, 72–74, 80–82, 83–84,
    90–91, 92, 94, 95, 97, 99, 100,
    104n33, 108, 115, 116, 120–21, 125,
    127–28, 130–31, 147, 153, 166–67,
    169, 178, 180, 198
Confederate press, 80–82, 83–101;
    attitudes toward labor, 91–99,
    102n6; criticizes aspects of Southern
    society, 88–91; criticizes the North,

85–86; glorifies the Confederate
    poor, 94–100
Confederate States of America, 3, 10,
    23, 26, 28, 35, 36, 37, 38, 39, 47, 50,
    60, 69, 73, 92, 95, 96, 107, 112, 113,
    123, 126, 129, 166, 167, 168, 169, 170,
    173, 177, 182, 183n4, 190, 191, 194, 195,
    196, 203, 209, 210; capital of, 2, 168;
    Clothing Bureau of, 93; Congress
    of, 120; currency of, 107, 108, 112,
    117, 121, 123, 125, 129, 146, 169; divi-
    sions within, 81, 84, 199; Engineer
    Bureau of, 112, 119, 123; House of
    Representatives of, 128; impress-
    ment of slaves, 112, 113–14, 116, 119,
    120, 130; Medical Department of,
    119; memorialization of, 165–82;
    Mining Bureau of, 112, 119; Nitre
    Bureau of, 119; seal of, 4, 6n4; Senate
    of, 127; Virginia state legislature of,
    29, 119, 120; War Department of,
    104n29, 108, 111, 119, 120, 147. *See
    also* Confederate army; Confederate
    nationalism; Confederate press
Congress. *See under* Confederate
    States of America; United States
Connelly, Thomas L., 7n7
conscription, 48, 97
Constitution. *See under* United States
Constitutional Union Party, 13
Continental army, 4, 48
Continental Congress, 48
conventions. *See* National Conven-
    tion; secession: Virginia secession
    convention; Southern convention
Cook, Dr., 141
Cooke, John Esten, 41
Cooke, John Rogers, 41
Cooke, Julia Turner, 41
Cooke, Philip St. George, 38, 41–42,
    43, 44, 46, 50, 56n42
cotton, 14, 17, 19, 25, 27, 110, 116, 138
Cox, James, 110